Greek History

A Captivating Guide to the History of Greece, from the Bronze Age through Classical Antiquity to Modern Greece

Free Bonus from Captivating History
(Available for a Limited time)

Hi History Lovers!

Now you have a chance to join our exclusive history list so you can get your first history ebook for free as well as discounts and a potential to get more history books for free! Simply visit the link below to join.

Captivatinghistory.com/ebook

Also, make sure to follow us on Facebook, Twitter and Youtube by searching for Captivating History.

Contents

Part 1: History of Greece

A Captivating Guide to Greek History, Starting from the Bronze Age in Ancient Greece Through the Classical and Hellenistic Period to the Modern Era

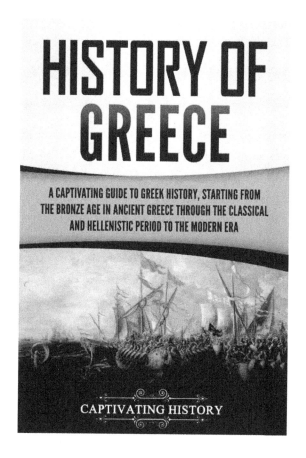

Introduction: It's All Greek to Me

Greece stands large in the minds of many as the epic spawning ground of Western civilization. It was here that philosophy, democracy, science, mathematics, and just about everything else that the Western world might take for granted was forged. Most scholars agree that we owe much to the culture of ancient Greece. But as high as we hold the Greece of the bygone past, we have to realize that Greek history did not end in the era of Socrates, Plato, and Aristotle.

After the Classical era, Greek history merged and melded with the Roman Empire in what would later be termed the Greco-Roman period. Even though Rome conquered Greece and turned the once free Greek city-states into subjects of Rome, the Romans had great respect for this subject people. So much so, in fact, that they adopted their customs as their own. Greek philosophy, religion, sports, and theater are just a few aspects of Greek culture that the Romans sought to infuse with their own.

Even the Greek language became popular and was one of the most widely spoken languages of the Roman Empire, second to Latin. It was during this timeframe that a previously unknown sect of Judaism called Christianity would rise up to influence and then ultimately supersede Greek philosophy. The combination of Roman roads and a common Greek language were the greatest facilitators for the preaching of the gospel.

Rome did indeed come to accept Christianity, and eventually, it would become the dominant religion, with Roman Emperor Constantine establishing a new capital all the way in the Greek East—Constantinople. Under the backdrop of a Christianized Roman Empire, Greek power grew in the east until the eastern half of the Roman dominion was distinctly Greek in flavor.

The Western Roman Empire would fall in the meantime, while the eastern half continued under the Greek-speaking and Greek-thinking Byzantine Empire, which was based out of the Greek capital of Constantinople. This phase of Greek culture would last until it was toppled by the Ottoman Turks in 1453. Greece itself would then be controlled by the Ottoman Empire until it finally wrested its freedom from the Turks in 1821.

It has been a long struggle since then, and Greece has survived two world wars, a civil war, a military junta, an economic collapse, and a worldwide pandemic. Yes, there is much more to Greek history than just Socrates, Plato, and Aristotle. As important as classical Greece is, it is important not to forget the continuing saga of Greek culture. Here is the history of Greece in full.

Chapter 1 – The Origins of Ancient Greece

"Fables should be taught as fables, myths as myths, and miracles as poetic fantasies. To teach superstitions as truths is a most terrible thing. The child mind accepts and believes them, and only through great pain and perhaps tragedy can he be in after years relieved of them."

-Hypatia of Alexandria

The mists of time hang low over Greece at its inception. And there is no way of knowing exactly what prehistoric Greece might have been like. We do receive some pretty good hints, however, in the form of Greek mythology and plenty of anecdotal lore. These myths, of course, should be taken much as they are perceived—as myths. But even if they are fictitious renderings, they impart crucial details of what Greek life at the very dawn of human history must have been like.

The legends of old describe motivating factors for Greek society and imbue Greek culture with its own sense of manifest destiny. Although most are not likely to take, for example, the epic journey of Odysseus, literally, the indomitable spirit and courageous virtues portrayed within the tale would be a sounding board for future Greek temperament. Greek researcher and writer Thomas R. Martin refers to this as the "concentration on excellence" displayed in the Greek imagination. The epic characters portrayed in these narratives represented the Greek ideal of what they longed for themselves and their society as a whole to achieve.

The *Odyssey* and the *Iliad* come down to us from the so-called Archaic period of Greece as tales that were passed down orally, meaning they were spoken or sang in front of an audience. The *Iliad* actually takes place before the *Odyssey* and revolves around the Trojan War. The *Odyssey*, on the other hand, occurs after the events of the *Iliad*. The tale of heroic Odysseus, who returned home after an absence of twenty years, would have been particularly stirring to Greek ears. And the fact that his wife Penelope had remained faithful to him after all of those years would have elicited reactions of admiration for her loyalty and dedication.

Besides these echoes of the primordial past, the real spark began when the Greeks first learned to express themselves in the written word. The Greeks are believed to have reached this epoch around 770 BCE, for it was at this time that the Greeks first began to record their own history.

Prior to this, much of what prehistoric Greece was like is largely unknown. Even once the Greeks started to write things down, it took a while for the ancient Greeks to become prolific writers. With this deluge of material, it can be hard to separate legend from reality, but one must at least try to discern the difference, for even the fabrications tell us a little something about the mentality of ancient Greek civilization.

One thing that is certain is that the early Greeks were a people fixated on those who came before them. Today, folks who are interested in their ancestors might go to an ancestry website, look up their family tree, and leave it at that. Such things are perhaps just a passing curiosity—nothing more and nothing less. Back in the days of ancient Greece, however, who came before you could mean just about everything.

From potentates to the average citizen, groups of early Greeks categorized themselves based upon their lineage from a powerful figure from the past. These descendants were often the heroes and, in some cases, even the demigods of legendary lore. It was through this lineage that the Greeks declared themselves to be the progeny of greatness. The most popular of these patron patriarchs is that of Hellen.

Although those of us in the West are more familiar with Hellen (or rather Helen) being used as a feminine moniker, the Hellen of ancient Greek lore was the bold son of Deucalion, who, in turn, is the son of the Greek Titan Prometheus. In Greek mythology, the Titans were a class of celestial beings who ended up waging war against the Greek gods of Olympus, otherwise known as the "Olympians."

As Greek myth tells us, the Olympians ultimately won in this struggle, and the Titans were defeated. However, two of those Titans, Prometheus and his brother Epimetheus, had remained neutral during the conflict, so they managed to escape punishment. After the war was over, in fact, they were recruited by the head honcho of the Olympians, Zeus, to do a bit of divine work on Earth.

According to legend, the Titan Epimetheus was tasked with designing all of the animal life on Earth. His brother Prometheus, in the meantime, was given the special assignment of creating an intelligent lifeform to reign at the top of the food chain: human beings. It is said that Prometheus formed human beings from the very mud and muck of the earth. And since all of the baser biological attributes, such as sharp teeth, claws, and shells, were given to the animals for defense and offense, Prometheus had to contemplate an alternative means of giving this higher lifeform distinction over the other creations.

He determined to create these beings as nothing short of the very "image" of the gods. For anyone familiar with the Book of Genesis in the Bible, you might be a little stunned at the similarity. Here we have two creation stories that speak of human beings being made of the "dust" of the earth and also made in the "image" of the divine. As to what "image" might mean, though, has long been debated. Some take it as a literal interpretation that humanity was made to have a similar appearance to divine beings. Others who wish to delve deeper into the metaphysics of it all theorize that the legend is referring to the human soul being imaged to the mortal clay of the human form. Just like a computer is "imaged" with data, Prometheus sparked within us a divine program of sorts—or at least so this myth would have us believe.

At any rate, according to Greek myth, shortly after Prometheus forged man, he began to pity him. Despite their divine software, physically speaking, human beings just seemed too weak and defenseless to hold their own in the world. As such, Prometheus wanted to give humanity something that would give them an edge. Even though it was not permitted, Prometheus decided to intervene on man's behalf by giving them the gift of fire.

Another interesting parallel from Judeo-Christianity is the extra-biblical narrative found in the Book of Enoch, which claims that fallen angels transgressed against God by teaching human beings certain arts that God felt they were not ready for. In Greek myth, the Titan Prometheus is said to be playing a very similar role. He was trying to aid humanity, but he broke a prime directive in doing so.

And according to Greek legend, Prometheus paid a terrible price for going against Zeus's orders. He is said to have been stretched out against a rock and chained in place so that a giant bird of prey could peck at him (in particular, at his liver) for all of eternity. Sounds like a pretty terrible fate by any stretch of the imagination.

At any rate, it was Prometheus's son Deucalion who supposedly fathered Hellen with his wife, Pyrrha. Interestingly enough, Deucalion is sometimes known as the Greek "Noah" because the myth surrounding Deucalion is a flood story, very much reminiscent of the one in the biblical Book of Genesis. In this account, Zeus is angry and disgusted with the depravity of humans and orchestrates a flood to wipe them off the face of the earth. However, Deucalion was warned of what would happen, and taking refuge in a giant "wooden chest," he and his family survived the deluge.

Deucalion's son Hellen is said to have given rise to the first Greeks through his sons Aeolus, Dorus, and Xuthus. Greek ancestry is said to have split between these three sons, giving rise to the Aeolians, Dorians, and, by way of the two sons of Xuthus—Achaeus and Ion—the Achaeans and Ionians. It was these four main tribes, which were ultimately descended from Hellen, that were said to make up the Hellenes of the ancient Greeks.

Another major part of ancient Greek tradition was to create incredible backstories to certain geographic locales. In the region of Greece known as "Hellas," for example, it is said that Hellen himself resided there as a king in the shadow of Mount Othrys in Thessaly. According to the mythological backstory, when Hellen's reign came to a close, he was replaced by his heir, Aeolus. It was then the children of Aeolus who ended up spreading out from Thessaly to form a greater Greece that stretched all the way to Corinth in the south and Peloponnesus in the west. This branch of Hellenes was said to have traveled far and wide as they populated the far reaches of ancient Hellas (Greece).

Those who are said to have hailed from the Achaean branch played a major role in the so-called "Heroic Age," in which they perfected the art of war in Sparta, Argos, and Mycenae. They were the stars of the great Trojan War, a tale of which it has only recently been discovered must contain some kernels of truth in the midst of all of its grand myth-making.

The Trojan War, you see, revolved around the city of Troy. Troy was long believed to be entirely fictional, but excavations on the western shores of modern-day Turkey have revealed a city that seems to have been the mythical backdrop of this epic struggle, with several Greek artifacts unearthed from the time period in question. At any rate, it was the Achaeans who fought in the Trojan War who filled up much of ancient Greece's lore, with the blind poet Homer often calling the sum total of the Greek population simply "Achaeans."

The Ionians and Dorians, in the meantime, initially played a lesser role in ancient Greece, but eventually, they would come to take center stage by helping to give rise to both the Athenians and Spartans, the latter of which are perhaps the most famous military arm of the Greeks. For the Spartans, martial defense was everything, and people were recruited and trained to fight in the Spartan armed forces as young as seven years old.

Today, the notion of a child soldier would be complete anathema to most of us. But for the Spartans, fighting was simply a way of life, and they taught their youth that they had to learn the skills of warfare from a young age. Even infants were not immune to this critique since it wasn't uncommon for newborn children to be left to die if they were deemed to be somehow deficient and therefore not suitable to grow up to be a fighter. Again, such things today would be absolutely abhorrent from a modern perspective, but for the Spartans, such drastic measures were just part of who they were as a people.

The Spartans eventually clashed with the Athenians in the 5th century BCE, besting their foes around 404 BCE in what was known as the Peloponnesian War. As fiery as their spirits were, the Spartans' decline began to set in by 370 BCE after the Spartans lost out to another Greek group called the Thebans. And since the Spartans did not leave much of cultural value other than their art of war, their actual influence on the shape of Hellenization can be said to be fairly minimal.

The most enduring bond of any nation, of course, is its language. So, where did the Greek language come from? This question by itself opens up the door of yet another fascinating facet of not only Greek but also world history as a whole. Historians have traced the Greek language back to a large, mysterious people group from the distant past referred to as the Indo-Europeans.

The Indo-Europeans were said to have originated somewhere in Eurasia before swooping down on lands as far afield as Greece, Iran, and even India (hence Indo-European). It is said that the first wave of Indo-Europeans arrived during the Early and Middle Helladic periods around 2000 BCE. The fact that these Indo-Europeans were most likely not on a mission of peace is evident by the archaeological record, which seems to bear witness to the sudden destruction and dislocation of those who were already in the region upon the arrival of the Indo-Europeans.

If groups were not altogether pushed out, they seem to have intermingled and eventually intermarried with the newcomers. It seems that the Greek language as we know it today was forged in this cultural melding of the Indo-Europeans and the older inhabitants who had crossed paths with them thousands of years ago. The Greeks themselves referred to the original peoples who lived in Greece in the primordial past as being the "Pelasgians." Not all of the Pelasgians lost their original identity, and some pockets are said to remain in Attica and Arcadia.

At any rate, it was during the Middle Helladic period, around 1600 BCE, that the majority of Greek and Indo-European descendants began to create a complex civilization, complete with citadels, temples, and palaces. Since much of this civilization is found in the southern Greek city of Mycenae, this ancient Greek society is often called Mycenaean.

According to Greek myth, Mycenae served as the backdrop of the killing of the Mycenean King Agamemnon at the hands of his wife, Clytemnestra. During the Trojan War, King Agamemnon came back with the spoils of war, which just so happened to include a certain Trojan priestess named Cassandra (also spelled as Kassandra). Agamemnon's wife was apparently not too happy about all this. She was unhappy enough, in fact, that she conspired to have her husband killed.

Although this story is generally viewed as the product of myth-making, there are those who have tried to argue that perhaps at least some of this tale is true. A researcher by the name of Heinrich Schliemann, in fact, even claimed to have found the burial site of this long-dead Mycenean king, a site full of buried artifacts and even a "golden death mask." But subsequent inquiries into this archaeological find revealed none of the artifacts were from the time period in which King Agamemnon is said to have lived. So it is that the veracity of this tale remains a mystery.

The very real footprints of the Mycenean civilization, however, remain clearly distinct, with outposts stretching to Athens and Thebes. The Myceneans were also the first Greeks to develop writing, coming up with what is known as Linear B around 1000 BCE.

Before the rise of epic Greek literature, most of these early writings contain notes of everyday life, such as the listings of foodstuffs and the like. Although the Myceneans had the Indo-Europeans as ancestors, they were clearly influenced by their Near Eastern neighbors, such as the nearby Minoans of Crete. Artwork, pottery, and other sculptures that have been recovered show a deep similarity between the two cultures. Much of this influence most likely came from seaborn commerce between the two regions.

As rapidly as the Myceneans had risen, their downfall was even faster. It seems that around 1200 BCE, the whole civilization faced a sudden collapse. The reasoning behind this remains unclear, with some historians speculating about everything from possible intrusion by outside forces to civil strife among the Myceneans themselves.

This left Greece in what has been termed a "dark age," followed by what has been called the Dorian invasion. This was when the Dorian sect of Greeks from the north came down and took over what little remained of the Mycenean settlements. This invasion, in turn, prompted some of the older settlers to cross over the Aegean Sea and create new settlements on the west coast of Anatolia (modern-day Turkey).

The Dorians, too, crossed the sea, except not in the direction of Anatolia but toward Crete, Rhodes, and Lycia. Over the next few centuries, not a whole lot is known. The Greek Dark Ages lasted until about 750 BCE before the brilliant light of the Hellenes began to shine forth once again.

Chapter 2 – Coming Out of the Dark Ages

"On a summer's night, I have sat on the balcony drinking Ouzo, watching the ghosts of Greek heroes sailing past, listening to the rustle of their sail cloths and the gentle lapping of their oars...and lain alongside Pythagoras watching him study the myriad of triangles in the constellations twinkling above us."

-Phil Simpkin

Around 750 BCE, Greece is believed to have come out of the Dark Ages, and once again, it embarked upon a marked advancement of civilization. This period, known as the Archaic Age, saw renewed commercial ties with the already thriving nations of the Middle East and Anatolia. These contacts allowed for the Greeks to adopt, among many other things, advanced metallurgy and an improved alphabet, the latter of which came by way of utilizing the Phoenician script to make improvements upon classical Greek writing.

As conditions began to improve on the Greek mainland, Greece experienced a kind of baby boom. Archaeological records show that there was a great increase in the population at this time, and this increase led to a renewed interest in the settlement of neighboring lands. As Greece became more crowded, those seeking more room to grow left for locales in the east, as well as settlements as far west as Sicily and Italy.

The term "Greek" itself came from the Italians, whom the Greeks came into contact with in Italy. Supposedly, it all stemmed from an incident in which Greek visitors were asked by Romans from where they had traveled, and the Greeks who had previously hailed from a settlement called Graia replied that it was from this town that they had come. The Romans, not realizing that these few Greeks were referring to one puny town rather than their entire homeland, thenceforth called all Greeks "Graeci," which in Latin simply meant "the people of Graia."

During this period, several prominent city-states began to dot the Greek landscape. The actual origin of the concept of the city-state is still a matter of argument for historians. Some have speculated that such a polis became desirable for the Greeks due to the nature of Greece's terrain, which featured flat plains nestled among majestic mountains. For them, it only made sense to form a centralized base in which people could forge a unified defense just in case someone happened to drop down from the highlands and attempted to ransack their settlements. And the fact that each of these city-states seems to revolve around already existing features of the environment seems to lend credence to this hypothesis.

These city-states were developed so that each city could stand as a strong, individual unit while also entering into commerce and communication with other neighboring city-states. And what was forged for the sake of common defense eventually became major commercial hubs and administrative centers.

On the other hand, the Myceneans, as great as they were, did not rely on the city-state structure but instead took top-down orders from their king. After Greece left the Dark Ages, the city-states came to prominence, and they were generally administered by the landed elite. This, of course, led to inevitable conflict between the upper class, landed gentry, and the poor, landless peasants who tilled their fields.

The Greek poet Hesiod made a note of this disparity in wealth in his piece, "Works and Days." Here, Hesiod illustrates just how hard life is for the toiling peasants and explains the growing animosity toward the landed elites. However, the major shift occurred when the city-states began to send emissaries across the seas and ushered in maritime riches that did not depend upon how much land one controlled.

By the 7th century, all of these factors led to tremendous societal upheaval in which the city-states came to be controlled by the so-called "tyrants." Although Greek in origin, the term is now quite familiar to English speakers, and no one in the English-speaking world would have any trouble at all understanding what a tyrant is. And as one might imagine, these original Greek tyrants were the same kind of power-hungry bullies, attempting to lord over everyone else through whatever tyrannical means were at their disposal.

Tyrants were typically members of the landed elite who had come to enough prominence to control city-states by force. This tyrannical leadership was naturally resented by the Greek people, but tyrannical control was not always so easily done away with. One famed tyrant, a man named Cypselus, ruled the Greek city of Corinth, and he was followed by an equally tyrannically ruler: his son, Periander. The two ruled for around seventy years, from 655 BCE to 585 BCE.

The people certainly groaned under their tyranny, yet at the same time, Corinth developed into a wealthy port city under the leadership of these two tyrants. So as tyrannical as they may have been, much of the city's wealth was due to their decisive actions. Such things were certainly not rare to the Greeks, and they have been repeated in other parts of the world throughout history.

Besides an occasional bent toward tyrannical rule and the consolidation of resources, another development of the city-state was the use of local militias. This phenomenon came to prominence due to the inability of city-states to sustain large armies. The best that could be done was to have citizens of the city being able and ready to take up arms when needed rather than having a huge professional army, which would need food and shelter on a regular basis.

In an effort to keep the volunteers for the city-state's militias in good fighting form, athletic contests were developed. During times of relative peace, members of the city's militia would compete in games of physical endurance with each other. These feats of endurance were localized, and they were primarily between individual citizens of that particular city-state.

In order to survive, the city-state forged ties of patriotic duty among its members for mutual defense. These militiamen became known as hoplites, and the average city-state could boast anywhere from three thousand to ten thousand of these hoplites at any given time. Along with defending the city-states, the hoplites actually became an important safeguard against encroaching tyranny. The city-state in which the hoplites most crucially performed this role was Sparta. It is said that Sparta was essentially tyranny-proof due to the efforts of its "hoplite government."

Yes, in Sparta, the hoplite warriors were more than just a mutual defense force; they actually became a part of the government itself. Sparta, which was situated on the flat plains near the Eurotas River, was actually an assortment of four closely connected settlements. And each of these settlements was run under a so-called "Spartan constitution," which featured an actual hoplite assembly that would meet to discuss matters important to the community. The Spartans were highly successful in both military matters and in the governance of their own domain.

That domain soon began to expand as the Spartans conquered neighboring regions. But as Sparta expanded, the difficulty of fielding a militia in sufficient numbers became increasingly more pronounced. As successful as the Spartan city-state may have been, any hope that the Spartans would become empire builders was apparently doomed to failure.

Nearby Athens, in the meantime, was having some pretty serious problems of its own. In the mid-600s, a tyrant named Theagenes was lording over the nearby city-state of Megara. Around 640 BCE, Theagenes began to threaten Athens. He and his son-in-law are said to have plotted a takeover of the city and tried to push out the landed elites so that the two could lord over the Athenians themselves. The attempt failed, but it led to the infamous Draco of Athens, who forged his so-called "Draconian" measures that he believed were needed to keep Athena prosperous.

As you have no doubt noted, the commonly used term "draconian," which means something drastic and desperate, takes its meaning from this incident. It is rather ironic that a man put in place to safeguard Athens from tyrants would impose laws that would essentially be viewed as extreme and tyrannical.

At any rate, around 620 BCE, the Draconian laws were codified in Athens. The exact details of the laws are not entirely clear, but it seems that punishment by death for even the most minor of infractions was quite common. The harshness of the Draconian laws created a backlash by the time of Solon in 594 BCE. Solon was made an archon (chief administrator) in Athens around this time, and he soon legislated a brand-new set of laws that, unlike the Draconian ones, tried to create a social compact that was strong yet far fairer in its implementation.

The major issue of Solon's day was the fact that the peasant farmers were being made to supply one-sixth of all of their harvest to landowners. These Draconian measures were considered harsh and often resulted in the peasants becoming indebted and ultimately enslaved by the rich landowners for whom they toiled. Solon solved this problem by easing the debts of the peasants while weakening the monopoly of the landed elite. With the stranglehold of the affluent broken, Solon then proceeded to broker a new system of governance in which he forged the boule, an assembly of some four hundred representatives comprised of one hundred members of each of the four main districts in Athens.

The archonship role of chief administrator, however, became a disputed position among the Athenians. This role continued to be a contentious issue, and it ultimately culminated in a successful seizure of power by yet another tyrant—Pesistratos. Pesistratos established a military dictatorship that lasted from 546 BCE to 510 BCE, when his son and successor, Hippias, was kicked out of power, finally ending the regime.

Even though this was essentially a strong-armed dictatorship, Pesistratos's regime was successful, both commercially and domestically. Under this tyrant's willful commands, major construction works were undertaken, creating lasting monuments to the tyrant who ordered their undertaking. By the 400s, the situation had changed, and the oligarch Cleisthenes decided to enter into a partnership with the common man of the city or, as the Greeks called them, the demos.

Cleisthenes then established ten groups of people, which were grouped together by location, in an attempt to bypass already established dynastic roots. It was these humble beginnings of democratic reform that would lead to the first full-blown democracy the world had ever known, which first came to prominence in Athens.

Chapter 3 – Athens and the Classical Era

"Socrates gave a lifetime to the outpouring of his substance in the shape of the greatest benefits bestowed on all who cared to receive them. In other words, he made those who lived in his society better men and sent them on their way rejoicing."

-Xenophon

The Greek Dark Ages were clearly over when the enlightened democracy of Athens took root in the 5th century BCE. Although we refer to Athens as being the place where democracy was born, by today's standards, it most certainly wouldn't be the kind of democracy of which we would approve. For one thing, only men who were born from an Athenian mother and father were allowed to participate in this democracy. Still, considering the times in which basically all societies were patriarchal (meaning male-dominated), Athenian democracy was indeed a significant advancement in human governance.

All Athenian-born men of Athens had the democratic right to speak their mind before the council and could actively vote for legislation of which they approved. This was a direct democracy. Even though modern nations, such as the United States, often boast that they are democracies, they are most certainly not direct democracies such as Athens was. If you live in the United States, for example, just ask yourself when was the last time you marched down to Congress and voted for a piece of legislation. You didn't. This is because the US uses a representative form of government, in which representatives the people vote for on Election Day go off to the nation's capital to represent their constituents and vote on their behalf in favor of or against the proposed legislation.

Athens, however, sported a direct democracy in which the people directly participated. Imagine a bunch of men in the town square being asked, "Men of Athens! Do you want to go to war with Sparta? Yes, or no?" This would be followed by a cacophony of yeses and noes being shouted until it was determined what the majority of Athenians wanted to do. This is direct democracy, a form of government with no presidents, no senators, no congresspeople, or any other form of representation.

Such a tradition, of course, took citizen participation to a whole new level, as the average Athenian had to show up to vote on just about any decision made by their society. Even more taxing, they also were expected to engage in voluntary service as magistrates themselves. In addition, the Athenians voted on their military leaders, voting for a total of ten different military chiefs every single year. The generals, therefore, were the elected officials who wielded the most power.

The greatest flaw of Greek democracy is said to have been a lack of will for citizens to galvanize themselves to action during crisis situations. For instance, imagine if a war was looming on the horizon, and half of the citizenry either failed to show up to vote or was completely bewildered as to what kind of action to take. As beautiful as direct democracy might sound, it soon takes on the trappings of an unintelligent, bickering mob with no idea what should be done and who should do it.

And this indecision could be devastating. It would not be good to have a heated debate among citizens while enemy troops were on the verge of beating down the doors to the assembly hall. This sort of dilemma presented itself during the Ionian revolt. The Ionian revolt involved a group of Greeks known as the Ionians who had founded Greek colonial outposts on the west coast of Asia Minor. By the 5th century, these outposts had been swallowed up by the growing Persian Empire.

In 499 BCE, the Ionians staged a revolt against their Persian overlords while they pleaded with their Greek counterparts on the mainland for help. The Spartans, for their part, flat-out refused since, as far as they were concerned, the Persians posed too distant of a threat to have to move their troops so far away. The Spartans were far too fearful of what might happen to Sparta if they left it undefended to mobilize any of their troops abroad.

Athens and the city-state of Eretria were more helpful, however, and agreed to come to the Ionians' aid. Athens, as it turns out, had some ulterior motives in mind since its burgeoning population was dependent upon shipments of corn and other supplies from Anatolia. Furthermore, Athens already had a bone to pick with Persia since Persian aggression in 514 BCE, under King Darius I (also known as Darius the Great), had disrupted Greek coastal communities and overseas commerce.

At any rate, as the battle heated up between the Ionians and the Persians, things came to a head when the Ionians assaulted the Persian administrative outpost of Sardis. The settlement was largely burned to the ground by the Ionians, although the Persian troops and administrators managed to hole up in a citadel and survive the onslaught. The whole effort proved to be rather fruitless, however, because shortly after, the Persians rallied and sent reinforcements that were easily able to dispatch the Ionian rabble-rousers.

Any self-respecting Athenians present at this point decided to head back to the mainland. Nevertheless, the Ionians continued to struggle with the Persians until they were decisively put down in 494 BCE. In the aftermath, the Athenians were kicking themselves over the relatively weak response of their fellow Greeks for the Ionians. This feeling of inadequacy was only reinforced a few years later in 490 BCE when the Persians decided to strike out against the Greek mainland itself.

The Persians hit Eretria first; the Eritreans held out for almost a week before they were forced to submit. And during the course of this struggle, no other Greek city-state took decisive action to defend them. They remained befuddled and indecisive in their assembly halls, unsure of what to do. Without facing any serious resistance, the Persians were then able to make their way to the Bay of Marathon to threaten Athens itself. Athens, realizing that it would need some help in repulsing the Persians, naturally sent emissaries to nearby Sparta to request aid.

Ridiculously enough, the Spartans refused the request on the grounds that they were celebrating a religious holiday. It sounds almost like a joke, but it is the truth. The completely unsympathetic Spartans refused to lend a hand to their neighboring city-state simply by stating that they had better things to do. This left Athens virtually by itself, with only the meager support of an obscure nearby settlement called Plataea (also spelled as Plataiai) to fend off the might of Persia.

But unlike the callous Spartans and despite their smaller stature in the Greek world, the Plataeans were determined to make a vigorous effort in coming to the aid of Athens, which had been a loyal ally to Plataea in the past. According to Greek historian Herodotus, lest the Athenians lose their nerve, they were all led out of the city to meet the threat head on. This meant marching from the gates of Athens some twenty-five miles to Marathon.

This twenty-five-mile stretch between Athens and Marathon is significant for another reason, as the modern-day meaning of a marathon is derived from an event that took place there. During the Battle of Marathon, a Greek soldier by the name of Pheidippides ran those twenty-five miles from Marathon to Athens to deliver the message that Persian forces had been bested in battle. According to legend, this messenger was so out of breath that he only had one word to shout to the Athenians, "Niki! Niki!" which is Greek for "Victory!"

Modern readers will note the similarity between "Niki" and a certain brand of running shoes called "Nike." Yes, Nike footwear does indeed take its name from the Greek word for victory. But the soldier-turned-messenger Pheidippides did not have long to celebrate the feeling of being victorious. According to legend, he was so exhausted after his marathon run that he keeled over and died! At any rate, it is from the events of this account that the term "marathon" has become associated with "long-distance running."

During the Battle of Marathon, the Athenians set up shop right on the road to Athens. Here, it is said that some ten thousand hoplites stood their ground, each holding a sword and a javelin, prepared to fight to the death. These ten thousand men were ultimately outnumbered by three to one when a force of some thirty thousand Persian troops marched right into their encampment.

But even though the Athenians were outnumbered three to one, they fought ferociously, and they were able to deliver an incredible number of casualties upon their attackers, forcing them to flee. This victory was spoken of with great pride many years later, and around 447 BCE, when the Parthenon was created, it was built with the defeat of the Persians in mind.

Interestingly enough, the Spartans who had refused to fight on the day that this ultimate showdown occurred actually arrived on the scene the next day when their services were conveniently no longer needed. One can only imagine the contempt the ancient

Athenians must have felt for this belated show of support. Nevertheless, the Spartans themselves were most certainly overawed by what the Athenians had done. And it was after the victory of Marathon that the Athenians took the lead over the rest of the Greek city-states.

Chapter 4 – United They Stand

"Anybody can become angry—that is easy. But to be angry with the right person and to the right degree and at the right time and for the right purpose, and in the right way—that is not within everybody's power and is not easy."

-Epicurus

After their advances were rolled back by the Athenians, the Persians bitterly plotted their revenge. It would be the Persian who took the helm after Darius—Xerxes—who would next lead an assault not just on Athens but also the Greek civilization as a whole. And this time, nothing would be given to chance. Every aspect of the campaign would be meticulously planned.

The Persian warriors were heavily armed and well provisioned. Even so, it was made sure that plenty of "supply dumps" would be buried under the ground all along the way to Athens. Several naval craft, in the meantime, were massing along the Bosporus in Anatolia, preparing for an invasion. However, the Greek city-states of the mainland initially seemed to take little notice amidst their squabbling with one another.

But as the threat continued to grow, clearer heads finally prevailed. And in 481 BCE, an assembly of Greek city-states managed to gather together at Corinth to discuss a joint strategy against the Persians. This alliance would become known as the Hellenic League. The dominant power player of this league was Sparta, which, despite its previous dithering, carried the most obvious military might. But even once the league was brought together, there was still quite a bit of bickering as to what the best path forward would be.

The Spartans wished to stand their ground in Corinth, but such a move would leave the entire center of the Greek mainland defenseless. Athens, on the other hand, wished to pursue the Persians on the northern front of Greece. After many arguments were made, it was finally determined that a unified army would be sent to the Vale of Tempe in the northern reaches of Thessaly.

Upon reaching Thessaly, however, it was understood that the Persian forces could easily outflank the Greeks. The strategy then shifted again, and it was decided it would be better to shut off access to the south of the country instead. This led to some seven thousand Spartan troops being placed at Thermopylae. Led by the famed King Leonidas of Sparta, the Spartan forces held off a much larger Persian army for about two days. However, the Persians were tipped off about a secret path, which enabled them to go around the amassed Spartans. Leonidas, realizing that he and his men were doomed, allowed those who wished to flee to leave, but he remained with some one thousand loyal troops to fight the Persians to the death.

Those Spartans were destroyed, all of northern Greece was in peril, and, once again, the Athenians were forced to face the Persians alone. The average Athenian citizens were evacuated to higher ground. The Persians showed up in Athens only to find a meager residual force who fought to defend the Acropolis. This group was easily put down, and the city was looted.

However, the Greeks weren't completely beat yet. The Greek navy managed to lure the Persian forces into waging war in the waters between Greece and the Isle of Salamis, and the Persian ships became trapped, allowing the Greek naval forces to pick the Persians off one by one.

This was a major setback to the Persians, but the war was far from over. Winter was setting in, and the Persians decided to hold the ground they had in Greece and wait until spring to reengage the remaining resistance. The final showdown occurred in Plataea, where resurgent Greek forces were able to drive the Persians off the mainland completely. It was only through the unification of the remnants of Greek power that the Persians were finally defeated.

With all the Greek factions united and with the mighty Spartans leading the pack, they marched right up the Isthmus of Corinth to meet the Persians on land. It was near the city of Attica that this climactic fight erupted. The Persians were able to charge the Greek formations on horseback, and Persian arrows inflicted terrible losses, but in the end, the Greeks were able to stand up to the Persian threat and halt their advance. Not only that, in the immediate aftermath, the Greeks were able to regain the lost Ionian colonies in Anatolia.

This sequence of events would prove to be a powerful lesson to the early Greek democracies of just how important unity was for survival, and it would lead the way toward uniting the city-states into one single polity. It was for this reason, after all, that the powerful Hellenic League was formed in the first place. It was established in order to create a stronger compact between all of the Greek city-states in common defense against outside aggression. And predictably enough, it was Athens that would take the lead in this charter.

Persia would again threaten the Greek lands in 466 BCE when a fleet was sent to skirmish with Greek troops in the Aegean Sea near the coast of Anatolia. Known as the Battle of the Eurymedon River, here, once again, the Persians were defeated. Thanks to the cooperation of the Hellenic League, the Persians had been checked on both the land and the sea. As a result of this triumph, the Persians would not be able to menace the Greeks again for several more decades.

The fact that the Greeks were able to stop what was then the world's greatest empire in its tracks was an impressive feat, and the glory of the Greeks' triumph was not lost on them. They would long celebrate the victories of Marathon and Salamis, instilling themselves with an unbridled sense of national pride. Also, the fact that the league was maintained even after the Persian threat was eliminated demonstrates that the strength of solidarity was deemed to be crucial for Greek survival.

But even though the Greeks managed to stand toe to toe with the Persian Empire, as soon as their unity dissolved, they would be at each other's throats. With the defeat of the Persians, the Greeks had shown that they could stand strong when united together. But as the years progressed, cracks in their social compact would emerge, and it would prove increasingly difficult for them to hold it together. Early on, one of the first points of friction occurred when some members of the union attempted to break away due to what was perceived as an overreach by Athens.

The primary reason that Athens was able to maintain dominance was due to the city-state's powerful navy. If anyone fell out of line, it would not take much for Athens to scramble a fleet together to poke and prod the rebels back into conformity. And in some cases, members were even forced into the compact against their will. This happened with Karystos and the island of Skyros, which were both forcibly coerced into the union. Even more infamous was the subjugation of the Cycladic island of Melos, which was forced into Athens's orbit around the year 416 BCE. This coercion resulted in the massacre of countless inhabitants of the island and others being outright enslaved. Most historians would agree that this was a clear overreach of the Athenians, who otherwise have often been painted as the idyllic forgers of democracy. Yes, they may have created some aspects of the democratic ideal, but the actions of this democracy were often less than ideal for those on the periphery.

Relations with Sparta had greatly deteriorated by this time, giving rise to the Peloponnesian War, which lasted from 431 BCE to 404 BCE. The war was called as such because, during this great rift in Greek relations, Sparta had rallied the city-states of the Peloponnesian League in the Peloponnesian region of Greece. The Spartans and the Peloponnesians had decided to stand up to what they perceived as the "imperialism" of Athens.

The Spartans also wanted to make sure that they maintained control of the mainland and stayed strong in case of revolts from within their sphere of influence. And they could only stay strong if Athens was kept in check. Hostilities actually erupted when Corinth fought back against Athenian pressure. In 432 BCE, Corinth began to have trouble with the nearby Greek settlement of Corfu (also known as Kerkyra). After hostilities between these two settlements commenced, Corfu asked Athens for help. Athens agreed, but it angered Sparta in doing so since the Spartans were allied to Corinth.

During the war, both sides had their own advantages. Athens's major advantage was its naval power, whereas Sparta's advantage was the size of its hoplite infantry forces on land. In 425 BCE, Athens managed to take 120 Spartan troops as prisoners of war. This might not seem like much, but since Spartans had pledged to fight to their deaths, the fact that so many were captured managed to erode the reputation of Spartan prowess in battle.

This was then followed by a group of Athenian naval craft heading around the western shores of the Peloponnese. The Spartans feared that this would be used as a launching pad to attack Sparta and took decisive action. They sent a group of Spartans to face the threat and attempted to lay siege to the Athenians stationed on the Peloponnese. However, the Athenians simply sent another fleet of ships to intercept them, and pretty soon, the Spartans themselves were being overwhelmed by the Athenians.

Sparta continued to struggle in the larger war, and in 418 BCE, the Spartans struck a victory of their own by knocking Athens's ally Argos out of the war. The Spartans then continued to rack up gains against Athens, and in 412 BCE, they even managed to forge an alliance with the old Greek foe of Persia through the local Greek satrap (a local ruler) Tissaphernes, which enabled Persian Emperor Darius II to sweep down into western Anatolia to reclaim the Greek cities in Ionia. Darius II then sent his own son Cyrus to the region to oversee Persian efforts in person.

The next major turning point in this war occurred in 405 BCE when the Athenian navy was destroyed. Bereft of a navy, food and other goods soon ceased to arrive in Athens's ports. The Spartans were now well positioned to starve their enemies into submission. And so, with pressure building on all sides, the city of Athens was finally forced to surrender in 404 BCE.

But even though Athens was defeated, the power politics of the Greek city-states managed to save the city from total annihilation. The supposed allies of Sparta, namely Thebes and Corinth, still wanted Athens around as a check against the strength of Sparta itself. They did not mind weakening Athens and stripping the city-state's extraterritorial lands from it, but they wanted the city itself to remain mostly intact as a bulwark against total domination by Sparta.

In the end, like an unruly child called to task, Athens was forced to become a partner with Sparta and the other Greek city-states once again. Athens had seemingly grown too powerful for its own good, only for it to be knocked back in line with its fellow city-states. This could have been a chance for a renewed sense of unity, but it would not be long before an outside power would rise up to take advantage of the lingering instability.

Chapter 5 – The Dangers of Democracy

"For myself, I think that those who cultivate wisdom and believe themselves able to instruct their fellow-citizens as to their interests are least likely to become partisans of violence. They are too well aware that to violence attach enmities and dangers, whereas results as good may be obtained by persuasion safely and amicably."

-Xenophon

In the aftermath of Athens's defeat by Sparta, the democratic institutions that had flourished in the city-state were dismantled. In its place rose what can only be termed an oligarchy, which was controlled by just a few of the landed elites. This ushered in a period that would become known as the time of the Thirty Tyrants. These brutish enforcers were backed up by the power of a small Spartan encampment stationed right in the middle of Athens's Acropolis.

Completely devolving from a democracy to a petty oligarchy, many of Athens's brightest, pro-democracy minds began to form a sort of exiled intelligentsia. These renegades eventually found a home in Attica, where they were protected by Thebans who were unhappy with the heavy-handedness of the Spartans. They also managed to flourish in the nearby town of Piraeus, where they gained support from the locals. When it became widely known that these pockets of resistance were developing, the tyrants of Athens and their handlers from Sparta began to mobilize themselves to purge the democrats from their midst.

They were initially successful, but due to pushback against the subsequent harshness and austerity, a middle-of-the-road approach was developed, in which more moderate forms of democracy were allowed to take root once again in the city of Athens. If anyone was viewed to have stepped outside the bounds of this newfound moderation, however, they were quickly punished.

Shortly after this restoration, one of the greatest of Greek tragedies is said to have transpired. For it was around 399 BCE that the Greek philosopher Socrates suffered persecution and was ultimately executed by Greek authorities.

Socrates himself is not known to have written anything down, and what we know of this great teacher actually comes down to us from one of his later protégés—Plato. Socrates taught his pupils to think freely, but the Athenian authorities soon became alarmed and felt that he was teaching them to think just a little bit too freely. And after some of his teachings were uncovered by the powers that be, he was actually charged with the so-called crime of "corrupting the youth," as well as general "impiety."

The impiety charge was apparently on the grounds that he was accused of worshiping false deities while failing to adhere to the proper state religion. Socrates did not deny these charges since he was indeed one to openly criticize the anthropomorphic nature of Greek's old belief system. At any rate, these alleged "crimes" landed Socrates in the courtroom. Socrates didn't have an attorney; he defended himself.

During the course of the trial, he clearly expressed his beliefs and the reasons behind his actions. His efforts would become known as a Socratic apology, and his methods, as described by Plato, would later be known as the Socratic method. This is a method of debate that employs a question-and-answer, conversational format in order to prove a point and provide critical analysis of a subject.

Despite all of his skills of reason, Socrates was ultimately unable to turn the tide against him. Socrates was found guilty, and he was sentenced to death. He was forced to drink a cup of poisonous hemlock. It is said that one of the constant threads of Socrates's teachings is to embrace death without any fear or hesitation. Socrates apparently wanted to practice what he had been teaching and gladly took the cup he was given without any sign of fear or trepidation. And when others around him began to cry, he was quick to tell them to wipe away their tears. Socrates assured them that death was not a big deal but rather just a normal transition that we all must undergo at some point in our life.

It was Socrates's noble death that made him a martyred icon in the eyes of his students and the subsequent followers of his philosophy. The most important thing that Socrates's life and teaching exposed about democratic societies is the realization that just because the majority of the people in a democracy decide to do something, it does not mean their decision is a good one.

Socrates was killed by the unanimous consensus of a mob mentality. Yes, a jury of his peers democratically decided to kill him, but just because the majority of those operating the levers of Athens's democracy decided to end his life, it does not mean that this decision was an ethical one. Interestingly enough, the Founding Fathers of America were also very much afraid of developing a democracy with a mob mentality, and they looked toward the lesson of Socrates as a great warning against the dangers of such things. America's Founding Fathers knew full well that all manner of horrible things could occur when a huge mob of people get caught up in the moment and decide to do something. James Madison, for one, had actively read up on the example of the direct democracy of Athens and clearly saw how unbridled, dangerous passions of a momentary majority could wreak untold havoc on society. After all, in a moment of passion, it takes a while for the cooler heads to prevail.

Yet, if decisions were made by six hundred citizens screaming in an assembly immediately after a call to action is made, the cooler heads would never get the chance to consider the possibilities. The Founding Fathers knew that this could lead to disastrous and completely wrong decisions on the part of the democratic masses. What if, for example, in ancient Greece, the Acropolis mysteriously burned down one night, with a rumor emerging that Corinth was behind it? Before the facts are even known, you could have the assembly packed with an entire mob of citizens demanding action being taken against Corinth. In a direct democracy like Athens, this could lead to an authentically democratic decision being made to wage war against Corinth. Yet, suppose that right after much bloodshed against the Corinthians had ensued, the Athenians learned that Corinth actually had nothing to do with the fire at the Acropolis and the whole thing was all just a big accident.

Well, this is exactly what the Founding Fathers' fears were when they shuddered at the notion of a "mobocracy" run amuck. Or as James Madison stated in the *Federalist Papers* at America's founding, "In all very numerous assemblies, of whatever characters composed, passion never fails to wrest the scepter from reason." He then even went on to note, "Had every Athenian citizen been a Socrates, every Athenian assembly would still have been a mob."

In other words, even if assembled citizens were of the best character, they could—as the above example demonstrates—become very easily confused and inflamed in the passion of the moment, leading to bad decisions being made. It was for this reason that the Founding Fathers eschewed direct democracy for a representative republic in which democratically elected representatives are (hopefully) enlightened enough to understand what is in the best interest of their constituents. And if they fail to vote for legislation that benefits their constituents, they can be democratically voted out in favor of other representatives who promise to do so.

At any rate, immediately after the death of Socrates, the mob rule of Athens was pushed aside when the Spartans decided to clamp down and take on greater control. As one might expect, the other Greek city-states soon grew resentful of this overreach by Sparta, just as they did when it was Athens lording over them. And by 394 BCE, Thebes and Corinth were teaming up with Athens to wage against Sparta in what became known as the Corinthian War.

The war ended up being a big, bloody stalemate, with neither side gaining any real advantage. But perhaps the oddest part of the whole thing was the fact that the old enemies of the Greeks, the Persians, were the ones who actually mediated a truce between them in 387 BCE. This cessation of fighting became known as the King's Peace, so named after the Persian king at the time, Artaxerxes II.

The King's Peace, however, would not be the final say in who would dominate the Greek world. For shortly thereafter, Athens joined a new alliance with other city-states and rose up to challenge its antagonists. Called the Second Athenian League, this union consisted of Athens along with a smattering of city-states of the Ionian and Aegean Seas. This alliance was markedly different from previous ones since Athens, apparently learning lessons from its past, made a real effort to not lord over its allies.

But although this was indeed more considerate for its partners, it also created a vacuum of leadership, and the Second Athenian League quickly proved to be too indecisive to make any real difference in the power politics of the Mediterranean world. The next attempt at peacemaking occurred in 371 BCE when Athens and Sparta, along with Persia, brought about plans for a general peace.

Sparta's rival Thebes initially indicated that it would sign off on the agreement, but it was only willing to do so if it was allowed to represent the Boeotian cities. Boeotia is a region of central Greece of which Thebes is a part. So essentially, the Thebans wanted to be recognized as the main player from their district.

The Spartans, however, did not want Thebes to take a leading role among the Boeotian cities and rejected the offer outright. Instead, the king of Sparta, Cleombrotos, decided to march directly on the region to subjugate it. The Thebans and Spartans then faced off against each other on the plain of Leuctra. The Thebans were able to defeat the Spartans, and King Cleombrotos was killed during the course of the conflict. This marked the end of Spartan dominance in the region.

Interestingly enough, however, in a virtual replay of what had happened to Athens many years before, the significantly weakened Sparta ended up aligning itself with its old nemesis of Athens so that the two could present a united front against the suddenly resurgent power of Thebes. But it wasn't Thebes that Athens had to worry about but rather a surprise incursion from neighboring Macedonia when a man named Alexander wished to make himself great.

Chapter 6 – The Rise of Macedonia

"You see—Oh Greeks! The Enemy already acknowledge the country to be ours; for when they made peace with us, they stipulated that we should not burn the country belonging to the king, and now they set fire to it themselves, as if they looked upon it no longer as their own."

-Xenophon

Even while the Greek city-states were weakening each other with all of their intermittent skirmishes, Macedonia to the north of Greece proper was steadily increasing its might. Unlike the Greeks, the Macedonians did not reside in city-states and loose confederations but rather in an autocratic kingdom with centralized authority over the entire nation state. Although Macedonia has at times been considered a Greek-influenced region, actual Greeks did not consider the Macedonians a part of their heritage.

Since the Macedonians did not have a good handle on the Greek language and did not have a form of governance with which the Greeks were familiar, such as a democracy or an oligarchy, the

Greeks considered the Macedonians as hopeless outsiders. So, it is a little ironic that it was these "outsiders" who would come to spread the Greek language and culture all over the known world.

Nevertheless, the Greeks had long looked down on Macedonians as being their backward, uncivilized, and unenlightened neighbors. And for much of its early history, Macedonia was also known to be militarily inferior to its Greek neighbors. But by the 300s, all this was steadily changing. The Macedonian monarchy was growing in strength, and so, too, were its armies. The first truly promising and strong Macedonian leader came in the form of King Philip II in 357 BCE.

Philip would build Macedonia's military up to be the most formidable in the region. Later Greek historians would attribute this accomplishment to the force of Philip's own personality. It seems that Philip was able to unite Macedonia even while the Greek city-states remained divided. He was then able to use this united front to take full advantage of his hopelessly divided neighbors.

It wasn't always smooth sailing for King Philip, however, and he had to work to gain the dominance that he eventually achieved. At the beginning of his reign, he had inherited a divisive and fractured kingdom. But through Philip's skill as a politician, he was able to bring the factions of his kingdom together. He also wasn't above bribing or even assassinating those with whom he didn't see eye to eye. Whatever it took, Philip muscled and manipulated his way to unquestioned authority.

And once he was at the top, he made sure that Macedonia's troops were well trained and ready to fight. He built up his army primarily on the lower classes, with whom he had developed a cult of personality in which he was at the center. Along with military might, Philip also recognized the importance of culture, in particular, Greek culture. He knew that the Greeks had forged a very unique and powerful form of civilization, and he wished to emulate it within his own kingdom.

As such, he established a brand-new Hellenized capital in Macedonia, which he called Pella. He also recruited some Greek advisors into his own inner circle. The Greek city-states, in the meantime, began to take notice of Macedonia's ambition. Greek politician Demosthenes was particularly astute as to what Philip was up to, and he openly warned people about it in several lectures called the *Philippics*.

Despite this early warning from the likes of Demosthenes, the tidings of impending doom were mostly ignored. In the meantime, Macedonian King Philip was on the march, waging war and taking territory by force. And soon, he had incorporated several of Greece's northernmost city-states into his empire. He then surprised everyone by annexing territory to his east, which gave him direct control of Mount Pangaeus, which had valuable silver and gold mines.

Philip now had not only a sound army but also sound finances with which to consolidate his base even further. With his fortunes even further secured, he managed to pressure Thessaly into entering a partnership with him and then pushed his influence onto several other Greek city-states. Throughout all of this, Thebes had become considerably weaker after several years of battling its neighboring city-state of Phocis, a struggle that often revolved around who had access to the sanctuary of Delphi, which was located in Phocis.

Even though Phocis was smaller than Thebes, the fact that they oversaw the sanctuary of Delphi, where many Greek pilgrims visited and left offerings of gold, silver, and the like, meant they had tremendous resources at their disposal to hire outside fighters to engage their enemies. Thus, Phocis was able to fight off the more powerful Thebes for several years. It was only in 346 that Philip decided to put his thumb on the scale in this seemingly never-ending conflict between the two city-states and coerced them both into coming to terms.

It was only after this direct and obvious foreign interference from Macedonia that Athens became truly alarmed and entered into an alliance with Thebes. These developments ultimately led to a showdown between Philip and these two Greek allies when the Macedonian king sent his army to Athens in 338 BCE. The forces of Athens and Thebes were ill-prepared to stand up to what amounted to the most well-trained military force in the region. Philip's troops moved in machine-like precision, moving forward in a solid formation with their long pikes with which they steadily tore through their enemies.

In addition to the pike-wielding infantry, the Macedonians also employed a cavalry that could quickly strike out at the enemy before pulling back. At the onset of the battle, the Greeks actually had the numerical advantage, fielding a force of about thirty-eight thousand troops compared to the Macedonians' thirty-two thousand, but the ferocious pikemen of Philip very rapidly bridged that gap. The cavalry, which was led by Philip's soon-to-be-famous son Alexander, was also quite good at decimating the Greek defenders.

At one point during the battle, the Theban forces had stretched themselves too thin, and Alexander was able to lead the cavalry full-force into the vulnerable section of the Theban line, smashing right through their ranks. This cut the army in half and allowed Alexander and his men to completely decimate the cornered Thebans. The entire Greek defense fell apart shortly after that, and soon, the Macedonians were in complete control of the situation.

But unlike the worst fears of Demosthenes, who predicted the complete destruction of the Greek city-states if Philip took over, Philip showed a surprising amount of benevolence to those he had just vanquished. No petty retributions were conducted; instead, the Greek city-states were simply asked to become partners with Macedonia. In order to show their respect for the Athenians, Philip even went as far as to have Alexander personally deliver the ashes of those Athenians who had perished in the conflict.

The Greeks were almost relieved at the results of their defeat, and only Sparta would remain hesitant in accepting the dominance of Macedonia. To make things official, one year after his successful military campaign, Philip brought the Greek leaders together in Corinth and had them swear their undying support to Macedonia in what would become known as the League of Corinth, also sometimes known simply as the Hellenic League.

This Hellenic League would become the unified force that would spread Macedonian-led conquests far and wide. For all of the freedoms of democracy, it was the top-down nature of Macedonia's centralized government, headed by a Macedonian king, that enabled the consistency necessary for true empire-building. First Philip and then his son Alexander would come to steadily dominate much of the known world.

But not everyone in the Greek-speaking world was so thrilled about being a part of this dynamic imperialist machine. The Macedonians were viewed as outsiders, and the idea that the independent city-states would have to follow the mandates of this outside force was, in their eyes, the worst kind of tyranny. Even worse than the thirty tyrants was the tyranny of this foreign influence from Macedonia.

Philip himself was well aware of this lack of trust, and the crafty and cunning politician in him wanted to find a way to bring his Greek subjects into a more authentic allegiance. An Athenian political leader by the name of Isocrates brought Philip the key he was looking for to unify the masses. Isocrates urged Philip to bring the Greek city-states together on a campaign to take on the old enemy of the Greeks—the Persians. Having a common enemy certainly does tend to bring folks together, and Philip readily agreed with this strategy.

And so it was at the dawning of the League of Corinth that Philip made clear his plans of sending the whole Greek-speaking world once again on a crash course with the Persian civilization. A year after this pronouncement, Philip sent his general Parmenion to make his way to Anatolia so that the first stepping stone toward an all-out invasion could be made.

All of the machinery for this great conquest was already in place, but the man behind the wheel would soon be taken from the helm. Philip, as powerful as he was, had become surrounded by much intrigue in his personal court. Philip had a total of six women whom he called his wife, but only one of these brides was considered his queen—Alexander's mother, Olympias.

Queen Olympias was of royal stock; she had formerly been a princess of Epirus or what today would be considered the country of Albania before she married King Philip. Initially, Alexander was Philip's only potential successor, and he had been groomed as such. Alexander had what in those days amounted to the finest in education, being personally tutored by the great Greek scholar Aristotle. But in 336 BCE, Philip took yet another woman to be his bride, which caused a rift between him and both Alexander and Olympias.

Philip ultimately divorced Olympias and had her sent back to her homeland of Epirus, which was a part of the ancient Greek world that today constitutes part of Albania. But even though King Philip had divorced his wife, she was still the mother of the heir to the throne and, therefore, held some considerable clout. However, there were some decidedly nasty rumors floating about that threatened to take even her claim as the mother of the heir apparent away from her.

At the heart of the drama seems to be insinuations that Olympia had been unfaithful to Philip, and there was even gossip that Alexander might be illegitimate. Although these rumors seem to be unfounded and perhaps were purposefully started by Philip himself, there was some fear that Alexander could be demoted. Alexander and his mother knew that any potential offspring from his father's new union could somehow disrupt Alexander's own destiny.

However, most historians dismiss this since Alexander was the oldest son, and he was already well on his way to becoming Philip's heir. Nevertheless, there was tension in regard to Philip's new wife and what might result from their pairing. Despite the drama, Philip and Alexander managed to reconcile for a time, and Alexander even attended his father's wedding. But things quickly got out of hand when one of Philip's generals allegedly gave a toast to Philip and his new wife, wishing their union to produce a "legitimate" heir for Macedonia.

If this event really did occur (historians are still unsure if it did or not), it would have been an obvious snub to Alexander and his right to succeed his father. And Alexander wasn't going to take such an insult sitting down. According to tradition, he jumped right up onto his feet. Staring down the general who dared to say such hurtful words, he took the cup of wine he was holding and hurled it into the general's face. Philip was apparently ready to side with his general over his own son and immediately stood up with his sword drawn.

But Philip only managed to take a few steps toward Alexander before he stumbled, tripped, and fell to the ground. Philip had apparently drunk way too much for his own good and lost his footing. Some might speculate that it is possible that Philip only pretended to be drunk as a means of avoiding a full-blown confrontation with his son. As crude as such a ruse was, it would have saved Philip some face. No one present could say that he did not answer his son's challenge, yet at the same time, he could avoid actually hurting his son by blaming his inaction on being drunk.

At any rate, after his dad's stumble, Alexander angrily ridiculed his father, declaring, "Look, everyone! The man who wants to cross Europe to Asia can't even make it from one couch to the next!" After this dramatic event, Alexander went to live in Epirus, where his exiled mother Olympias was staying at the time. While he was away, Philip's new wife gave birth to a baby.

However, this child was no threat to Alexander since she was a female, and as was the case with just about all monastic dynasties of the day, the male typically inherited the throne. New tidings then came to Alexander shortly thereafter that his father was planning to marry Alexander's sister, who was also a child of Queen Olympia, to an uncle of his in Epicurus.

Back in those days, it wasn't at all uncommon for a niece to marry an uncle, a nephew to marry an aunt, or cousins to marry each other. Today, such things would be viewed as bizarre, but back then, it was considered acceptable, especially within royal families that were attempting to solidify dynastic bonds. And this arranged marriage to a relative in Epicurus was apparently Philip's attempt to build some new bridges over the previous ones he had burned.

As was customary, Philip once again staged an elaborate wedding banquet, and of course, Alexander was invited. Alexander, seeking to mend fences, obliged his father and attended. But there would be even more drama afoot, this time not involving Alexander at all but rather a spurned courtesan by the name of Pausanias. The exact details of what led to this assassin's grievance against Philip are a bit murky, but it seems that a deep personal animosity had developed.

At the king's court, Pausanias is said to have been a personal favorite of King Philip, and according to some accounts, the two were even said to be lovers. Philip, however, had a roving eye and started seeking the favors of another male paramour. Pausanias was upset about all of this, and he began a vicious gossip campaign against the new lover, slandering him in all kinds of ways. But what apparently hurt the man the most was the slanderous remarks in which he was accused of being a coward.

In the rough-and-tumble world of ancient Macedonia, bravery meant everything. And to prove his bravery, the ridiculed young man went to the front lines of the Macedonian army. He ended up being killed in battle as a result. Both Philip and his top general, Attalus, were upset with what had transpired.

Attalus, for his part, was beside himself with rage that Pausanias would commit what he viewed as being an entirely dastardly and cowardly act. The man who died as a result of Pausanias's machinations also happened to be a friend of his. So, it was with this frame of mind that Attalus decided to take justice (albeit his warped sense of it) into his own hands and punish Pausanias.

And Attalus would do so with the most insidious of intrigue by initially befriending Pausanias. He actually invited Pausanias over to a get-together with some of his other friends. They plied Pausanias with alcohol until he was incapacitated. And when Pausanias was too drunk to resist, his utter humiliation began. The men took off Pausanias's clothes and proceeded to gang-rape him.

As soon as he had recovered enough to do so, Pausanias sought out King Philip in order to punish Attalus and his other attackers. Philp is said to have genuinely felt sorry for his former friend, but since he needed his trusted general on the front lines, he opted not to pursue any charges. It is said that this humiliation burned in Pausanias's mind so much that he decided to take Philip's life.

Of course, all of this is ultimately speculation since Pausanias was struck down and killed shortly after he committed the act. Pausanias would not live long enough to give his own personal account for his actions. After stabbing Philip right through the heart, Pausanias attempted to make a break for it. There was nowhere for the killer to run, however, and he was quite easily intercepted. And rather than arresting him and questioning him as to his motives, he was simply killed right there on the spot.

For some, things appear to have happened a little too conveniently. Could it be that there was a larger plot afoot that involved Queen Olympias? What if she had hired Pausanias to kill the king? If she had, it is possible that she covered her tracks by ordering those close to her to immediately kill the assassin after he carried out the hit. Dead men don't talk after all. This is all just conjecture, of course, and much about what really happened to King Philip remains a mystery. The sudden rise of Philip's son Alexander to greatness, however, is not.

Chapter 7 – Enter Alexander the Great

"Those who intend on becoming great should love neither themselves nor their own things, but only what is just, whether it happens to be done by themselves or others."

-Plato

After Philip II's sudden demise in 336 BCE, his son Alexander was named king of Macedon at just twenty years of age. Alexander wasted no time in getting his house in order. Knowing that loyalty was everything, he made sure to reshuffle the deck of courtesans to those who were most sympathetic to him. Alexander then looked abroad, where whispers of rebellion began to surface among the recently conquered Greek city-states, which wished to test the will of the young new ruler.

Alexander knew all too well that he had to present a strong face to these subject nations if he was going to be able to keep the Hellenic League together. The first to test the new king was Thessaly, which had begun its rebellion by blocking off certain roadways in and out of the region. It was not the worst offense that the Thessalonians could have engaged in, but Alexander knew that if he didn't come down on them—and come down hard—this trespass would only lead to more.

Thus, Alexander was determined to march right over to Thessaly to knock some heads. And the way he did so was rather ingenious. For even though the Thessalonians had blocked the roads into the region, Alexander simply had his engineers build a new road through the rear of the mountain passes. The Thessalonians, who were actively guarding the other side of the mountains, were horrified to find Alexander and his army suddenly drop on top of them. The battle quickly turned into a rout, and the desperate Thessalonians were forced to quickly come to terms.

With the Thessalonians groveling at his feet, Alexander then marched south to Thebes. Ever since Philip's death, the Thebans had been restless and were considering an open rebellion just like the Thessalonians. All it took to change their minds was the sight of Alexander at the head of his massive army, galloping up to the outskirts of their city. Without any struggle at all, the Thebans agreed to recognize Alexander's authority.

After subduing Thebes, Alexander went over to Thermopylae and found them to be already compliant. And every region he visited seemed equally compliant until, finally, Alexander reached Corinth, and in full sight of the representatives of the League of Corinth, he was proclaimed as the "leader for life."

Shortly after this proclamation, a rather conspicuous incident is said to have occurred. While Alexander was camped in Corinth, a man wandered into the city, claiming to have been attacked by Persian troops who were harassing the neighboring city of Ephesus. It would later be learned that the man was actually someone Alexander had hired to pretend to be a war-torn refugee in order to stoke the flames of Greek resentment against the Persians. But it worked. The League of Corinth was indignant that the Persians would attack one of their own. Fully confident in the might of Macedonia, the city-states agreed to throw in their lot in a renewed war against Persia.

Early on, fractures in this alliance would emerge. And predictably—if not outrageously—enough, it was the Thebans who once again began to rebel against Alexander. It is a bit hard to fathom how Thebes could consider rebelling against Alexander so soon after a previous rebellion had been put down, but it seems that the Greek politician Demosthenes might have had something to do with it. Demosthenes was a popular speaker and was making his rounds in Athens. He was known to stir folks to action just by the sound of his voice. This time, however, he was apparently spreading outright falsehoods, for he started to circulate the claim that Alexander had perished on the front lines.

When this bit of fake news reached Thebes, the Thebans got excited and decided to rebel once again. It must have come as quite a shock when the Macedonian monarch showed up on the outskirts of their city alive and well. This time, there would be no fighting but rather outright annihilation. Alexander burned the city to the ground. The rest of the Greek city-states took the lesson of Thebes to heart, and attempts at rebellion soon ceased.

With everyone else falling in behind him, Alexander could finally focus on what he really wanted—a Pan-Hellenic conquest of the East. Alexander and his armies reached Anatolia around 337 BCE, and with an army of some forty thousand troops—one-fourth of which were likely Greek—the march toward the Persian Empire commenced. Initially, Alexander's forces were greeted as liberators since they were primarily encountering the Greek settlements on the Anatolian coast.

The first encounter with Persian forces occurred farther east at Granikos River, just outside of the outskirts of a city called Priapus. Alexander's forces were outnumbered by the Persians, but he urged his comrades on. Upon making contact with the enemy, a pitched battle ensued in which both sides fought with ferocious desperation. Alexander himself quickly became a target due to his brightly shining armor. It seems that he was easily recognized as the leader of the group, and due to the gleam of his regalia, Persian arrows were quick to find their mark.

At one point, even a Persian swordsman was able to get close enough to the Macedonian to strike the back of his helmeted head. The sword cut right through Alexander's helmet and went through skin and bone. It was just a flesh wound, but it was a gruesome one at that. Fortunately for Alexander, this was the closest the Persians would get to him. And it was not for lack of trying.

Alexander's ostentatious armor made him stand out, so the Persians began zeroing in on him. They became so obsessed about it, in fact, that they opened themselves up to being butchered by making blind charges toward Alexander's heavily guarded position. Macedonian troops cut down Persian after Persian as they forgot all else and threw themselves headlong at Alexander. They must have thought that by taking out the leader, the battle would end, but after they were unable to do so, all they had to show for their efforts was the wasted lives of countless Persian troops. Soon, the Persians death toll was too high for them to continue their efforts, and they decided to make a run for it.

After this first victory against the Persians, Alexander famously ordered his men to gather up about three hundred suits of armor from slain or captured Persians, and he had it sent off to Athens. He proclaimed that these trophies were dedicated to Athena as some kind of good luck charms to bring him further victories. Alexander then marched on to Ephesus, the very place from which news of a false flag attack had originated. The Ephesians did not welcome Alexander with open arms; on the contrary, the town, despite its heavy Greek population, initially attempted to put up a resistance. It was a fleeting one, however, and in rather short order, Alexander's mighty army convinced them otherwise.

Since this is a book on Greek history and not a book on the deeds of the Macedonian Alexander the Great, delving too much into his exploits can be distracting. So as not to get too off track, Alexander's conquests can be summarized as follows. After bringing Anatolia to heel, Alexander headed south to Syria, which was also a part of Persian Emperor Darius III's domain. It was there, in Syria, that Darius himself led his army to a colossal confrontation with Alexander and his men.

The two forces collided near the town of Issos (also spelled as Issus). The wide, open terrain proved beneficial to Alexander's forces, but the Persian cavalry was still able to inflict devastating losses. Nevertheless, Alexander's forces were able to finally break through the Persian lines, and not only that, Alexander managed to make contact with Darius himself. The two began to clash openly with each other.

Alexander's leg was injured in the fray before they both tumbled to the ground and fought hand to hand. Darius, knowing that the battle was lost, is said to have "torn off his royal robes" and retreated with the remnant of his forces. But in his haste, he did not bring his own wife and mother with him. Even though his advisors had warned him against bringing members of the royal family to the fight, Darius had brought them regardless.

He would regret it. Now, Alexander had two important royal hostages in his custody. Darius probably figured that Alexander was going to use them for leverage, but he never did. At one point, Darius even gave Alexander an extremely generous offer for a truce. Darius proclaimed that he would allow Alexander to keep all of the lands in Asia Minor that he was already in possession of, along with certain financial compensation and the hand of his daughter in marriage. Alexander could have all of this if he simply returned Darius's wife and mother to him unharmed.

However, Alexander revealed just how cold and callous he could be by refusing to enter into any negotiations. Instead, he headed farther south to the city of Tyre (in what is modern-day Lebanon) and besieged the city. The siege lasted for about seven months, but Alexander was ultimately victorious. During the siege, it is said that the city's defenders actually used a form of Greek fire on Alexander and his men.

This was essentially a sticky, napalm-like substance that was poured down from the city walls on top of Alexander and his troops. This terrible onslaught forced Alexander to make a tactical retreat. But it wasn't long before he and his military machine charged right back into place. This time around, they broke through the walls of Tyre and then laid waste to the city, killing some seven thousand of its residents.

After this rampage, Alexander went to Egypt, where he furthered his conquests, adding the Egyptians to his column and even founding a new city named after himself—Alexandria. This city would become a Greek metropolis and an international commercial hub of the Mediterranean. Alexander's next major campaign took him back up through Syria and then into what was then called Mesopotamia, which was a region comprised of parts of modern-day Syria, Turkey, Iraq, and Iran.

It was here, out on the Nineveh Plains in 331 BCE, that a climactic battle between the forces of Alexander and the Persian Empire would unfold. For this rematch, Darius had fielded an even larger force, greatly outnumbering Alexander's army. If Alexander had been your average person, he might have been kicking himself at this point for not accepting Darius's earlier generous offer for a truce since, for all intents and purposes, it looked as if all of the Macedonians were about to be annihilated.

But Alexander was not your average person. Even though he was greatly outnumbered, he pushed his army forward. By using an ingenious technique, he had his troops approach in a diagonal fashion so that the right flank would make contact with the Persian forces first. This allowed the Macedonian army the defensive advantage of collapsing into a protective square formation if the Persians threatened to surround them. The right flank could work like a battering ram against the Persian lines and then pull back to a defensive position when things became too much to handle.

Alexander himself led the decisive cavalry charge that broke through the enemy lines. Not only that, but Alexander also managed to launch an assault on Darius's own chariot. The driver was actually killed by one of Alexander's comrades, and in the confusion of the battle, many of the nearby Persians mistook the slain driver for being Darius. This caused great discord and distress in the Persian ranks, and some began to openly desert the fight, thinking that it was all over.

Darius, in the meantime, once again made a break for it, and he fled from the scene with whatever of his entourage he could get. At this point, Darius had basically lost control of his whole empire, and he was a man hunted, hounded, and in hiding. Alexander was able to step into just about any Persian capital and claim himself to be in control. A short time later, Alexander received an update on Darius. He learned that the Persian king had actually been usurped by a Persian general named Bessus, who was now claiming to be the new emperor.

Of course, Alexander could not allow such a challenge to go unopposed. He sent in his troops, and Bessus's forces were defeated. However, before they could reach Darius, he had already been fatally stabbed by Bessus. Alexander managed to see his old nemesis right before he expired. Although Alexander no doubt would have liked to have slain Darius himself, seeing him in such a pathetic state actually made the Macedonian feel sorry for him. In fact, he had Darius buried with full honors.

Alexander was now recognized as the new Persian emperor, as well as the titular king of several other countries and principalities. This was not enough for him, though, and he eventually pushed on into regions as far as Uzbekistan, Afghanistan, and even western India. Alexander is said to have wanted to push even farther east, but his own army threatened to revolt if he did so.

It was for this reason that Alexander finally decided to settle for the territories he had gained, and he began to consolidate his holdings. His number one goal now was to find a way to unify all of the Macedonians, Greeks, Persians, Mesopotamians, Egyptians, and the like into one coherent empire. These plans were interrupted, however, when Alexander came down with a terrible fever and perished in 323 BCE.

The man who could not be bested on the battlefield succumbed to a viral infection. With his death, his empire splintered into several factions. But even so, Greek culture had already spread far and wide, and thanks to Alexander, the world would never be quite the same again.

Chapter 8 – The Aftermath of Alexander's Empire and the Beginning of the Greco-Roman Civilization

"If something were brought about without an antecedent cause, it would be untrue that all things come about through fate. But if it is plausible that all events have an antecedent cause, what ground can be offered for not conceding that all things come about through fate?"

-Chrysippus

At the time of his death in 323 BCE, Alexander the Great had spread Greek culture far and wide. And in many ways, the seeds that he planted would eventually give rise to that later Hellenistic-inspired conglomeration of nations—the Roman Empire. In the immediate aftermath of Alexander's demise, however, what would have been his Pan-Hellenic empire fractured into what could be termed as being several different Hellenistic kingdoms, which were ruled by his generals.

It must be stressed that although the generals were themselves Macedonian, they adopted the Greek culture and typically had Greek officials in their administrations; most of them even ruled over sizeable Greek populations. The general who ruled over the largest piece of territory was a Macedonian man named Seleucus. He ended up controlling Persia and Syria, and it was from his name that the Seleucid dynasty sprung.

Another successful former general of Alexander's was Ptolemy. Ptolemy famously set up shop in Egypt and essentially became a Hellenized pharaoh, whose line would only end with the death of the famous Cleopatra in 30 BCE.

Antigonus, another one of Alexander's generals, o would eventually take control of Macedonia and much of Greece. After Alexander the Great's death, it was actually the fate of Macedonia that would be in the greatest dispute.

Before Alexander had died, he had taken a wife by the name of Roxanne. Roxanne was pregnant when Alexander perished in 323 BCE. Shortly after Alexander's death, Roxanne gave birth to a son who was Christened Alexander IV. Since this child was obviously not old enough to rule, a regent by the name of Perdiccas was placed in charge of the day-to-day affairs until Alexander IV came of age. Alexander IV, however, would only get to live to be thirteen years old, as he was brutally murdered in the summer of 309 BCE.

After much infighting, one of Alexander's old generals, Antigonus, finally managed to set up a successful successor state. Although Alexander's empire had splintered, the Greek kingdoms that emerged (at least when they weren't fighting with each other) developed great economic, commercial, and cultural ties with one another. The doors had been pried open for extensive trade. Wine from Syria, papyrus from Egypt, spices from India, and gold from

Greece were all available commodities, and they were shipped back and forth between the kingdoms of this suddenly Hellenized world.

And it wasn't just goods that received traffic far and wide but also ideas. Greek philosophies, such as stoicism, cynicism, and epicureanism, were suddenly circulating to other regions. It seems that since the Greeks no longer had to focus so much on defending themselves since they were under the protection of Macedonia, it gave them much more time to think—and think they did. Greek philosophers set up whole schools of thought, and many of these ideas found a place within the halls of none other than the Great Library of Alexandria, which had become the decided repository of the Hellenistic knowledge that had thus far been accumulated.

The first of these Hellenized kingdoms to fall was the one founded by Antigonus, which revolved around Macedonia itself. This occurred during the time of Antigonus's grandson, who was also named Antigonus or, as it were, Antigonus II Gonatas. The Gonatas part of his name was actually a nickname that translates as "kneecap." The reason behind this odd nickname has been subsequently lost to history. At any rate, it was during Antigonus II Gonatas's reign that Greece suffered a massive invasion around 270 BCE by a band of roving Celts.

These invaders were successfully repulsed, and they were forced to flee to Anatolia, where they were brought to task by Pergamon, who was the Hellenistic potentate of the region. Pergamon exiled the defeated Celts to Galatia. Shortly after the Celtic invasion, Antigonus II Gonatas had to fend off an invasion sent by the neighboring Kingdom of Epirus. Epirus was ruled by King Pyrrhus, from whom the famed expression "Pyrrhic victory" comes. Gonatas stayed the course in Macedon until he died in 239 BCE.

Antigonus II Gonatas would be succeeded by his male heir, a son by the name of Demetrius II. Demetrius would then reign supreme over Macedon over the course of the next ten years. At the very end of his tenure as king, the kingdom began to splinter. Demetrius II was succeeded by his son Philip V. Philip II of

Macedon may have begun Macedonia's rise to prominence, but ironically enough, Philip V of Macedon reigned over its demise.

This was due to a growing power to the west—the Roman Republic. The Romans, with their capital in Italy, had previously waged war with their powerful Carthaginian neighbors in North Africa. In 201 BCE, the Romans successfully put the Carthaginians down. With their southern front clear, the Romans began to look toward their eastern frontier, and soon, Macedonia fell into their sights.

Rome desired conquest, and as it pertained to Macedonia, it certainly did not help matters that the king of the Macedonians, Philip V, had previously aligned himself with Carthage. The Romans used this as a pretext for a punitive expedition. This charge was led by Roman commander Quinctius Flamininus. Initially, the Macedonians were able to hold their own, engaging in a classic phalanx formation, but it did not take long for the Romans to break the Macedonians' lines.

With the Macedonian army defeated, Philip was forced to follow the directives of the Roman who had bested him. It came as some surprise, however, when the Roman commander directed the Macedonian ruler to grant autonomy to the Greek city-states that had been under his dominion. It is unclear what Flamininus thought this would accomplish, but it seems he opened up Pandora's box. For as soon as freedom was restored, the Greeks went back to their old ways of fighting amongst each other, and not only that, they also began waging war against the Romans who had just freed them.

Soon, the most rebellious of the Greeks—Sparta—was in open conflict with the forces of Flamininus. This Spartan rebellion was led by a man by the name of Nabis, who was going around Greek city-states and stirring up the local populaces with promises of land redistribution should they stage a successful revolt. Such tidings were particularly alarming for the senators of the Roman Republic since they were primarily made up of the landed elite. As such, any mention of a major redistribution of land was perceived as an enormous threat to the social order, and not just for Greece but also the rest of the Mediterranean.

In order to contain this revolutionary ferment, the Roman senators did not hesitate to authorize military action, and soon, Roman troops were in Sparta putting down the political uprising.

Philip, in the meantime, eventually managed to wrestle back control of Macedonia, but it was short-lived. After another climactic battle with the Romans in 167 BCE, the Romans were able to assert their dominance once again in the region.

Initially, Rome sought out a hands-off approach with the Greeks, but when it was clear that this would not be tenable, Rome increased the reach of its direct control. First, the northern portions of Greece were lumped together with Macedonia, and they were referred to as the Roman province of Macedonia. Soon after this, southern and central Greece were lumped together into what was termed the province of Achaea.

After Roman dominion was assured, the regular Roman citizens began to show up in Greek lands to do business with the Greeks. It is said that the island of Delos, in particular, was transformed into a great financial hub for business. Sadly enough, much of this business was in literal human capital since Delos had a large slave trade operation, in which as many as ten thousand slaves were trafficked out of Greece every single day. The signs of the affluent Romans that came here to do business are still evident in the form of ancient Roman villas, whose interiors are decorated with elaborate mosaic tiles.

The Romans were not always welcomed, however, and internal discord and rebellion were frequent occurrences. One of the most impressive rebellions against Rome occurred in 88 BCE when Mithridates, a Hellenized king who reigned over the Kingdom of Pontus on the southern shores of the Black Sea, began to strike out against Romans in the region. These acts inspired the neighboring

Greeks to commit likewise acts, and soon, Mithridates was viewed as their own personal champion of freedom.

However, this march to freedom wasn't a pretty one. When several Greek city-states rose up to throw off the yoke of their perceived oppressors, it is said that thousands of visiting Romans were caught completely unaware and were slaughtered. The Greeks would face a severe backlash, and in 84 BCE, Roman general Lucius Cornelius Sulla (better known simply as Sulla), with the full might of Rome behind him, marched over to the Aegean and crushed Mithridates's army. He then marched on Athens itself, taking the city by force.

Over the next few decades, both Greece and Rome would see great shifts in the political sands. A man named Julius Caesar would rise up as a leading figure of the Roman Republic only to be assassinated in 44 BCE. This would mark the end of the Roman Republic, and it was followed by a period of turmoil that would ultimately result in the birth of the Roman Empire around 30 BCE, which was headed by the first Roman emperor—Augustus.

Roman rule managed to bring an end to the constant infighting between Greek city-states. Now everyone was under the same Roman administration, and they more or less fell in line with what their Roman procurators asked of them. There was no more wondering what the hot-headed Thebans might do come spring or if Sparta would launch a sneak attack on Athens—all of this incessant fighting was a thing of the past under direct Roman control.

The peace and security that the Romans provided allowed the Greeks to not worry about the potential for outside conflict and instead focus internally on themselves. This allowed philosophy and intellectual endeavors to flourish once more. And the Romans, despite their conquest of the Hellenized world, seemed to genuinely respect Greek culture and philosophy, adopting much of it themselves.

It was this symbiosis that gave rise to what is often termed to be Greco-Roman sensibilities. The admiration of Greece was a common occurrence in Imperial Rome. And some Roman emperors, such as the infamous Nero, put Greece on the top of the list when it came to palaces outside of Rome to pay homage to. He may have gone down in history as a crazed and bloodthirsty tyrant, but Nero knew great culture when he saw it. In 66 CE, he famously visited the region to personally participate in Olympic-styled sports, theater, and musical performances. Nero being Nero, of course, would have always received the gold medal in the Olympics since anything less could have resulted in the execution of those giving out the awards!

Other Roman emperors, such as Marcus Aurelius, were deeply steeped in Greek philosophy. Emperor Aurelius was a fervent practitioner of stoicism, the Greek philosophy that stresses self-control and moderation. But, of course, the biggest and most defining influence to hit the Greek-speaking world during the Pax Romana ("Roman Peace") wouldn't be stoicism, cynicism, or epicureanism; instead, it would be a new strain of Judaism imported from the Middle East called Christianity.

Chapter 9 – Christianity in the Greek-Speaking World

"For I choose to follow not men or men's doctrines, but God and the doctrines [delivered] by Him. For if you have fallen in with some who are called Christians, but who do not admit this [truth], and venture to blaspheme the God of Abraham, and the God of Isaac, and the God of Jacob; who say there is no resurrection of the dead, and that their souls, when they die are taken to heaven; do not imagine that they are Christians."

-Justin Martyr

Greece had always been a crossroads of ideas. Having said that, it is only natural that a vibrant new religion called Christianity might eventually make the rounds. Leading this charge was Paul the Apostle, who toured a string of Greek communities around 50 CE. Before we get into Paul's ministry in the Greek-speaking world, let us delve into his background a little bit.

Paul, who in his early life went by Saul, was born in a Hellenized Jewish community in Tarsus. He grew up with his foot in two worlds—that of the Hellenized Greeks and that of traditional Jewish culture and belief. Paul was a serious student of the Torah from a young age, and immediately after his bar mitzvah, he trained under the pharisaical Rabbi Gamaliel. He became a zealous believer in rabbinical law and sought to stamp out any deviation from Judaism. So, when Christianity became popular in Jerusalem, Paul looked at the nascent movement with worry and concern. And soon enough, he was moved to try and stamp it out, lest all of Israel became infected with what he viewed as false teachings.

In his passion to drive the Christians out, Paul became relentless in his persecution of them. According to New Testament scripture, he even stood watch while one of the apostles—Steven—was stoned to death. According to the Bible, Paul then made a trip to Damascus, Syria, with the intention of rooting out Christian gatherings that had formed there. It was on the road to Damascus that Paul allegedly encountered the supernatural. He later claimed to have seen a vision of a radiant light in the middle of the road, from which a voice inquired, "Saul! Saul! Why do you persecute me?" Paul asked, "Who are you, Lord?" At which the figure is said to have replied, "I am Jesus, whom you are persecuting." Without getting into too much of the details of Paul's visionary experience, it was after this road to Damascus moment that Saul the persecutor changed his name to Paul and went from persecuting Christians to being the most active spreader of the gospel. Of course, there are those who might debate the merits of the accounts in the New Testament, but as far as history goes (as well as Paul's letters stating the same), it was this moment that changed Paul's life forever.

And now that we have briefly looked at Paul's background and what allegedly led him to become a missionary, let us delve into his missionary exploits in the Greek-speaking world. Paul's first major mission abroad was actually in the city of Antioch in Anatolia. From here, he departed to Cyprus. In Cyprus, Paul and his fellow missionary Barnabas stopped at Salamis before heading to the Greek city of Paphos. It was in Paphos that Paul had a rather interesting encounter with a man named Bar-Jesus.

In the Jewish world, the name "Jesus" was actually a variation of Joshua. The name itself was not unusual. And the Hebrew prefix of "Bar" simply means son. So, someone named "Bar-Jesus" would literally be someone known as "Son of Jesus." Despite the similarity of his name, this man was nothing at all like Jesus Christ. In fact, it was said that he was a "sorcerer" and that he viciously heckled Paul at one of his speaking engagements.

According to the Book of Acts in the New Testament, Paul eventually grew so sick of the harassment that he shouted at the man, "You son of the devil, full of every sort of deceit and fraud, and enemy of all that is good! Will you never stop preventing the true ways of the Lord?" Paul then followed up his outrage with one of the few times that an apostle actually cursed someone. For it is said he shouted at the troublemaker, "Watch now, for the Lord has laid his hand of punishment upon you, and you will be struck blind, you will not see sunlight for some time." And sure enough, at least according to the biblical narrative, the man went blind.

Besides blinding folks, scripture tells us that Paul was able to get many of the local Greek-speaking population to convert to Christianity. Paul then headed back to Anatolia, where he ended up at the Greek settlement of Perga. Paul was once again able to spread his message to the populace, and many became acquainted with Christianity. Paul then went to the nearby Greek settlement of Iconium, and once again, Paul was well received. However, due to antagonism by local authority figures, he wrapped things up rather quickly before heading over to the settlement of Lystra.

Here, scripture tells us that Paul managed to heal a man who was unable to walk. Upon seeing this miracle, the Greeks who were present began to proclaim in astonishment that Paul and his partner Barnabas were gods. Yes, you heard that right; instead of considering the men as being messengers of the divine, their Greek audience was convinced that Paul and Barnabas themselves were divine beings. And as they talked amongst themselves in astonishment, they insisted that Paul must be a manifestation of Hermes and Barnabas a manifestation of Zeus.

As one might imagine, Paul was not too pleased with this sudden turn of events. As the crowd began to admire him and Barnabas in worshipful reverence, a disturbed Paul rebuked their efforts. He shouted at them, "Men—why are you doing these things? We also are men, of like nature with you, and we bring you good news, that you should turn from these vain things to a living God, who made the heaven and the earth and the sea and all that is in them."

At this point, Paul had only visited Greek settlements on the periphery of the Greek world, but around 50 CE, he left for Athens in Greece proper. It is said that Paul immediately immersed himself in the great discussions of religion and philosophy that were constantly bubbling to the surface in this intellectual cauldron. In particular, he showed up at a place called Mars Hill, where people participated in open discussions about all manner of metaphysical topics. On this hill, Paul famously addressed a crowd with the words, "Men of Athens, I notice that you are religious in every way, for as I was walking along, I saw your many shrines. And one of your altars had the inscription on it: 'To an Unknown God.' This God, whom you worship without knowing, is the one I am telling you about."

Paul was very smart in his approach. He was in the midst of all sorts of pagan worship, with idols and shrines set up to just about every deity conceivable. It was the Greek custom at the time to leave an additional shrine out to the so-called "unknown god" that they might have forgotten about. It was not really done with too much thought; really, it was just an afterthought to ensure that the Greeks had all of their metaphysical bases covered.

However, Paul used it to his advantage to break the ice with them and state that the unknown god they were worshiping was actually the God of whom he spoke. Paul then showed just how erudite he was when it came to Greek philosophy by seamlessly tying the words of a famous Greek poet with his own biblical beliefs. Paul stated, "He is the God who made the world and everything in it. Since He is the Lord of heaven and earth, He doesn't live in man-made temples, and human hands cannot serve His needs, for He has no needs. He himself gives life and breath to everything, and He satisfies every need. From one man He created all the nations throughout the whole earth. He decided beforehand when they should rise and fall, and He determined their boundaries. His purpose was for the nations to seek after God and perhaps feel their way toward Him and find Him though He is not far from any of us. For in Him we live and move and exist. As some of your own poets said, 'We are his offspring.'"

Paul was actually quoting the words of the Stoic philosopher Aratus of Soli, who, in his philosophical treatise, "Phaenomena," described his views on the nature of the universe and humanity as the offspring of divinity. Paul had also paraphrased the words of another Greek philosopher, Epimenides. Paul borrowed from him the words, "For in him we live and move and have our being."

Epimenides had actually written those words about the Greek god Zeus. He wrote them at a time when many Greeks were casting away their belief in the old gods as if they had buried them in a tomb. The full quote from Epimenides actually reads, "They fashioned a tomb for you, holy and high one, Cretans, always liars, evil beasts, idle bellies. But you are not dead: you live and abide forever. For in you we live and move and have our being."

But even though Epimenides wrote this about Zeus, anyone familiar with Christianity can see the parallels to Christian thought since Christians believe that Jesus was buried in a tomb only to be resurrected and "live and abide forever" after the third day. And Paul no doubt had Jesus in mind when he thought of the words of this Greek poet, simply substituting Zeus for Jesus.

Paul's preaching in Greece was indeed successful, and several local churches began to take root. However, these early churches had to remain underground since local authorities often frowned upon the new religion. In its early beginnings, Christianity was largely misunderstood for a variety of reasons. The practice of communion, for example, in which Christians passed around wine and bread and repeated the words of Christ, "This is my blood. This is my body." had Christian believers being accused of cannibalism.

Christians were so secretive in the early days—much of this secrecy borne out of necessity—that these common misunderstandings turned into gross exaggerations. The early church in Greece faced a vicious cycle of having to be secretive in order to avoid persecution, only for this very secrecy to produce further gossip about them and further misunderstandings of the faith. This led to the rise of many so-called Christian apologists, who would attempt to explain and argue extensively about the true nature of the Christian faith, the most famous of which was Justin Martyr.

Justin was born around 100 CE in the region of Samaria in northern Israel. Justin was actually of Greek origin, although he grew up around Samaritan culture. Early on in life, he immersed himself in Greek philosophy, but he was unable to answer certain philosophical questions, so he turned to Christianity. Justin Martyr wrote lengthy apologetic texts, attempting to explain his reasoning for converting to Christianity until he was beheaded in 165 CE.

Christianity would continue to suffer from various waves of persecution until Roman Emperor Constantine issued the Edict of Milan in 313 CE, which officially "legalized" Christianity. This edict allowed Christians to come out into the open and practice their faith without fear of repercussions. From this point forward, Christians in Greece and much of the rest of the Roman Empire would flourish.

Soon, rather than merely being tolerated as an acceptable religion, Christianity would become the official religion of the empire itself. Emperor Constantine would also eventually become a Christian. He would also establish a new Christianized capital for the Roman Empire, not in the Latin West but in the Greek East, on the grounds of the old Greek settlement of Byzantium, which was located on a narrow strip of land that connected the European continent to Asia Minor (Turkey).

Once the old site of Byzantium was rendered into the new Roman capital, it was renamed in honor of Constantine himself; it was called Constantinople. As good as all these things were for Christians, the fact that Christianity had suddenly become the main religion of the Roman Empire kick-started a major ideological shift among the faithful.

In the past, when Christians were horribly persecuted by Roman authorities, it was widely believed among Christians that the Roman Empire would soon face God's wrath. It was a common belief that Rome would be destroyed in the events of Armageddon mentioned in the Christian Book of Revelation. But once the Roman Empire itself became Christian, it obviously caused many Christians to second-guess that assumption. However, it would not be long before Christians would look elsewhere for potential harbingers of the apocalypse.

Chapter 10 – The Rise and Fall of the Greek Byzantine Empire

"You see that even the enemy did not dare to declare war against us until they had seized our generals, for they were sensible that, while we had commanders and yielded obedience to them, we were able to conquer them; but, having seized our commanders, they concluded that we should, from a want of command and discipline, be destroyed."

-Xenophon

The Roman Empire, in many ways, had become too big for its own good. And under its top-down authoritarian regimes, the ever-expanding territory of the Roman Empire had become increasingly hard for one Roman emperor to govern. Constantine had successfully ruled the Roman Empire as the sole emperor, but his successors would not be quite as capable. And by 395 CE, the Roman Empire was once again split in two, with one emperor ruling the Greek East while the other ruled the Latin West.

The western half of the Roman Empire was frequently besieged by roving bands of Germanic tribes, such as the Ostrogoths, Visigoths, Franks, and Vandals. As the name of the Germanic Vandals might imply, these aggressive warriors specialized in smash-and-grab tactics of attacking, looting, and fleeing. Initially, the Romans were able to stand up to the incursions, but over time, the constant fighting finally broke Rome's back, and the western half of the Roman Empire ended in 476 CE.

The eastern, Greek portion of the Roman Empire based out of Constantinople would go on to last another one thousand years, and it would be rechristened the Byzantine Empire. As the Western half of the Roman Empire lay in ruins, the eastern half would remain strong with a series of successful emperors, as well as a powerful Greek Orthodox Church apparatus. Similar to the Western Roman Empire's development of Catholicism and the pope in Rome, the Byzantines would establish the office of the patriarch in Constantinople for their top bishop, who is often referred to in the Orthodox faith as the "first among equals."

In the immediate aftermath of the Western Roman Empire's fall, the Greek half of the empire was primarily on the defense, fending off and sometimes bribing troublemakers who were threatening their borders. It was not until the reign of Byzantine Emperor Justinian I (also known as Justinian the Great) that the Greek half of the empire sought to reclaim some of the lands that had been lost. Justinian rose to the Byzantine throne in 527, and he wasted no time on embarking upon his plan of *renovatio imperii Romanorum*, or as it were, the "restoration of the empire of the Romans."

In order to do so, however, Justinian knew that he had to placate his greatest threat to the east—Persia—so that he would be able to focus the full might of his forces in the west. It was with this express purpose in mind that Justinian came to terms with Persian King Khosrow in 532. The terms of the agreement were not that great since it entailed the Byzantines having to pay tribute to the

Persians, but it was enough to get them off of their backs, allowing them to focus on reclaiming the lost lands of the Western Roman Empire.

But before Justinian could focus on his project of reclamation, he also had to ensure the stability of his own capital. For in that very year, Justinian had to put down the so-called Nika riots. In order to understand the Nika riots, one must understand the popularity of chariot racing in the Roman world. The Greek East had created a tremendous pastime in which spectators watched teams of chariots competing against each other. These teams were known by colors associated, and by the time of Justinian, the two most prominent teams were the Greens and the Blues.

These teams represented more than just sports; they also represented political and even military power. The Blues had powerful backers, and so did the Greens. These two teams were usually opposed to each other, but in light of Justinian's sudden taxing of his citizens to fund his impending conquest, as well as his decision to pay tribute to the Persians, they actually joined forces to show their disdain.

This popular uprising broke loose during a chariot race in which Justinian was in attendance. During the course of the races, spectators began to shout, "Nika! Nika!" over and over. The word "Nika" means "victory." This word was shouted in between angry remarks made about Justinian himself. In this hostile atmosphere, thousands of Greeks came out onto the street to attempt an outright overthrow of the government. Emperor Justinian was understandably shocked at these developments, but he regained his senses fast enough and sent in troops to quell the unrest. He was indeed able to restore order, but it has been estimated that tens of thousands were killed in the ensuing melee.

So, after the eastern frontier was stabilized and his own people were under control, Justinian began to send his Greek forces into the former Western Roman Empire to retake lands that had been conquered. First, he sent an army led by Byzantine general

Belisarius to take back territory in North Africa, which the Vandals had seized in 429 CE. The territory was reclaimed with relative ease. General Belisarius then turned north and managed to capture the southern Italian town of Naples before marching on Rome itself.

By the 550s, the Byzantines had managed to reclaim much of the former western portion of the Roman Empire. Justinian's territory stretched through the Middle East, all across North Africa, to southern Spain and a smattering of Mediterranean islands, leading to the reclaimed Italian Peninsula and then back to the Greek heartland itself. But Justinian's successors would steadily lose this reclaimed territory.

In fact, his immediate successor, Justin II, lost most of Italy to an invasion of the Lombards—a Germanic tribe that would control almost the entire Italian Peninsula for the next two centuries. Justinian II was followed by Byzantine Emperor Tiberius II, who ended up fighting a losing battle against Slavic invasions of the Greek Balkan territory. It was around this time that the people groups of the Slavs, Avars, Patzinaks, and Bulgars, in particular, began to appear in the Greek territory.

The next emperor, Maurice, found a unique way to solve the problem of the Balkans. The old Byzantine foe of Persia had erupted into a civil war, prompting the Byzantines to intervene. Maurice was able to successfully put his thumb on the scale, and he tipped it in favor of Khosrow II. Khosrow thanked the Byzantine emperor, which led to closer relations. Emperor Maurice even married the Persian king's daughter, shoring up relations even further. With the Persians suddenly in the Byzantine's back pocket, Maurice could finally focus on driving out the Byzantines' enemies from the Balkans—a feat that was achieved in 602 CE.

You might think that Emperor Maurice would be loved by his Greek subjects for his success, but due to the fact that the Slavic Avars had stolen thousands of Greek citizens, with Maurice essentially ignoring this, he was not particularly popular. Dissension broke out in the ranks, and a Byzantine soldier, whose name comes down to us as Phocas, led a rebellion on the capital and had the emperor killed.

Phocas turned out to be even less popular than Maurice, and he could not escape the stigma of being seen as a usurper to the throne. Complicating matters for him was the fact that the Persian king now considered all the previous treaties null and void since Phocas had assassinated his former brother-in-law.

Phocas was ultimately removed from power by a popular Byzantine general named Heraclius in 610. Right around the time that Heraclius came to power, a prophet by the name of Muhammad had begun his ministry in the lands of Arabia. At the time, he was just one lone figure, slowly gathering a following of like-minded believers. But one day, Muhammad's successors would build up an army that would march on Constantinople itself.

However, during Heraclius's reign, the number one threat to Byzantium would remain the Persian Empire. In fact, shortly after Heraclius came to the throne, the Persian forces stormed into the Byzantine territory in the Middle East, seizing both the cities of Jerusalem and Damascus. Heraclius was able to rally his forces, and during the Battle of Nineveh in 627, he was able to soundly defeat the Persians.

The Byzantines managed to reclaim the territory they had lost, but both the Byzantine Empire and the Persian Empire had fought each other to a standstill as a result. This led to both empires becoming significantly weakened. And it was during this moment of weakness that the Muslim armies began to rise up and chip away at both of these former juggernauts. Muhammad, at this time, had successfully taken over all of the Arabian Peninsula (modern-day Saudi Arabia, Yemen, United Arab Emirates, Qatar, and Oman).

With this power base secure, the forces of Islam began to threaten Byzantine holdings. The first major confrontation occurred in 629 at the Battle of Mu'tah, which took place at the selfsame village of Mu'tah just to the east of the Jordan River. This opening battle did not go well for the Muslim fighters, and the Byzantines were easily able to drive them out. Not only that, three important Muslim military commanders were killed, one after the other. This was a terrible defeat for Muhammad's forces, but it would not be enough to deter him or his followers.

The Battle of Yarmouk in the borderlands of Syria and Jordan would prove to be a decisive one. Muhammad had already passed away at this point, having died in the summer of 632. His successors, however, would carry on the fight for him, and zealous jihadists scored a decisive victory against the Byzantines in 636. In a matter of decades, all of Palestine was in Muslim hands, which allowed the Islamic armies to permanently station themselves in Syria.

From this base, these warriors would send further incursions into the Byzantine heartland of Anatolia and threaten the Greek Byzantine capital of Constantinople. The city was besieged from 674 to 678. The Greeks were ultimately able to repel the Muslims by using the secret art of Greek fire. Although some minor raids would continue to occur off and on, this victory managed to keep major onslaughts at bay. It was not until 717 that Islamic forces would once again try their luck with a direct attack on Constantinople.

A combination of factors helped the Byzantines drive off this latest incursion. Sure, Greek fire was employed, but so was a whole lot of diplomacy with the Bulgar tribes that had settled in the Balkan region today known as Bulgaria. The newly allied Bulgars were a great help in augmenting the Byzantines' might. Even the weather proved to be favorable for a Byzantine victory since the stormy conditions nearly wiped out their opponents' ships.

It was really this victory that bought the Byzantine Empire some much-needed time, as it resulted in the Muslim caliphate changing its aims and looking elsewhere for territorial gains. The Byzantines, in the meantime, began to question if perhaps they had fallen out of God's favor. Interestingly enough, they began to consider the fact that the Muslims eschewed all manner of icons, as they refused to have any paintings of religious figures, no matter their importance. This is the reason why there are few depictions of Prophet Muhammad. Muslims did this because they felt that paintings of religious figures took focus away from God (Allah) and actually amounted to a form of idolatry.

Somewhere along the way, some leading thinkers in the Byzantine Empire began to wonder if God was, in fact, displeased with the Byzantine habit of having rich and elaborate religious icons. These sentiments kick-started a religious struggle that took place from 726 to 842. This was a pitched ideological battle between those who revered the religious icons of the Greek Orthodox faith and those who wished to see them removed. The Greeks were always known for their artwork, so, of course, Christian Byzantium was full of all kinds of religious works of art, including grand mosaics of religious scenes, sculptures, and other religious icons.

But as mentioned, those who were against the icons—the so-called iconoclasts—wished to have these revered works of art removed as quickly as possible. It is said that it was mostly the non-Greek residents of the far eastern regions who had to deal with Muslim incursions who were the most opposed to the icons, whereas the much more integrated Greeks tended to embrace them.

But no matter what side of the debate the Byzantines fell under, the rising tide of Islam still battered against its shores. By 900 CE, much of the Byzantines' frontier regions were lost. They lost their grip of Sicily in 902, and they nearly lost Thessaloniki in 904. Over the next couple of centuries, the situation would look increasingly dire for the Byzantines. It was so bad, in fact, that by the 1090s, the Byzantines began to seek help from the pope in Rome, even though the pope had previously excommunicated the Greek Orthodox patriarch due to doctrinal differences.

At this point in time, the Germanic tribes that had succeeded the Western Roman Empire had melded with the remnants of the Romans to form the medieval kingdoms of western Europe. As the medieval Europeans grew stronger, the once-mighty Byzantines were growing weaker until they were actively seeking out help from the westerners. This, along with accounts of Christian pilgrims being harassed in the Holy Land, is what led Pope Urban II to call for the First Crusade.

Christians in the west readily answered this call, and soon, European armies were sent crashing into Muslim forces in the Middle East. The First Crusade managed to wrest much of the Holy Land from the grasp of the Islamic power brokers of the region. But over the next two centuries, these gains were steadily reversed, and by 1291, the last of the Christian Crusaders had been expelled from the Middle East.

This left the Byzantine Empire once again alone on the front lines, facing off against an ever-expanding Muslim force. And soon enough, the latest Muslim power to gain prominence—the Ottoman Turks—would prove to be the Byzantines' undoing. The Byzantine Empire ultimately fell to the Ottomans in 1453 after a prolonged siege that saw the Ottoman Turks blasting the great walls of the city with powerful cannons.

Even faced with this onslaught, the Byzantines managed to hold off the Turks for about two months. The walls of Constantinople were thick and strong, and the fact that they withstood the Turks' firepower for several weeks is a testament to that. The sultan's cannons were cumbersome and time-consuming to reload, so during those breaks in between firing and reloading, the Greeks did everything they could to repair any damage that had been inflicted.

Nevertheless, the Turks did indeed eventually break through the walls of Constantinople, and by all accounts, what happened next was a terrible bloodbath. The Greeks were greatly outnumbered by the invaders, and despite the many acts of heroism that were displayed that day, they were quickly overrun by the Turks. It is said that Byzantine Emperor Constantine XI Palaeologus (it is perhaps ironic that the last Byzantine emperor shared the same name as the first) personally led the last desperate charge against the Ottomans, perishing in the onslaught.

With the defeat of the Byzantine troops, the Greek citizens of the city were massacred, tortured, and horribly abused at the hands of their enemies. Neither priests, nuns, nor small children were spared. Thousands of residents were enslaved. The rape and pillage of Constantinople went on for three whole days until Ottoman Sultan Mehmed II ordered a cessation of the violence.

An eyewitness to this devastation comes down to us from a man known to history as Leonard of Chios. Chios, of course, was a Greek island within the Byzantine Empire, from which Leonard had hailed. Leonard was a Greek scholar, and he was apparently in Constantinople that day and somehow managed to live to tell of the horrors he saw.

Leonard reported, "All the valuables and other booty were taken to their [the Turks] camp, and as many as sixty thousand Christians who had been captured. The crosses which had been placed on the roofs or the walls of churches were torn down and trampled. Women were raped, virgins deflowered and youths forced to take part in shameful obscenities. The nuns left behind, even those who were obviously such, were disgraced with foul debaucheries."

In the aftermath, even the great Christian Orthodox church, the Hagia Sophia, would be transformed, although it would not be destroyed. Still, many Greek Christians saw the act of transforming the church as a defilement, as the conquerors of Constantinople converted it into a mosque. This towering piece of Byzantine architecture would now be accompanied by minarets, which were installed by the Ottoman Turks.

After the dissolution of the Ottoman Empire, the Hagia Sophia was later turned into a museum. But in recent years, hard-liners in Turkey have called for it to be reconverted back into a mosque. This would be a controversial move for sure since such an act would most certainly open up the old wounds of the past.

At any rate, after over one thousand years, the great Christian empire of Byzantium had fallen. Constantinople, the imperial capital of Christianity, would become Istanbul, Turkey. All of Christian Europe was shocked to hear of these developments. The loss of this Christian bulwark in the east sent a seismic shift throughout all of Christian Europe, but none were affected more than Greece itself, which was essentially now on the front lines of the Muslim advance. With Constantinople gone, many feared that Athens would be next.

Chapter 11 – The Struggle for Greek Independence

"Cut away all that is excessive, straighten all that is crooked, bring light to all that is overcast, labor to make all one glow of beauty and never cease chiseling your statue, until there shall shine out on you from it the godlike splendor of virtue, until you shall see the perfect goodness surely established in the stainless shrine."

-Plotinus

The capital of the Byzantine Empire was overrun by Ottoman forces in 1453, leaving Greece itself wide open to invasion. Only the so-called Despotate of the Morea, which made up most of the Peloponnese of southern Greece, was left. It was the last outpost of the former Byzantine Empire. Defenders of this land fought hard to fend off the Ottomans, but it proved to be an impossible task.

Athens fell to the Ottomans just five short years later, in 1458. The cradle of Western civilization was now officially in the possession of the east, and the rest of the Peloponnese would follow by 1460. As destructive as the Turkish military was and as horrible as the bloodthirsty pillaging of Constantinople, in particular, had been, the rule of the Ottomans was in some ways surprisingly benevolent, especially when it came to the Christian clergy.

The conquering sultan of Byzantium, Mehmed II, officially appointed a new patriarch in Constantinople, who was a Greek named Gennadius II, in 1454. It is said that at the patriarch's swearing-in ceremony that the sultan urged him to "be Patriarch, and good fortune be with you. Count on our friendship in whatever you will, possessing all those privileges which the Patriarchs enjoyed before you."

Many conquering Muslims were willing, to some extent, to follow the precepts of the Quran as it pertained to Christians and Jews. The Quran (also spelled as Koran, the central religious text of Islam) refers to Christians as people of the book and advises Muslims to treat them well as long as they pay a tax to Muslim authorities. Yes, Christians essentially had to pay a protection racket to stay safe. They were essentially considered to be second-class citizens, but the terms were more favorable than many would-be Christian conquerors would have dictated.

After all, Christian kingdoms during this period were likely to demand subject people immediately convert to Christianity. The Muslims, on the other hand, gave the conquered people a choice to either convert to Islam or retain their original faith and pay a special tax called jizya. But money was not the only thing that the Turks taxed. Shockingly enough, they also demanded a tax of children, as they required Greek families offer up one of their boys to be taken and raised by the Ottomans and groomed for a special military auxiliary force called the Janissaries.

In Turkish, this practice was called devshirme, but for the Greeks, it was known as *pedhomazoma* or "child collection." These young boys were brought up to be fierce fighters for the Ottomans. They actively fought for Islam and were made to be zealous believers in the faith. One can only imagine the agony of their Greek Orthodox parents in having to deal with all of this.

However, not all of the kidnapped boys became fighting men, as some were trained in more specialized tasks. Some even reached high administrative positions within the Ottoman government. According to one account, a Greek child by the name of Sinan was carried off by the Ottomans in 1491. He was raised in "palace schools" and ultimately succeeded in becoming the chief architect of the empire, building colossal structures. Some of his works are indeed perceived to be the best achievements of Ottoman architecture. But the individual who designed and built them was not Turkish but rather a transplanted Greek ripped from his family in his youth and made to serve the Ottoman Empire.

The Ottomans divided up Greece into six districts, with each one governed by a local administrator who was loyal to the sultan. Even though the Ottomans controlled Greece, there remained pockets of unruly resistance in Greece's mountainous terrain. These rebels would periodically rise up against the Ottomans, but the damage done to the regime was always minimal.

A few other outliers of resistance remained, but they were steadily pushed back. In 1522, the Ottomans besieged the island of Rhodes in the eastern Mediterranean, driving out the Knights Hospitaller—a vestige of the Crusades—who had been stationed there. The Greek island of Cyprus, which at this point was controlled by the Republic of Venice, held out for a while too, but it was ultimately taken by the Ottomans in 1579. It was only by virtue of the Republic of Venice and its control of the Ionian Islands that enabled any portion of Greek-speaking lands to be free of Ottoman domination.

Some Greeks accepted their fate of being under Ottoman dominion, but others, especially in the rural mountainous regions, kept up periodic resistance throughout Ottoman rule. Others took advantage of the situation and moved to the more cosmopolitan cities of western Asia Minor, such as Constantinople and Smyrna. Here, skilled Greeks could often make a lot of money by gaining work as merchants and administrators. Those who did not wish to be under the Ottoman yoke, however, also had the choice to flee. And many decided to depart their ancestral homes for western Europe.

Italy, in particular, received a large influx of Greek refugees. This sudden deposit of Greek culture in Italy would eventually germinate into the intellectual movement known as the Renaissance. It was the sparks set by the transplanted Greek intelligentsia that sparked this thirst for knowledge in the west. But even as the west became enriched by this influx of Greek refugees, Greece itself became increasingly backward and poor. Greece's industry suffered, and what little money the people had was taxed by the Ottomans.

As historian David Brewer put it, the Greeks were subject to "increasingly complex, arbitrary, and oppressive taxes." They were taxed for farms, vineyards, and even the raising of sheep—all of this on top of the general jizya tax that had to be paid simply to exist as Greek Orthodox Christians in the Ottoman Empire. By the 1600s, Greece had been reduced to an impoverished state, and many Greek towns saw a rapid decrease in population, which was brought about by those fleeing the harsh economic conditions that were being imposed.

During these dark times, the citizens of Greece clung to the Greek Orthodox faith. For the Greeks, their religion was everything, and thankfully enough, their Muslim overlords did not take it away from them. Although non-Muslims were forced to pay a tax for the continuation of their faith, they were mostly allowed to adhere to their religious beliefs. The hardest part of Greek life under Ottoman rule, no doubt, was the fact that the Ottomans could come and take a Greek family's children at any time.

As mentioned above, boys could be groomed for service in either the military or an administrative position. Many Greek young men made up an entire legion of the Ottoman army known as the Janissaries. These young men would be raised to be religious fanatics, and they would often return home to pressure their former families to convert to Islam just as they had. But as bad as things were for Greek boys, they were perhaps far worse for Greek girls. If the Ottomans so pleased, Greek girls could be snatched up and placed in harems. As romantic as such things were sometimes made out to be, this was nothing short of sexual slavery being imposed upon Greek women and girls.

There were some instances in which the Greeks refused to hand over their children to the Turks. One of the most notable incidents occurred in 1705 when a Turkish administrator came to northern Greece to collect fifty boys for the Janissaries. The administrator was immediately met with a hostile crowd of parents who began defiantly insisting that under no circumstances would they hand over their children. Rather than turn over their sons, the crowd mobbed the administrator and killed him on the spot. As bold as their resistance was, it was not long before Turkish retribution visited them. As a result, all who were involved in this resistance were rounded up and beheaded.

There have been some Ottoman apologists that have tried to downplay these abuses in later years, but no matter how one might try to sugarcoat it, life under the Ottoman rule was often not a very happy one for the Greeks. Despite the dark clouds hovering over the Greeks, by the 1750s, the illumination of the Enlightenment of western Europe began to make its way over to Greece. Soon, Greek translations of the works of Rousseau, Montesquieu, and Voltaire were surfacing in Greek cities.

The latter of which gave the Greeks the most hope since Voltaire was himself a lover of Greek civilization, and he openly encouraged the European powers to intervene on Greece's behalf. In 1770, Voltaire even pleaded with Greece's powerful fellow Orthodox nation to the north, Russia, to directly aid in the liberation of Greece. Russia's Catherine the Great did attempt as much after the outbreak of the Russo-Turkish War, which took place between 1768 and 1774.

This war was initiated due to hostilities between the Polish and the Ottomans. As the situation escalated, Russian troops parked themselves in the borderland between Poland and the nearest reaches of the Ottoman Empire. The war ultimately proved to be a great success for a resurgent Russia. The Russians managed to gain territory in the Caucasus region, and Romania, Serbia, and Montenegro achieved liberation. In the backdrop of all of this, Empress Catherine the Great sent Russian diplomats to Greece to engage in secret discussions about staging a revolt against the Ottomans, pledging Russian support for the Greeks.

The Russian Navy, under the leadership of Alexei Orlov, arrived off the shores of Mani in southern Greece in February of 1770. The turnout of Greek rebels was lower than expected, with less than two thousand participating. Soon, extra help arrived from Crete, and the Greek rebels were able to go on the offensive against the Ottomans. This resulted in Ottoman troops being pushed out of the regions of Laconia and Morea, but soon after that, the offensive stalled.

However, the worst was yet to come. As soon as word of these developments reached the ears of the Ottoman sultan, the Ottoman Empire engaged in a punishment of the worst kind against all Greeks throughout the empire. Whether they had participated in any revolutionary activity or not, every Greek resident of the Ottoman Empire was suddenly subject to persecution, abuse, and quite possibly death for no other reason than the fact that they were Greek.

This "anti-Greek pogrom," as it were, was enough to frighten the Greeks into submission. But as bad as things were, it was not a complete disaster for the Greeks. For after the Russians won the war and concluded a treaty with the Ottomans, the Ottoman Empire pledged to allow the Russians to place Greek Orthodox Christians and churches under Russian protection. It was a rather vague sense of protection, especially in the aftermath of the massacre the Turks had just finished against the Greeks, but the idea that a great power such as Russia was officially taking the Greeks into consideration meant a lot at the time.

At any rate, it was this nascent rebellion that planted the seeds of what would ultimately become the Greek War of Independence several decades later. By the late 1700s, both the French and American Revolutions were able to serve as an inspiration for a similar Greek revolt. And the mindset that was developing in the Greek intelligentsia was made clear in 1806 when a Greek patriot penned an anonymous treatise entitled, *The Rule of Law for Greece: A Discourse on Freedom.*

The paper expounds upon the Enlightenment thinker Jean-Jacques Rousseau's concept of man's original nature being one of "primitive happiness" and that it was only the contrivances of oppressive social structures that had robbed man of his joy. The writer then argued that the tendency of humanity is always to improve the state that they are in. The treatise stated that since the Ottoman Empire was already in decline, the Greeks should be able to break free. It was reasoned that there were two main obstacles that prevented the Greeks from doing so, and they were the rich Greek merchants and the Greek Orthodox clergy. It was argued that rich Greek merchants were happy with the status quo and did not want to rock the boat, while the clergy was completely beholden to the Turks and unable to think for themselves.

Shortly after this work was circulated, the Greek Orthodox Church began to strike back, and it condemned these Enlightenment-inspired ideals as nothing short of sinful and something that would ultimately lead the Greek faithful astray. These feelings were best expressed in an encyclical issued in 1819 by Patriarch Gregory V, which was called "Enlightenment as the Handmaid of Irreligion."

Here, he argued that the so-called knowledge of the Enlightenment would only lead to irreligion and, as he phrased it, "false patriots" who were "unworthy of their ancestral calling." In other words, how much would the Greeks profit to gain the ideals being proffered upon them by the Western world if in so doing they compromise their traditions and lose their ancestral soul?

This was the argument being made by the Greek Orthodox Church at the time. Yes, they knew that the Turkish regime was horribly oppressive, but, as the treatise rightfully stated, they did not want to risk losing their faith in a pursuit of liberation. The Greek Orthodox Church had come to view the so-called progress of western Europe as a threat to old traditions and philosophical outlooks. By clinging to the old way of doing things, the Greek Orthodox faith influenced schooling, and it avoided the modern sciences of astronomy and mathematics in favor of teaching long, outdated musings by classic Greek titans such as Aristotle. Although the west certainly still revered Greek figures like Aristotle, it accepted that many of his theories were off-base and needed a more modern interpretation.

Aristotle, for example, did not understand gravity, and he spoke of rocks falling to the ground simply out of an innate desire to return to the earth, as well as flames of fire moving upward because they wished to return to the air. Aristotle believed that nature had a place for everything, and phenomena such as these were simply a result of objects returning to their natural place. Aristotle had no evidence to support this theory; it was basically just something he surmised from pure speculation. In the 1700s, Isaac Newton, of course, dispelled all of this nonsense with his mathematically proven theories of gravity. However, Greek schooling still embraced Aristotle's and other great ancient Greeks' teachings wholeheartedly, and as a result, Greece was behind its European counterparts.

As Greek-speaking people were debating the merits of old tradition and newfangled ideas, the movement for Greek independence suddenly received help from an unexpected source. Ali Pasha, the viceroy of Ioannina, was flirting with open rebellion from the Ottoman Empire.

Ali Pasha had expanded his control to include southern Albania, the Peloponnese, and much of western Greece. By 1812, Ali was in a powerful position, as he controlled the prosperous town of Ioannina, taking full advantage of its rock-solid economy. It was only in 1820 that it all came crashing down when the Ottomans decided to rein in the rebellious province. Ali was a crafty politician, and in order to thwart the Ottoman attempt to knock him back in line, he reached out to the Russians to recognize his domain as an autonomous region.

In exchange for this favor, he enacted several reforms that were favorable for the Greek populace. He reduced taxation, wrote off debts, and abolished enforced servitude. The Turks, in the meantime, were closing in on Ali Pasha, and by the fall of 1820, they had pushed deep into his territory. Everywhere they went, they burned down villages, terrorized Greek citizens, and generally left the place in ruins.

Ali Pasha was forced to escape to the citadel in Ioannina, and he prepared to dig in for a long siege. But if the Ottomans felt that they had restored order in the region, they had another thing coming. By the spring of 1821, all of Greece seemed to be in revolt. In February there was an uprising in the Danubian principalities of Wallachia and Moldavia led by a Russian officer who was originally of Greek extraction—Alexander Ypsilantis. Soon thereafter, the Greeks of the Peloponnese rose up and openly declared war.

The first major gains happened in the fall of 1821 when Greek rebels, led by one Theodoros Kolokotronis, started to besiege Tripolitsa. At the same time, Greek ships were put together and sent on a crash course to smash into the Ottoman Navy in the Aegean Sea. This was crucial since it literally kept additional Ottoman troop arrivals at bay, preventing them from making landfall.

Back in the Peloponnese, the Turks were being completely driven out. A huge victory was scored on October 5th when the Greek rebels managed to take over Tripolitsa. The capture of this town was important since it consisted of the major administrative center for Ottoman control of the region. The dreadful massacre that ensued, however, was nothing short of terrible. It is said that tens of thousands of Turkish inhabitants of the city were put to death even after surrendering. Yes, as much as the Greeks had suffered for centuries under the Ottomans and had atrocities inflicted upon them by the Turks, Greek freedom fighters were not always immune to descending into murderous mayhem.

It is important to note that although some Greeks butchered Turks, it does not mean that all Greeks were responsible. Such a thing would seem like common sense, yet this logic was completely lost on the Turkish sultan when he heard of what had happened at Tripolitsa. Since Christian Greeks were involved, the sultan immediately blamed all Christian Greeks. The first thing he did, in fact, was have the Greek Orthodox patriarch of Constantinople killed; he was executed that Easter Sunday.

Even though the patriarch, who was in far off in Constantinople, had nothing to do with the rebellion in the Peloponnese—in fact, he had excommunicated those involved—the Turks held him responsible since he was the leader of the Greek Christians. Yes, even though the sultan gave the patriarch great privileges, the sultan could end his life at a moment's notice if he so desired. Yet another reason for the Greek Orthodox faithful to want to throw off the Turkish yoke.

After killing the patriarch, another mass persecution (if not outright mass extermination) of Greeks within the Ottoman Empire commenced. Prominent Greeks were grabbed up by mobs of Turks and killed on the spot in Smyrna, Adrianople, and Constantinople. In the city of Kydonies alone, it is said that about thirty thousand Greeks were killed. In the Greek communities in

Rhodes, Kos, and Cyprus, the situation was even worse, with whole communities being annihilated.

Even more atrocities occurred on the island of Chios, in which thousands were decimated. Not only were they killed, but the killers were also depraved enough to desecrate their remains. They would take bags of human body parts back to Constantinople simply so they would have the pleasure of dumping them in the street. These outrages soon reached the ears of western Europe, and the European nations were in an uproar, with many rattling their sabers to aid Greece in its time of need.

Northern Greece, in the meantime, saw its gains rapidly rolled back by the Turkish forces. The rebels here were soon pushed south, where they linked up with the rebels in the Peloponnese. The besieged Ali Pasha met his end in January of 1822 when his compound was stormed by Turkish troops, although the exact details of his demise remain unclear.

With Pasha eliminated, Turkish troops headed south later that spring to put down the rebellion still brewing in the Peloponnese. Without direct outside aid and with tensions building among the rebels themselves, it seemed as if the Turks were poised to snuff out the entire revolt. A Turkish contingent of about twenty thousand troops was able to march on the city of Thebes before heading across the Isthmus to Corinth, easily taking both cities.

But the Turks made a big mistake by crossing through the "narrow defiles" of the Dervenakia, allowing Greek fighters to carry out a wildly successful ambush that left around seventeen thousand of the Turkish soldiers dead. Another Turkish disaster occurred in the city of Missolonghi, where a Turkish contingent, riddled with rampant sickness, was similarly ambushed by Greek guerrilla fighters.

The Turks were decimated, and the commander was so disheartened that he ended his own life. Also in 1822, the Greeks forged their own constitution. The Greek intelligentsia knew full well that in order to have the nations of the world recognize and take their proclaimed independence seriously, they needed the rightful apparatus of an independent state, such as a coherent system of government enshrined in a constitution. Despite this social compact being developed, by 1824, the volunteers were more fractured than ever.

Different rebel leaders seemed to have different aims, and no one could come together well enough to present a unified front against the Ottomans. The Greek revolution then faced a severe challenge in 1825 when armed forces from Egypt were deployed by Ibrahim Pasha, the son of Muhammad Ali, the regional administrator of Egypt. At this time, Egypt was one of the most prosperous and militarily advanced of all of the regions of the Ottoman Empire.

Ibrahim Pasha landed a sizeable force at the harbor of Modon (sometimes known as Methoni) in the western Peloponnese that January. Faced with these odds, the Greeks reached out to the British for aid. The British foreign secretary, George Canning, who was posted in Greece at the time, was handed off the so-called "Act of Submission" by Greek delegates. The document was rather explicit in its aim, stating, "In virtue of the present act, the Greek nation places the sacred deposit of its liberty, independence, and political existence under the absolute protection of Great Britain."

Since the initiative was not in line with Britain's foreign policy at the moment, Canning ultimately declined to pass the missive on. All he could do was advise the Greeks to continue the struggle. One of the primary reasons that the great powers, such as Britain, were hesitant to openly support Greece was that they feared that Russia would become heavily involved, seize territories, and then precipitate a complete collapse of the Ottoman Empire. And the great powers were not yet ready for the massive disruption to the status quo that such an event might bring.

However, by the Spring of 1826, after the fall of the city of Missolonghi, it began to look increasingly likely that the Greek resistance would be snuffed out and that Greece would soon be an Ottoman territory administered by the Egyptians. It was only when the Greeks seemed to be right on the brink of collapse that the foreigners finally came to Greece's aid.

But it must be stressed that in these early days, rather than foreign powers, it was foreign citizens who initially became involved. Due to the great romantic views of Greece among the intellectuals of Europe and America, individual European citizens began to actively support Greece even before their governments sanctioned aid. These zealous volunteers from abroad became collectively known as the "philhellenes," which in Greek basically means one who loves or has a great admiration for Hellenistic culture.

In the Greek War of Independence, droves of volunteer philhellenes came to the lands of Greece to take up the fight for its freedom. But not only did they send people to fight, these philhellenes also raised considerable sums of money to help fund the cost of waging a war against one of the world's most expansive empires. This influx of cold hard cash was especially crucial when it came to healing the fractures of the Greek revolutionaries since much of their infighting could be blamed on a desperation borne of a lack of funds.

With adequate financial assistance, the Greek rebels were able to focus on the real objective—driving out the Turks—rather than squabbling amongst themselves over who was using what resource. The most famous philhellene who arrived on Greece's shores to fight was British poet Lord Byron. Byron was definitely a man in love with Greek culture, and when he heard of Greece's distress, he did not hesitate to lend a hand.

Lord Byron showed up to fight alongside the Greek patriots in January of 1824. Sadly, Byron would perish just a few months later from an illness he had contracted. Even though Byron didn't do much on the actual battlefield, the high-profile nature of his presence alone was a tremendous boost when it came to bringing recognition to the cause. In fact, Byron's death led the public to clamor for a more robust support of Greece.

Soon, the European heads of state—especially Byron's native Britain—were forced to listen. Russia, for its part, was already heading in that direction. The Russian tsar, Alexander I, was initially fearful of what revolutionary chaos might mean for the region, but after hearing of various Turkish massacres and especially the cold-blooded murder of the patriarch of the Greek Orthodox Church, he could no longer ignore what was happening. Russia, after all, viewed itself as the guardian of Orthodox Christianity, and it could not stand by while their Orthodox brothers and sisters were being slaughtered. Another European head of state drawn to the cause was King Charles X of France.

In 1827, these powers came together in London to sign the treaty of the same name—The Treaty of London.

Chapter 12 – The Outside World Gets Involved

"Every man of action has a strong dose of egoism, pride, hardness, and cunning. But all those things will be regarded as high qualities if he can make them the means to achieve great ends."

-Giorgos Seferis

In 1827, Britain, Russia, and France signed an agreement called the Treaty of London in which they recognized the right of Greece to be independent. Furthermore, the treaty stipulated that the Ottoman Empire should recognize Greece's independence as well. The sultan wasn't ready to just lay down after all this fighting, and predictably, he refused to agree to any such terms. It was this refusal that set the stage for the climactic Battle of Navarino.

During this battle, which was waged on October 20th, 1827, the combined might of the European allies decimated a joint Turkish/Egyptian fleet. The Allies located the fleet parked in Navarino Bay. As they approached, the Turks opened fire. Moments later the Allied ships let loose with everything they had.

The Turkish craft were stuck in the bay, and they were literally blown out of the water by the heavy artillery fire that was unleashed.

With the destruction of this fleet, Greek independence seemed all but assured. Yet not everyone in the participating Allied countries was all that happy about what had happened. There were some in Britain, for example, who felt that the Allied fleet had overstepped its bounds. In January of 1828, there was a shakeup of the administration, and Britain's Tory Party came to power, charging that England had no business being involved in Greece's struggle. These feelings were later echoed by the king of Great Britain himself when he remarked that the incident was an "untoward event."

Nevertheless, Greece was on the road to statehood, and that January, a man named John Capodistrias (also known as Ioannis Kapodistrias) was poised to become the first head of that newly established state. Capodistrias had been a lifelong bureaucrat, and he was used to some sense of order. Out of a desire to wrest order from what had been a rather chaotic situation, he called for the new constitution to be temporarily suspended so that he could directly control affairs.

Capodistrias was famous for his distrust of Greek's young democracy, stating that the Greeks were not yet ready to make their own decisions. He felt that the most important thing was to have a strong centralized government focused on reversing the damage and decline inflicted on the country by the Ottomans. Capodistrias argued that the Greeks should only focus on democracy when they were on a good enough economic and social footing to do so.

The kind of government that would form in Greece would ultimately be determined by outsiders. Shortly after their intervention at Navarino, Britain, Russia, and France began to debate what should be done with Greece. None of the powers wanted their counterparts to gain a decisive foothold in the region. A British protectorate, a Russian client state, or a French colony would have been anathema to all but the one in control.

So, thankfully for the Greeks, it was rather unanimously agreed that Greece should be an independent state. The great powers, as it turned out, were just as distrustful of Greek democracy as John Capodistrias was, and they began conniving on how to install an authoritarian monarchy in Greece instead. Capodistrias, in the meantime, did not have much longer for this world, as he was assassinated by his rivals on October 9th, 1831.

In the following year, 1832, the European allies finally installed their handpicked monarch on the Greek throne. Seventeen-year-old Otto (the son of King Ludwig I of Bavaria) became the first king of the independent Kingdom of Greece. However, the kingdom that Otto was to rule over was essentially bankrupt. Things were so bad, in fact, that roving bands of Greeks could be found foraging in the wilderness just to keep from starving to death.

Otto was faced with a devastated economy and social unrest, and the situation only continued to deteriorate until massive protests, which were ultimately embraced by large factions of the Greek military, broke out in 1843. These protests pressured the king to forge a new constitution and to create a "two chamber parliament," which consisted of the *Gerousia* (the senate) and the *Vouli* (the lower house of representatives).

National elections would now be held, although rampant corruption in office positions and fraud at the ballot box would become commonplace. In what was perhaps one of the greatest ironies of Greek history, the conditions of the free and independent Greece had become so unbearable that many began to immigrate to the Greek-speaking communities within the Ottoman Empire!

This was a great embarrassment to Greek revolutionaries, and it helped to give rise to what Greek patriots called the "Megali Idea," which translated basically means, "Big Idea." Greek revolutionaries felt that the smaller rump state of the independent Kingdom of Greece was not big enough and that much more of the former

Greek territories, including the old Byzantine capital of Constantinople, should be restored.

The concept was first introduced in 1844 by Greek Prime Minister John Kolettis (also known as Ioannis Kolettis). Kolettis famously stated, "A Greek is not only a man who lives within this kingdom, but also one who lives in Janina, in Salonika, in Serres, in Adrianople, in Constantinople, in Smyrna, in Trebizond, in Crete, in Samos, and in any land associated with Greek history or the Greek race. There are two main centers of Hellenism: Athens, the capital of the Greek Kingdom and 'the City' [Constantinople], the dream and hope of all Greeks."

These patriotic feelings were also, perhaps surprisingly, encouraged by the reigning monarch, King Otto. At this point in time, Greece was still a constitutional monarchy, with King Otto at its head. However, Otto's reign would come to an end in 1862 when revolutionaries took to the streets and demanded a new constitution be forged for Greek society. The outside powers would then appoint George I of Denmark as the new monarch, and a new constitution and representative government would be formed.

King George I had to contend with a popular movement that craved both domestic reform and expansion abroad. Britain helped satisfy some of these cravings by handing over the Ionian Islands to the Greek mainland shortly after George was placed on the throne. With the desire for territorial expansion satiated, King George focused on constitutional reforms, which were completed in 1864. The Senate, which was considered unrepresentative, was tossed out in favor of a more representative single legislative body.

This move gave more direct democracy to the Greek population, but the king still had veto power, as he was able to select and reject ministers at will and even dissolve whole legislative bodies outright. But despite these changes, corruption and voter fraud, especially around election time, remained high. Nevertheless, the bright spot in all of this was the fact that the

Greek economy began to improve. And by the late 1800s, Greece had developed a distinct middle class.

International intrigue was afoot once again in 1866 when the former Greek island of Crete rose up against the Ottoman Empire. In this struggle, the Crete revolutionaries looked toward their fellow Greeks of the mainland for help. Individual Greeks answered the call, and like the philhellenes who were present during the Greek War of Independence, these Greeks managed to add to the military might of those on the ground, as well as raise money for them from abroad.

The great European powers, however, did not want to upset the balance of power by giving too much to the Greeks and disrupting the Ottomans. As such, the Greek government was informed in no uncertain terms that the Greeks would be punished if they did not cease and desist all aid to Crete. This was an embarrassing development for revolutionary-minded Greeks, and it served to remind them that they were still being forced to do the bidding of foreign powers.

In the meantime, the Ottoman Empire began to shift its strategy against the Greeks by seeking to inflame tensions between the Greeks and their Bulgarian neighbors in the Balkans. One of the masterstrokes of this strategy emerged in 1870 when the Ottoman sultan approved the creation of an independent church for the Bulgarians, one that was separate from the main Greek Orthodox Church of Constantinople. The Bulgarians no longer had to look toward the Greeks; they could now dictate the tenants of their faith on their own.

Many Greeks saw this as nothing short of a "divide and conquer" technique. These developments were followed by the so-called Great Eastern Crisis, which rocked Greece and its neighbors in 1875. The crisis began when Montenegro and Serbia launched an assault on Ottoman holdings in Anatolia. The situation then really came to a head when the Russians decided to aid the insurgents. This led to the Russo-Turkish War of 1877.

During the course of the conflict, the Russian forces drove deep into Ottoman territory and parked just outside of Constantinople. Many people back in Greece thought that perhaps this was the moment that would finally fulfill their "Megali Idea" and that the old Byzantine capital of Constantinople would soon be restored. But these hopes were dashed when the parties involved in the war signed the San Stefano Treaty.

Instead of the treaty enabling a larger Greece, it actually created a larger Bulgaria. It seems that Russia was more interested in what was termed "Pan-Slavism" than it was Pan-Hellenism, as it helped its Slavic counterparts expand their base. However, the other European powers did not agree with Russia's aims, and a hastily convened congress was formed, which came up with an international settlement. The larger Bulgaria plan was then scrapped.

Still, a resurgent Bulgaria would become an increasingly competitive element for Greece to take into consideration. Greece would make some gains soon enough, though. In 1881, the British had the Ottomans hand over Arta and Thessaly to Greece. However, these gains were seriously threatened in 1897, with the next round of fighting between the Turks and Greeks.

This latest conflict totally backfired on the Greeks, as the Turks gained the upper hand and came close to taking Athens. Before the Greeks were delivered a knockout blow, the great powers intervened and put an end to the fighting. Although this saved Greece from complete destruction, it was a humiliating defeat, and Greece had to agree to relinquish its recent gains, as well as pay the sultan a fixed indemnity. This setback would put the Megali Idea on hold until the First World War broke out.

Chapter 13 – Greece during the First World War

"When General Allenby conquered Jerusalem during World War I, he was hailed in the American press as Richard the Lion-Hearted, who had at last won the Crusades and driven the pagans out of the Holy Land."

-Noam Chomsky

At the dawn of the 20th century, the Ottoman Empire was tottering at the edge of collapse. Sick of foreign interference, a group called the Young Turks came to prominence, seeking to correct the course of the failing empire. The Young Turks were more nationalists than imperialists, and they left many of the non-Turkish members of the empire wondering what their ultimate fate would be.

Also alarming to some was the fact that the Young Turk movement was closely aligning itself with the rising European power of Germany. The Balkans, too, were a source of great turmoil at this time, and after Austria made the decision to incorporate Bosnia and Hercegovina into its empire, the stage was already being set for World War One.

Back in Greece, dissatisfaction with the status quo had once again reached a fever pitch. In 1910, the newly elected prime minister, Eleutherios Venizelos, led this charge. He was a populist leader, who, among other things, championed the idea of reclaiming the Greek island of Crete from the Ottomans, and his support was only increased when his Liberal Party won the majority of seats in the Greek Parliament in 1912. Venizelos was a charismatic politician, and he was able to shore up support from an important figure on the international stage—British chancellor of the exchequer, David Lloyd George.

At this time, the British were increasingly suspicious of the Ottoman Empire due to its increasing coziness with the Germans. Venizelos was able to use this distrust in order to gain more leverage for the Greek cause. With the British in his back pocket, Prime Minister Venizelos began a dialogue with Greece's Balkan neighbors and established what was known as the Balkan League, which was basically a "defensive" pact between Greece, Bulgaria, Serbia, and Montenegro.

Then, the Montenegrins began the onslaught by waylaying a Turkish troop detachment in Albania. A little over a week later, the Greeks, along with the Bulgarians and Serbs, joined the fray. The Turks stationed in Albania were overwhelmed, and they were pushed back to Turkey. After this occurred, the Greek navy then went to action, blocking the sea lanes. With the sea lanes under the control of Greek naval craft, the Bulgarian troops marched on Turkey.

By November 8th, 1912, the Greeks had poured into Thessalonica, retaking the city for Greece for the first time since the Ottomans had seized it in 1430 CE. But this was all just a prelude to what was to come. Soon after this, a Serb from the Balkans would assassinate the archduke of Austria, Franz Ferdinand, and the whole world would erupt into war as a result.

A year prior to the archduke's assassination, King George I of Greece had been killed while on a sightseeing tour of Thessalonica. King George, who had ruled for nearly fifty years, was already making plans for his son and heir, Constantine, to succeed him. So, as traumatic as his assassination was, the monarchy was already primed for his replacement.

The fact that the new king was named Constantine and that the Greeks felt they were on the verge of claiming Roman Emperor Constantine's old city of Constantinople was certainly not lost on the imagination of the Greek public. It now seemed like the Megali Idea could really happen.

It was while all of these stirring notions were afoot in Greece that the First World War erupted. After Archduke Franz Ferdinand of Austria was killed, Austria demanded that Serbia do something about it. However, the demands were too draconian for Serbia's tastes, and the Serbs refused to acquiesce to all of the listed demands. This led to Austria declaring war on Serbia on July 25th, 1914. As soon as Austro-Hungarian troops appeared on the Serbian border, the Serbs naturally looked toward Russia for help. And as Russian troops mobilized and prepared to intervene, Austria's German allies mobilized as well.

The Germans called for the Russians to back off, but the Russians absolutely refused to do so. This led to Germany declaring war on Russia. The Ottoman Empire, eager to both get revenge on Russia for past wars and to further cultivate its growing relationship with Germany, immediately sided with the Germans and declared war on Russia. Shortly thereafter, Britain and France declared war on Germany.

World War One is generally known as a war fought between the Allied Powers of Britain, France, Russia, (and later the United States) and the Central Powers of Germany, Austria-Hungary, and the Ottoman Empire. But such categorization is confusing and largely inadequate in a variety of ways. For one thing, the Ottoman Empire wasn't exactly a "central power" as much as an eastern one.

The role of Greece, too, would have been ill defined. After all, Greece could be called a "central power," yet Greece most certainly would not have sided with the Central Powers that were active during World War One. Nevertheless, for the sake of clarity and continuity, for this section, we will go ahead and refer to Britain and its allies as the Allied Powers, and we will refer to Germany and its allies as the Central Powers.

Greece saw the war as a golden opportunity to pick apart the bones of the dying Ottoman Empire, so Greece naturally sided with the Allied Powers of Russia, Britain, and France. Venizelos, in particular, was convinced that British naval supremacy would allow for an easy win. And so, hedging his bets with Britain and its allies, Prime Minister Venizelos calculated that once the war concluded, Greece would be in a good place to ride the Allies' coattails all the way to Constantinople.

Venizelos's aspirations were greatly bolstered in January of 1915 when his British handlers informed him that there was talk of important concessions on the coast of Asia Minor (Turkey) that would be given to Greece should the Ottoman Empire be defeated. Venizelos, in turn, suggested that Greece might be able to part with some territory in Macedonia if it was allowed greater gains in Asia Minor. This disturbed some of Venizelos's opponents, and it even provoked a rift between the prime minister and the king, who felt that Venizelos was giving up too much, too soon, in return for Britain's empty promises.

This rift led to Venizelos resigning from his post. The king then went against the wishes of the public by appointing a new prime minister, one Dimitrios Gounaris. Thinking the war to be a folly, the king and his court then went against the popular sentiment of the times and did everything in their power to keep Greece out of the fight. This provoked the anger of the British and the French, who were counting on Greece to come into the war as their ally.

Nevertheless, Britain invoked its guardian status over Greece as outlined in the Treaty of Protection of 1853 and began to station troops in Greek territory. If the Greek people weren't going to fight, the British figured they would at least use Greek land as bases of operation for their own forces.

Greece, in the meantime, was in the midst of incredible turmoil. The majority of the Greek people wanted to join the fight against the Central Powers, but the king of Greece was just as determined to keep Greece out. It is rather rare when a whole nation seems clamoring to fight and a cautious leader is trying their best to keep them from doing so. Most of the time it is the other way around. Just think of the Vietnam War in which you had a string of United States presidents escalating the conflict while the public protested US involvement.

The politically exiled populist leader Venizelos set up what could be termed as a virtual opposition government within Greece, which became the center for his base of supporters. However, the greatest pressure on the king came from Britain and France. Infuriated at Greece's refusal to take part, these two European powers began to strip Greece's national government of any agency of its own. Part of the draconian measures included the immediate expulsion of anyone found to be a so-called "enemy agent." This meant that any Greek suspected of collaborating with or spying for the Central Powers could be immediately kicked out of the country.

Even more embarrassing than this overreach were demands for the Greek military to disarm. Naval ships were supposed to remove their guns, and even shore batteries had to be taken down. The king could not sit back and allow his country to be so thoroughly emasculated like this. King Constantine obstinately refused to meet any of these demands.

After his refusal, the Allies came down hard on Greece and demanded that the king step down from power. French and British soldiers came ashore near Athens at the port city of Piraeus, and a naval blockade was enacted over all of southern Greece in order to pressure the king to stand down. By January of 1917, the king had had enough, and he announced that he was going to resign in favor of allowing his son Alexander to become king in his place. As soon as King Constantine was gone and the new king was installed, the opposition party of Venizelos was put back into power.

Greece now had both the public will and the political apparatus to head into the war full force on the side of the Allies. However, things did not go well for Greece at the outset, with the Greek army taking a high number of casualties when they first entered the fray in the spring of 1917. A battlefield success was not achieved until the following year when, in May of 1918, victories were scored against Bulgaria in the Balkans. This again brought forth hope that perhaps Greece could ride the tide of the Allied Powers' success when the war ultimately concluded.

Greece faced another major offensive against the Bulgarians on September 14th, 1918, in which a joint force of Greek and British soldiers stormed into the Vardar Valley of Macedonia and engaged Bulgarian troops stationed around Lake Dorian. The battle was largely a stalemate, but after a prolonged onslaught, the Bulgarians were finally forced to retreat. With the Bulgarians on the run, the Allies shifted strategies and decided to mobilize British and Greek forces to the eastern Ottoman front.

At this point in the war, the situation had changed dramatically. Even though the Allies were gaining ground, they had been hit with the setback of Russia being knocked out of the war. Russia had been beset with internal turmoil from the beginning, and it suffered through a communist revolution in 1917 that overthrew the Russian tsar while Russian troops were still in the trenches. The new Russian/Soviet leadership then quickly moved to end Russia's involvement with the war.

This was a great victory for the Central Powers, but even so, the Ottoman Empire, for one, seemed to be on its last legs. The Ottomans put up a ferocious fight in the beginning phases of the war, but they were now running out of fuel. Greek advocates of the Megali Idea believed that the time to retake Constantinople from Turkey had arrived. But before the Greek army could advance farther, news was received that the worn-down Ottomans had already agreed to sign an armistice.

Once again, the Greeks were thwarted right at the gates of Constantinople, and they were forced to stand down. It was now understood that any further territorial gains for Greece would have to be hammered out through diplomatic negotiations rather than on the battlefield. Nevertheless, it was a great political victory for Greek Prime Minister Venizelos since his belief in the triumph of the Allied Powers had been fulfilled.

Greece also managed to arrive at the scene of this victory in very good shape. Since Greece had entered the war so late, unlike the other Allies, it had been largely shielded from heavy casualties, yet it was still able to claim a seat at the victor's table. In order to reconcile with his most vehement detractors in Greece, Venizelos needed to make sure that Greece was rewarded handsomely for its efforts. Knowing that his skills would be needed to pressure and cajole the Allies to give him the favorable terms he needed, Venizelos embarked on a grand tour of Europe to discuss Greece's post-war plans.

All of this finagling behind the scenes was done in the lead-up to the Paris Peace Conference, which was held in January of 1919. During this conference, the post-war order would be discussed. Venizelos believed that his aims for Greece would be achieved after meeting with the Allied nations to show them his way of thinking. Venizelos spoke before the Council of Ten (the heads of government of the major parties involved in the war) in February of 1919 and laid out his territorial claims.

Right in line with the Megali Idea, Venizelos's demands were indeed big—he insisted on Greek control of Epirus, Thrace, and the Turkish islands of the Aegean, as well as certain islands of the Dodecanese that had been previously claimed by Italy. But even more pressing, he insisted on regaining much of western Turkey where large Greek settlements existed. And although he stopped just short of demanding the return of Constantinople to Greek control, he suggested that Constantinople might become an "international" city. Most of the people present at the conference understood that the internationalization of Constantinople would simply be one further step toward Greece eventually claiming the city as its own.

As provocative as Venizelos's demands were, the Ottoman Empire was in no position to argue. With the whole regime on life support, it was all they could do to keep from completely collapsing. It was actually the Italians who caused the most trouble for these Greek demands since Italy had no intention of giving up any of the islands of the Dodecanese. The Italians were also insulted at the notion that they should concede anything in light of the fact that they had fought harder and longer than the Greeks during the war. The Italians expected to be rewarded with new territory rather than having to give anything up to anyone. In fact, the Italians were so incensed by these demands that Italian warships were sent off the coast of Smyrna in western Turkey in order to intimidate the Greeks.

This led Venizelos to request permission to land troops of his own to protect the territory, which he hoped would soon become part of Greece. He was granted this allowance, and in May of 1919, Greek soldiers arrived on Anatolian shores to prevent any unilateral action on the part of the Italians. This action was enough to deter the Italians, and Smyrna began to function as an unofficial part of the Greek state.

Matters were then made official on August 10th, 1920, when the Turkish government entered into the Treaty of Sèvres. This treaty granted Greece Smyrna, as well as a big chunk of the surrounding territory of western Anatolia. The Greeks were also granted the Sea of Marmara's northern coast, in addition to control of the Gallipoli Peninsula, Thrace, and the Aegean Islands.

The Megali Idea seemed to be alive and well, but like the best ideas of mice and men, it would not take much for this victory to come undone.

Chapter 14 – Greece in between World Wars

"Greece expects you not merely to die for her, for that is little, indeed; she expects you to conquer. That is why each of you, even in dying, should be possessed by one thought alone—how to conserve your strength to the last so that those who survive may conquer. And you will conquer, I am sure of this."

-Eleutherios Venizelos

The arrival of Greek troops in Asia Minor set off a cascade of resentment and fury within the Turkish populations of Asia Minor. Although the government of the Ottoman Empire had been defeated, many in the public did not wish to give up the fight for what they considered vital pieces of their homeland. A Turk by the name of Mustafa Kemal (also known as Kemal Ataturk) took up the banner of resistance and demanded that a new nationalistic Turkish government be formed to prevent the foreign encroachments that the defeated Ottoman state seemed incapable of fending off.

In the fall of 1919, Kemal, riding on a tide of popular Turkish sentiment, had already entered into a dialogue with the Allied Powers, insisting that the sultan had so disgraced himself that he no longer represented the true intentions of the Turks. The Allied Powers knew that this bold man's movement within the Ottoman Empire was indeed a strong one, and the tottering Ottoman government seemed entirely unable to rein it in.

This was of grave concern, as it meant that whatever agreements were reached with the Ottoman government would be rendered null and void if an internal revolution occurred and the Ottoman Empire collapsed outright. These fears seemed to come to fruition in 1920 when the Turkish parliament prepared to declare the emergence of a Turkish national state from the ruins of the Ottoman Empire.

Suddenly, there were two governments in the Turkish domain— the sultan's in Constantinople (Istanbul) and Mustafa Kamal's own seat of power in Ankara, Turkey. Riding on a wave of popular support, Kamal rejected the punishing Treaty of Sèvres entirely and made it known that he would not consider abiding by it for one second.

To the chagrin of the Greeks, the European powers seemed to lose the will to fight and instead began to enter into discussions with the Turkish nationalists. In a last-ditch effort for support, Venizelos reached out to his old British friend, David Lloyd George, to see if he could secure a pledge of British support for military action against the Turkish nationalists, but his requests were not indulged. Britain and the other Allied Powers were now ready to move on. Greece would be on its own.

Along with the threat of the mobilization of Turkish nationalists, Greece began to suffer from its own internal turmoil. First, King Alexander unexpectedly passed away, and in a decidedly bizarre manner. As ridiculous as it sounds, the young king was bitten by a monkey and died from an infection that resulted from the bite. It sounds like something straight out of a tabloid newspaper: "Greek King Bit by Monkey—Dies Terrible Death." But it is the truth.

Apparently, King Alexander was an animal lover, and he had his own personal zoo on the palace grounds. One of his monkeys had gotten into an altercation with his dog, and King Alexander tried to separate them. It was at this point that another monkey nearby jumped on the king and bit him. This bite led to Alexander perishing from blood poisoning on October 25th, 1920. This shock was then coupled with the even greater seismic shift of Venizelos and his party being voted out of power in the November 1920 election.

The party voted in supported bringing back the previous non-expansionist king—Constantine. They successfully voted for this action to be taken, and Constantine was back on the throne that December. Even if the public was still strongly supportive of the Megali Idea, the Greek political landscape was now unstable. And after Venizelos's party was booted out, the new political power players began to remove officials who had previously been loyal to Venizelos. Venizelos himself was deeply dismayed by this chaos, and in a state of depressed resignation, he left Greece entirely to live in what amounted to a self-imposed exile abroad.

Greece had a falling out with the European powers, which remained entirely disenchanted with King Constantine. Britain's most famous statesmen, Winston Churchill, had an interesting take on the whole matter. In light of the communist takeover of Russia, Churchill argued that the Turkish nationalists were the best bulwark against communism in the region. He further insisted that Greek control of the region would be weak and inconsistent, making Turkey vulnerable to communist insurgencies.

The Greeks now saw the writing on the wall, and they knew that their international partners were bailing on them. The Greek supporters of the Megali Idea felt that a repeat of Smyrna was in order. It had taken a show of military force to convince the world that Smyrna belonged to Greece, and if further acquisitions were to be had, it would take another strong showing.

It was with this strategy in mind that the Greek army launched a surprise attack on the capital of the Turkish nationalists, Ankara, on March 23rd, 1921. The attack did not go well, and at least part of the reason why can be attributed to the fact that King Constantine had purged the military of officers who had previously supported Venizelos.

The results of this fateful decision would become quite clear on the battlefield. At one point during the course of the conflict, a group of some 200,000 Greeks were repulsed by the Turkish troops. As the Greeks retreated, they left some twenty thousand dead Greek soldiers behind. The Greeks had found themselves in a very dangerous situation in Anatolia. Along with having to face the resurgent forces of the Turkish nationalists, the Greeks also had to deal with a largely hostile Turkish population who had found itself under Greek control.

Yes, even though the Greek residents of western Anatolia may have been happy with being annexed to Greece, the Turkish residents, who made up a significant number of the population, were not too pleased with the notion. In their eyes, the Greeks were not liberators but a hostile occupying force. As such, the Greek forces could expect nothing but antagonism and even outright attacks from the Turkish locals.

So, even if the Turkish national troops were kept at bay, it would be extremely challenging for the Greeks to administer a region in which a large segment of the population was vehemently against the Greek presence. Even more troubling was the prospect of what might happen to the native Greek residents if the Greek army was to leave western Anatolia. As had been the case for hundreds of years, the Greeks of western Anatolia were in danger of reprisals and even outright massacres at the hands of the Turks. If the Greek military was to suddenly leave, all of the anger and hostility toward the Greek occupation would undoubtedly be targeted at the remaining Greek civilian population. It is possible that a collective pogrom would have been carried out against them by the vengeful Turks.

Due to these fears, it was later determined by the cooler heads that prevailed at the bargaining table that a population exchange program would be the only means to stave off such bloody reprisals. This was a drastic measure for sure, but it would later prove to be the only means to prevent outright genocide from occurring against the Greeks who would ultimately be left behind.

At any rate, the moment of truth came on August 26th, 1922, when the Turks launched a massive offensive that sent the Greek troops in full retreat toward the western Anatolian coastlines. By early September, Greek forces were evacuating from the region. With the Greek troops gone, Turkish troops took control of Smyrna on September 11th, 1922. Almost immediately thereafter, a terrible massacre commenced in which scores of Greek residents were killed. This was followed a couple of days later by a large fire that ended up burning much of the town to the ground.

Coincidentally enough (or perhaps on purpose), the only section of Smyrna that survived the destruction was the Turkish quarter. It is estimated that about 25,000 people died in the inferno, and another 200,000 were left without any resources of which to speak. Many of those left destitute in the rubble actually made their way to the coast, desperately hoping for aid from mainland Greece. Greece, in the meantime, was forced to come to terms, and it hammered out a truce called the Treaty of Lausanne.

Although Greece was soundly defeated by the Turks, the terms were still fairly favorable to the Greeks. While they had to give up any claims to land in Anatolia, they were allowed to keep most of the territory it had prior to World War One. The most lasting impact of the treaty, however, was the aforementioned "population exchange" with the Turks, which was set into motion in May of 1923. The idea of exchanging entire populations based upon ethnicity is certainly controversial, but in light of the smoking ruins of Smyrna and the threat of subsequent massacres, it was viewed as the only way to prevent further reprisals against minority populations.

So, the Greek populations of Anatolia were exchanged for the Turkish populations of Greece. The only Greeks to remain were the 100,000 or so in Constantinople who had a guarantee of international protection, which allowed them to stay in the only home they had ever known. Greece greatly benefited from the importation of a highly skilled labor pool of Ottoman Greeks. Many of the new arrivals had been quite prosperous in the Ottoman Empire and began to lend their skills to Greece itself.

One major development was the introduction of Greek/Turkish-styled tobacco farming. Tobacco soon became the number one trading commodity for Greece as a result. But in the immediate aftermath of the war, few could see the positives that would later develop. At the time, it was a dark period of animosity and recriminations.

In the aftermath of the Smyrna disaster, the Greek king had dismissed parliament and formed a new party led by one Triandafillakos. This move was not popular with the general public or the Greek armed forces, the latter of which, led by Colonel Stylianos Gonatas, decided to let their voices be heard by dropping leaflets all over Athens by air on September 26th, explicitly calling for King Constantine to step down. Knowing that his time was up, King Constantine obliged, and he resigned as king the following day. Shortly thereafter, a provisional government was established in Athens by Greek General Theodoros Pangalos, along with his colleagues and fellow generals, Gargalidis and Mazaakis. With the support of some twelve thousand troops at their disposal.

Power was then given to a revolutionary committee, which had to sort out the state's affairs. King Constantine and his family were shipped off to their exile in Palermo. King George II was installed in his place. King George II's reign was rather short-lived, though; in April of 1924, the Greek public cast their votes at the ballot box in favor of the creation of the Hellenic Republic. It is said that 758,472 Greeks voted in favor of forming the Hellenic republic, while 325,322, voted to keep the constitutional monarchy.

Among those who voted for the republic was a considerable portion of recent Greek refugees. The Greek refugees associated the idea of a king with the failures of the Greco-Turkish War that had uprooted them from their homes. So, it is really no wonder they would have voted to abolish the monarchy.

The refugees also tended to be supporters of Venizelists. However, in June of 1925, a military takeover was orchestrated by General Theodoros Pangalos. This military government was, in turn, toppled by yet another coup, which was launched in the summer of 1926 by Colonel Georgios Kondylis. The only hope for the Greeks appeared to be the ballot box, and droves went to vote in 1928. After the 1928 election, Venizelos and his party were voted back into power.

Venizelos's first effort in office was to create strong relations with Greece's neighbors. He signed agreements with Italy and Yugoslavia, and he opened up dialogue with Albania. But perhaps most importantly, he sought to tamp down the discontent of the public by improving Greece's economy. He did this by focusing on improving agricultural production, as well as improving the nation's infrastructure. He also made sure that the school systems were modernized and made available to the populace.

Initially, the reforms went over well, for the Greeks now had enough food to eat, decent roads on which to drive, and good schools to which to send their kids. This was definitely an improvement, but these improvements were sharply curtailed in 1929 with the start of the worldwide economic downturn known as the Great Depression. The Great Depression affected many nations around the globe, but interestingly enough, one of the most negative impacts was the fact that Greeks in the United States found themselves unemployed and were therefore unable to send money back home to Greece. A large part of the Greek economy had been aided by these remittance payments, which collectively stimulated the Greek financial markets.

In many countries around the world, failed economies had become the playground of communist uprisings. Communists often used an economic collapse as a reason to point to the perceived failures of capitalism and to call for the centralized control of world economies by communist states. Fearing the same forces might try to take advantage of the economic troubles in Greece, Venizelos tried to head communism off at the pass by issuing the so-called "Idionymon Law," which made it illegal to have political association with groups that tried to undermine the social order. This meant, of course, that the communist party, which called for the overthrow of capitalism, would be entirely banned from Greece.

As fate would have it, Venizelos was voted out of office in 1933. Due to his electoral defeat, it seemed that his policies might be dead in the water. However, shortly after his defeat, Venizelos's supporters in the military attempted to launch a coup. The coup failed, and in the backlash against Venizelos and all who supported him, an attempt was made on Venizelos's life. Thankfully for Venizelos, this attempt failed just as the coup had, and in one of the most dramatic moments in Greek history, Venizelos was seen stepping out of a car filled with bullet holes, unharmed. This event seemed to set a fire in Venizelos's soul, and he tried one last uprising himself. In the spring of 1935, he staged a revolt against the government.

However, it did not go quite so well, and Venizelos was ultimately forced to flee to Rhodes. He would die roughly one year later in March of 1936 as an exile in Paris, France. This marked the end of the Venizelos movement. Not only was their leader dead, but those who had supported or even just sympathized with him were also steadily removed from any and all positions of power. Those who wished to restore the monarchy were now in a powerful position, and in November of 1935, they did just that, installing King George II back on the throne.

King George II then selected a Greek army officer—Ioannis Metaxas—as the next prime minister on April 13th, 1936. Metaxas was authoritarian in the extreme, and in what must have been one of the most comical sessions of parliament ever, he bullied parliamentarians to vote themselves out of existence, with 241 members voting for the suspension of parliament.

The only real resistance to Metaxas was the remaining communist element. This group managed to put together several labor strikes in May of 1936, the climax of which was a massive strike that hit the tobacco industry in Thessalonica. These efforts produced such a backlash that these subversive actors were completely shut down, as Metaxas convinced the king to censor the news media and curtail other constitutional rights. Soon, workers were no longer allowed to gather for strikes at all.

Metaxas was now the real power behind the throne, and he began to mobilize 1930s Greece into what could only be described as an authoritarian, fascist state. But although Greece was taking on the trappings of a fascist dictatorship, it would not fall in line with similar movements that were afoot in Spain, Italy, and Germany. Greek fascism would remain peculiarly isolated and even at odds with its similarly fascist counterparts. Part of the reason for this was the simple fact that Greece was still greatly beholden to Great Britain. Greece could not risk getting out of Britain's good graces, and unless Britain itself were to suddenly turn fascist, there was no way that Greece would risk its relationship with Britain by getting cozy with Italy, Spain, or Germany.

So, ideology aside, when World War Two commenced in 1939, Greece chose a course of pragmatism and did everything it could to stay out of the growing conflict. Greece's Mediterranean neighbor Italy would decide to push the issue. Italy invaded Albania in April of 1939, placing Italian troop detachments right across the Greek border. Fascist Italian dictator Benito Mussolini then delivered an ultimatum to Metaxas on October 28th, 1940, demanding that he allow Italian troops to move across the border to occupy certain strategic positions. And these demands had to be met in the next few hours.

It is said that when Metaxas was alerted to these impetuous demands, he declared, "I could not make a decision to sell my house on a few hours' notice. How do you expect me to sell my country? No!" As controversial as he was, Metaxas's "No!" would become Greece's rallying cry during the course of the conflict. Mussolini almost certainly knew that his demands would be rejected, and before the arbitrary deadline set for compliance had even run out, Italian troops were crossing over into Greece.

But even though Mussolini thought he was going to bully the Greeks into submission, he was in for a big surprise. Because as divided and chaotic as Greece had become over the last few years, the invasion of the Italians served to unite the Greeks together against a common enemy. And just about everyone was suddenly taking up Metaxas's rallying cry of "No!" The Greek forces quickly mobilized and managed to completely encircle the invading 3rd Alpine Division of Italy.

With this group of Italian troops neutralized, the Greek troops quickly turned the tables on the Italians and rapidly marched north to invade Italian-controlled Albania. This reversal was a severe embarrassment to Italy's ambition, but it did not necessarily mean that Greece would be pushed out of its position of neutrality. It was actually the British who would pull the Greeks into a war with Germany by insisting that the Greeks join them as an official ally in the struggle.

Britain began to suggest that the Greeks should allow British troops to be deployed in Greece. Knowing this would bring the full fury of Germany down on Greece, Metaxas refused to allow the British to do so. Metaxas soon would not have a say in the matter, though. On January 29th, 1941, he unexpectedly died of what has been described as a bad case of "phlegmon of the pharynx." He was then succeeded by Alexandros Koryzis.

Koryzis decided to take the British up on their offer, and he agreed to allow the British Expeditionary Force to land on Greek soil. The British arrived in March of 1941, and shortly thereafter, Adolf Hitler made the fateful decision to invade Greece. The reasoning behind this invasion was that he had already been planning a sneak attack on the Soviet Union, and having Allied forces to the south of German troops marching through the Balkans was viewed as an intolerable position in which to be.

So, predictably enough (and just as Metaxas feared would be the case), the Germans launched an invasion of Greece to clear out the Allies. If the British and Greeks had more time to solidify their positions, it is possible they could have repulsed the Germans, but as it was, the joint British-Greek forces had been hastily prepared and were not ready for the massive onslaught Nazi Germany was about to unleash upon them.

Chapter 15 – Greece during the Second World War

"Fascism, the more it considers and observes the future and the development of humanity, quite apart from political considerations of the moment, believes neither in the possibility nor the utility of perpetual peace."

-Benito Mussolini

Greece managed to stay out of World War Two for the first couple years of the fight, but in 1941, after Prime Minister Metaxas perished, his successor, Alexandros Koryzis, allowed the British to land troops on Greek soil, therefore ending Greek neutrality. Once Greece was officially in the Allies' orbit, Germany did not hesitate to invade. In April of 1941, the Germans, with some Italian auxiliaries, launched an invasion into the Greek heartland.

There was confusion from the start since the Greeks and the British had different strategies for the defense of Greece. The British wished for the Greeks to pull back so they could mobilize in the more defensible terrain of the Aliakmon Line. The Greeks, however, refused to give an inch of their territory to the invaders and stayed where they were. Thus, when the German army entered Greece, it found disorder and a lack of coordination in the ranks.

The Germans split into three main groups. One group drove south, pinning the Greek forces there, and the other two drove east to slam into Greek defenders in Thessaloniki. German forces managed to reach Athens on April 18th. As the Germans poured in, Greek Prime Minister Alexandros Koryzis made the fateful decision to take his own life. Martial law had been declared in the city, and the general public was informed that Koryzis had died of a heart attack rather than by suicide so as not to inflame tensions in the city even further. Greek politician Emmanouil Tsouderos would be appointed to succeed him.

The masterstroke came when the Germans cut off the British army, isolating them from the Greek forces. By the end of the month, British forces were retreating toward Corinth. The Germans would once again cut them off by deploying paratroopers onto the Isthmus of Corinth on April 26th, blocking their exit.

Despite the odds being stacked against their escape, the British and their commonwealth allies—some fifty thousand in all—managed to march north once again and make their way through the mountains of Roumeli They then made their way to the shores of the Peloponnese, where they were evacuated and taken to the island of Crete, which was still under Allied control.

The key word here is "still" since it would not be under Allied control for much longer. In the following month, on May 20th, the Germans launched an all-out assault on Crete. The Germans employed some four hundred bombers and dive bombers to blast the British positions to smithereens and then again used paratroopers and even their glider troops (German soldiers on hang gliders) to swarm the island. As daring as the German paratroopers and glider troopers were, some found themselves on a suicide mission because as much as German airpower had attempted to pound Allied defenses into submission, the defenders were still able to take pot shots at the Germans whenever they had a chance.

Others got caught on trees and other terrain and were massacred by angry villagers. But despite these losses, the Germans proved to be unstoppable. They had complete control of the skies and the surrounding area; it was only a matter of time before Crete fell. Before all was lost, the British did manage to evacuate King George and then Prime Minister Emmanouil Tsouderos, but Greek freedom itself was temporarily snuffed out. Once the Greeks were defeated by the Axis, Greek territory was divvied up between German, Bulgarian, and Italian zones.

This was certainly not what Italian dictator Mussolini had intended since he wanted to conquer all of Greece and incorporate it into his fascist Italian empire. But due to all of his previous blunders and inept abilities as a military commander, this was the arrangement for which he had to settle.

The Italian occupation zone was in western Greece, and it has been said that the Italian occupation was a fairly benign one. But the Greeks were still cognizant of the fact that it was the Italians who had started this whole mess, so they were most certainly not in the mood to make nice with the Italians. The German occupation zone, predictably enough, was the most brutal and oppressive.

It did not take much for the Greeks to end up on the wrong side of the Germans. They ran their sector as a totalitarian police state, and one wrong move could get a Greek resident hauled off to be imprisoned, tortured, or killed. In May of 1941 alone, it is said that two hundred villagers in the German-controlled village of Kastelli were shot and killed due to alleged insubordination. In 1943, an even worse incidence of mass murder occurred when 1,400 were killed in the town of Kalavryta.

Having said that, if the Germans were trying to win the hearts and minds of those they occupied, they sure had a funny way of showing it. And of course, for the Jewish residents, the consequences of German occupation were even more terrible. It is said that in Thessalonica alone, which had a Jewish community that dated back several centuries, over fifty thousand Jews were gathered up and sent to concentration camps. Due to the systematic removal conducted by the Germans, by 1942, the old Jewish quarters of Greece no longer existed.

The rest of the Greeks who remained faced starvation since many of the food imports that made up important staples of their diet were no longer available due to a blockade set up by the Allied Powers. The blockade was put in place to hurt the Axis Powers (Germany, Italy, and Japan), but it actually hurt the Greek civilians trapped under the Axis dominion more. In total, it is said that during the occupation of the Axis, an astonishing 8 percent of the Greek population perished.

Death by malnutrition was a serious threat. According to war historian Mark Mazower, those who were malnourished were easily spotted in the street due to the tumors and boils that would form all over their bodies. This is apparently due to the body's compromised immune system, which had been weakened from a lack of proper food. Bacteria apparently is able to grow unchecked in the pores of the skin when the immune system is significantly weakened from malnutrition. This frightening phenomenon could be seen in the pock-marked faces of many of those starving to death in Nazi-occupied Greece. It also was common for those near death to just suddenly collapse and die.

According to official Ministry of Health Data of in 1942, the rate of deaths in Greece shot up over the rate of births. As anyone can imagine, a society in which people are dying faster than they are being born is most certainly one that is in decline. Another sign was the local cemeteries, which were overwhelmed with a massive influx of dead to bury, especially during the winter months. And for those who did not die, the stress of the ordeal was certainly taking its toll.

The Greek populace was understandably under great strain, and many Greeks were at their wit's end. Many personal accounts have since emerged from survivors. One particularly poignant one comes down to us from a Greek woman by the name of Ionna Tsatsou, who was involved with some homegrown relief efforts at the time. She vividly recalled the desperation of the masses. She herself was more fortunate than most Greeks since she was the wife of an affluent college professor, but she often saw firsthand the havoc that food shortages had on the less fortunate.

She was particularly distressed by the starving children she encountered. The things she saw deeply affected her, and at times, they even haunted her dreams. And on one particular evening, one dream in particular stood out to her. She dreamt of "a large table laid with the most beautiful food and drink. At its head the Christ child was seated, and round him countless little Greek children. All ate compulsively and with gusto, smearing their faces. Among them many of my little friends. I awoke with the feeling of coming out of paradise and sinking slowly but consciously into a familiar nightmare." For her, waking up to the grim reality of Nazi occupation truly was a nightmare of the worst kind.

The Greeks did get some respite in the summer of 1942 when the British relaxed their blockade and allowed wheat to be shipped from Canada to those in need in Greece. This valuable aid was enough to relieve the famine and prevent a multitude of deaths due to starvation. As helpful as all this was, some could not help but blame the British for putting the blockade up in the first place.

But the British, in turn, blamed the occupying Axis Powers for refusing to provide resources to those whom they had conquered. But regardless of how much blame they shared for Greece's burdens, the greatest hope that the Greeks had, at least initially, was that the British would come to their rescue, and there were often rumors of the imminent arrival of a British fleet that would drive the occupiers out.

In the early days of the occupation, the Greeks even showed their defiance by actively fraternizing with British prisoners of war. There were more than a few accounts of Greeks surrounding German trucks loaded with British prisoners of war and loudly cheering and applauding them. Some were even offered cigarettes and beer. The Germans, of course, were none too pleased, and they would promptly chase the crowds off.

There were also many cases of Greek civilians taking in and sheltering British troops who still remained at large. They did this at great risk to themselves, for if the German authorities learned of what they were doing, they would no doubt be killed. But despite the Greek support of the British, as the days of the occupation wore on, hopes for an early rescue by outside forces increasingly dimmed.

The Greeks were determined to resist their occupiers, though, and it is said that immediately after the regular armies of Greece were defeated, homegrown bands of rebel fighters made their way to the remote mountainous terrain of the nation where they could prepare for the next phase of the war. Known as the "People's War," this phase had regular everyday Greeks prepared to engage in a long, drawn-out spate of guerrilla warfare against their oppressors.

Early on, a leading figure in this struggle for freedom emerged: Athanasios Klaras (also known as Aris Velouchiotis). Klaras was actually an active member of Greek's underground communist party, and he was a known left-wing ideologue. His National Liberation Front, which in Greek was called the Ethniko Apeleftherotiko Metopowhich, or EAM for short, would become the main focal point of resistance against the Axis Powers that occupied Greece.

He was said to have been a charismatic leader, and most importantly as it pertained to the armed resistance, he was a very capable military strategist. Although the roots of the EAM were communist, they were so successful that they ended up attracting

Greek people from all ideological backgrounds to their ranks. Not surprisingly, many Greeks were eager to join a common effort to resist the fascist occupation of their country. The group was so successful that in the fall of 1942, the British were able to use them to sabotage an important railway bridge to prevent the Germans from supplying forces farther to the south.

This was of extreme importance, as by this point, the Germans were actively sending supplies down this track of rail to southern Greece and then on to Axis positions in North Africa. The Allies were desperately trying to gain ground in North Africa, and they knew that cutting off this active supply line to the Axis would be of tremendous help. That September, the British actually dropped a small contingent into the mountain stronghold of the guerrilla fighters and helped orchestrate the operation directly from the ground.

Ideologically opposed factions of the resistance were convinced to put aside their differences for the common strategy of defeating the occupiers. The group struck on the evening of November 25th, 1942, successfully disabling the railroad by destroying the Gorgopotamos railway bridge. This was a great boon not only to the resistance but also to the greater war effort since it made Axis positions in North Africa more vulnerable and therefore easier to defeat, as the Allies attempted to use North Africa as a stepping stone to an invasion of Italy.

The Allies were indeed able to leap frog from North Africa to Sicily and then on to Italy. The Italians were unable to face the full force of the Allies, and they quickly came to terms and surrendered on September 8th, 1943. Interestingly enough, at least part of the Allies' success against the Italians was due to an elaborate ruse that had been perpetrated by the British. Known as Operation Mincemeat, the British pulled off a fairly morbid stunt in which they dressed a dead body up as a British officer and left it off the coast of fascist Spain for the Axis to find.

The British planted official looking documents on the corpse that detailed an upcoming Allied attempt to land in Greece and Sardinia. These plans were false, as the Allies were aiming for Sicily and then Italy. The Germans apparently took the bait, and even Hitler was convinced that the invasion would take place in the Greek theater. So, while the Germans were shoring up defenses in Greece, they neglected to fortify their positions around Italy, allowing the Allies to have a much easier time of things than they otherwise would have.

At any rate, as soon as news of Italy's surrender reached Greek ears, many Italian troops were murdered on the spot. The Italian government may have waved the white flag, but even with their hands up, some Greeks were ready for revenge. Although some Greeks sought vengeance on the deposed Italians, there were those who would just as soon celebrate with them. Some disillusioned Italians even began arming the resistance, selling guns, grenades, and other military equipment to the very groups that would continue the struggle against the Germans.

As soon as the Germans got wind of this, it created a predictable firestorm of wrath. The German liaison staff in Athens, General Heinz von Gyldenfeldt, told his Italian counterpart General Carlo Vecchiarelli in no uncertain terms, "If there were a rejection of a continuation of the fight [Italian surrender] then the German Army must, for its own security, be certain that Italian weapons would never be turned on the Germans, i.e., they must be surrendered to the German Army."

The Germans then systematically disarmed the Italians without incident. The German high command then gave the Italian troops the choice of either joining up with German troops or be evacuated from Greece. Most chose the latter. Sadly enough, for the Italians, they were deliberately misled into thinking that they were being evacuated back to Italy. This was not the case, as the Germans likely did not want to repatriate troops that could possibly turn on them later. Instead, they were put on a train that took them straight through the Balkans to Yugoslavia, where they were put in concentration camps and held as prisoners of war.

Not all of the Italians handed over their weapons peacefully. On the island of Rhodes, where the Germans were greatly outnumbered by the Italians, Italian troops refused to comply with German demands. This led to some pretty serious skirmishes between the two until the Germans finally forced the Italians to surrender, resulting in over forty thousand Italian prisoners of war being shipped off by the Germans.

Some Italians in mainland Greece opted for a third option. Rather than joining ranks with the Germans or risk facing deportation, they took to the hills and joined the Greek guerrilla fighters they found there. British intelligence actually estimated that by April of 1944, there were about ten thousand Italians who had joined ranks with the Greeks. At this point, the communist groups were controlling much of the rural countryside, and acting as a state within a state, they were even collecting taxes from the local villagers. It was claimed that these taxes were used to provide for the poor, but many believed it was just to line the pockets of the communists.

With the Italians out of the picture, the Germans redoubled their efforts to put down the Greek rebels, and—if it were even possible—they entered a new level of brutality. None other than German Field Marshal Wilhelm Keitel had advised, "This fight has nothing to do with a soldier's chivalry nor with the decisions of the Geneva Conventions. If this fight against the bands, in the East as well as the Balkans is not carried out with the most brutal means, the forces at our disposal may in the near future not last out to master this plague. The troops are therefore authorized and ordered in this struggle to take any measures without restriction even against women and children if these are necessary for success. [Humanitarian] considerations of any kind are a crime against the German nation."

This was the backward morality of the Germans during the war. Even while they were committing crimes against humanity, the German high command preached that showing the enemy any sense of compassion or "humanitarian consideration" was in itself considered a crime. Brainwashed with propaganda such as this, German troops acted as exterminators, engaging in the wholesale liquidation of rebels—male, female, young, or old—without any remorse or compassion.

The Italians, for their part, were notorious for fraternizing with the enemy, and many had Greek girlfriends on the side. The Germans, however, were strictly ordered to have no relations with non-Germans. They were simply told to ruthlessly root out and kill their enemies. For the most part, German soldiers seemed to abide by these chilling principles of unrelenting extermination. But no matter how many villages they burned, civilians they massacred, communist strongholds they leveled, the rebellion would not be stamped out.

Roughly a year after the Italians first folded, the German forces were on the run as well. The Soviet push into Romania led the Germans troops to withdraw from Greece in August of 1944 so that they could redeploy to face the more pressing threat of Russian troops storming through eastern Europe. In the meantime, the factions that had been working together in the Greek resistance began to split apart in a full-blown civil war, as communist forces and more conservative forces began to battle for the future of the post-war Greek state.

That October, even as British troops were landing on Greek shores, the communist Greek People's Liberation Army managed to gain the upper hand when they took over the Greek capital of Athens. Before World War Two was over, one of the major flashpoints of what would become the Cold War had already begun.

Chapter 16 – The Greek Post World War Order

"Beauty addresses itself chiefly to sight, but there is a beauty for the hearing too, as in certain combinations of words and in all kinds of music; for melodies and cadences are beautiful and minds that lift themselves above the realm of sense to a higher order are aware of beauty in the conduct of life, in actions, in character, in the pursuits of intellect; and there is the beauty of the virtues."

-Plotinus

In the immediate aftermath of the German withdrawal from Greece in 1944, the communist leftists initially had the upper hand and may well have taken hold of the entire nation if it was not for British intervention. Yes, Britain had long held Greece as a vital interest, and not wishing a communist takeover of the Greek homeland, the British decided to put their thumb on the scale in favor of the Greek nationalists.

In December of 1944, the Greek government in exile had returned, and with the support of the British, it was ready to do battle with the communist insurgency that had erupted in Greece.

Of course, a major objective of this was to retake the capital of Athens. During the course of this conflict, over ten thousand people were killed, and much of the city was damaged. In the spring of 1945, the British brokered a provisional government led by Greek General Nikolaos Plastiras.

As a means of securing peace, Plastiras enacted a national amnesty, in which former communists were promised that they would not be prosecuted as long as they laid down their arms. But this declaration of amnesty never really materialized. Instead, the White Terror was unleashed against all who were even suspected of having anything to do with the communist forces. In this sweep for communists and communist sympathizers, thousands were thrown in jails and hundreds were killed, some of them for offenses so petty and obscure as simply uttering what was considered inflammatory rhetoric.

It seems that out of sheer fear, either of communists or of being labeled a communist, the traditional factions of Greek politics, the Venizelist-styled populist liberals and conservative royalists, joined forces at the ballot box. General elections were held in March of 1946, and a right-wing candidate named Constantine Tsaldaris (also known as Konstantinos Tsaldaris) came to power, fronting the United Patriotic Party. Tsaldaris continued the crackdown on suspected communist subversives. The situation became so oppressive that, by the summer of 1946, an estimated eighty thousand Greeks fled the country.

The following fall saw the return of King George II to Greece, although he would ultimately pass away just six months later, with his sibling Paul being crowned king in his place.

Despite the support of the monarchy in Greece and the persecution of the communists, many budding Marxists were waiting in the wings for a communist takeover. Much of their hope lay in the fact that the Soviet Union was increasing in power in the region. Among other things, Soviet leader Joseph Stalin had insisted that the British make their exit, and many believed that the vacuum that would be brought about with the withdrawal of the British might allow communist Marxists to come in and fill the gaps. The underground Communist Party of Greece, the KKE, even actively called for partisans to prepare themselves for the next phase of the armed struggle against the Greek state.

And then, on October 26th, 1946, Markos Vafeiadis marked a new milestone in the struggle by declaring that he had formed a new Democratic Army, which consisted of tens of thousands of fighters. Up until 1949, this group harassed and alluded Greek's state military by hiding out in remote tracts along the Yugoslavian and Albanian borders. The tactics this army employed were not dissimilar to how the Viet Cong hid in the borderlands between Cambodia, Laos, and Vietnam during the course of the Vietnam War.

For the rebels, relations with Yugoslavia were important since it was believed that Josip Broz Tito's communist regime might lend a hand to help. It was with this in mind that the KKE and its Democratic Army holed up in the mountains of Greece, waiting for the next fortuitous time to strike. That moment appeared in the spring of 1947 when the British announced to the United States that its position in Greece was no longer tenable.

But if the communists felt that the departure of the British would give them free reign in Greece, they had another thing coming. Shortly after the British announced their decision to withdraw, United States President Harry Truman announced his Truman Doctrine, which vowed that the United States was committed to "fight communism wherever it might appear in the world." This meant that the Greek communists were now up against one of the most powerful nations on the planet. Not only would the Americans send tons of money to right-wing Greek politicians, but it also would not hesitate to send boots on the ground if they thought it could deter a communist takeover.

The United States wanted to stand as a bulwark against communism, but the effect that US policy had with the more draconian measures being taken by the Greek government was certainly a little more than for which it had bargained. For after the United States essentially handed the Greek authoritarians a blank check, they basically went ballistic on the KKE.

Greece's infamous minister of public order, Napoleon Zerva, arranged the imprisonment of countless Greek dissidents. Civil liberties were also snuffed out when certain communist-leaning newspapers were banned, and then in December of 1947, the KKE itself was made illegal. All of these crackdowns, which had the West's backing, culminated in the declaration of martial law in 1948, during which hundreds were summarily executed on the spot.

These startling developments obviously caused the communists to change tactics, and the so-called "hardline Stalinist" of the KKE, Nikos Zachariadis, began to retool what was left of the Democratic Army. If anyone could survive an onslaught, it was Nikos Zachariadis. Nikos had actually been interned at the Dachau concentration camp for several years until he was liberated by the Allies. He then arrived back in Greece to his comrades in the spring of 1945 in what was a rather dramatic scene.

And during the martial law crackdowns of 1948, it was Nikos who positioned himself as being the one who could somehow snatch victory from the jaws of defeat. It was with this mindset that some twelve thousand communist fighters faced off against some seventy thousand federal Greek troops in what the Greek national government had dubbed "Operation Koronis."

The battle was waged in the borderlands between Greece and Albania, which was mountainous terrain. The communist rebels held out for several weeks, but after sustained pressure and even a NATO (North Atlantic Treaty Organization) bombing of Mount Grammos, they were ultimately left with two distinct choices: fight to the last man, or leave the country. Many chose the latter and fled across the border.

More trouble for the Greek communists emerged in July of 1948 when their fellow communist strongman Josip Broz Tito of Yugoslavia (better known simply as Tito) had a falling out with Stalin. The two would remain alienated for the rest of the Cold War. But the Greek Marxists now had to decide whether they should align with the isolated Tito, who was nearby, or the main wellspring of Marxism, the Soviet Union, which was farther to the north. Although Tito was a powerful neighbor, they opted to stick with the big guy in the north. It did not do them much good, though, since Stalin did not consider Greece strategically important enough for Soviet ambition to rile the Western powers.

And spurning Tito certainly did not do the revolutionaries any favors either since Tito promptly shut down his border with Greece, cutting off one of the main escape routes in the mountains. Those who did not get slaughtered by federal forces were forced to accept defeat, and many lived as exiles in Albania. Although the Cold War, which was between the forces of capitalism and communism, would continue for the better part of the 20th century, communism was rather decisively vanquished in Greece.

Greece proved to be the first great victory of the Western capitalists' efforts in stamping out communism. Greece, for its efforts, was rewarded with a seat at the NATO table. But even though Greece was given a solid role to play in the free world, Greek politics would remain polarized between far right and far left ideologies. Nevertheless, life in Greece dramatically improved between the early 1950s and early 1970s. This era, which is sometimes referred to as the Greek Miracle, saw Greece beset with such rapid economic advancement that the only country to outpace Greece's rapid ascent was Japan.

But even though the domestic situation was improving in Greece, there was still more than enough political discontent to muddy the waters. And that discontent came boiling to the surface in 1967 when members of the Greek armed forces managed to topple the duly elected prime minister, Panagiotis Kanellopoulos, in a military coup. This kick-started the rise of the Greek military junta, which would rule the country until 1974.

This military government was established by a couple of Greek colonels, namely, Georgios Papadopoulos, Nikolaos Makarezos, and Stylianos Pattakos. This takeover blindsided both the international community and many Greeks alike. The motivations for this junta were multiple, ranging from preventing a liberal party from solidifying power to ensuring that military officers received a long overdue pay raise.

But like with most authoritarian regimes, the fact that this group had seized power—regardless of the reasons—made them on the hook to maintain it. They knew that the second they relinquished the power that they had gained, they themselves would be held accountable. The junta lasted for nearly a decade, and it was largely continued by strongmen who found that once they held fast to the reins of power, they were simply unable to let go.

Once in power, the junta presented itself as the guardian of Greece. Predictably enough, the members of the junta were vehemently against communism. This allowed them to avoid the ire of the United States. However, this military clique was not well groomed enough to suit the traditional intelligentsia, and their ham-fisted ways most certainly did not get them into the good graces of the Greek elite.

They did their best to harness a sense of Greek nationalism by promoting what they viewed as the best of Greek history. In fact, the generals strove to rewrite the history books just to better promote their views. Having said that, some of their views were most certainly rather narrow-minded, such as the notion that men should not have long hair (this was during the late 1960s hippie heyday) and that women should not be allowed to wear mini-skirts.

But although some of the ultra-conservative sensibilities of the regime were somewhat jarring, the colonels managed to continue the steady rise of Greece's economy. They also made sure that the general standard of living went up. So, even if a man could not wear his hair long, most of the people were kept content due to the economy's progress. And whatever dissidents did emerge were quickly shut down. Criticism was stifled in the press, and anyone deemed to be against the government was hauled off to prison. It was in 1968/1969 that one of the greatest purges of dissidents occurred. Within this timeframe, several military officials, as well as a whopping nine hundred government officials, were sacked from their positions.

As the junta progressed, one colonel rose above the others—Colonel George Papadopoulos. The king of Greece more or less sat back in a state of helplessness while all of this was going on around him. The monarchy would finally come to an end when Papadopoulos moved to abolish it in June of 1973. He also went ahead and proclaimed that Greece was a republic with himself as president.

However, it would not last, and in just a matter of months, Papadopoulos was booted out of power and replaced by Colonel Dimitrios Ioannides. Colonel Ioannides was a true revolutionary, and he soon attempted to instigate upheaval in neighboring Cyprus. The status of Cyprus had long been a contentious issue between the Greeks and their neighbors, the Turks. At one time, Cyprus had been a part of the Byzantine Empire. The Turks had conquered it, and they controlled the region until the British took it from them in 1878. All throughout this period, Cyprus was heavily populated by Greeks, and in 1950, Archbishop Makarios III became the so-called "Ethnarch" of the island, which was a religious as well as a cultural leadership role over the Greek Cypriots. Makarios led a popular movement calling for unification with mainland Greece, which would dominate Greek political discussions over the next two decades.

Britain, in the meantime, began to push back against the notion, and great tensions were sparked as a result. The matter was then complicated when Turkish nationalists began to argue that Cyprus should become part of Turkey. This point was made clear in 1955 when, during a conference in London, it was proclaimed that the moment the British should leave the island, it would immediately return to the Turkish domain.

It was only when the Turks began to assert themselves over the island that the situation truly became dangerous. And the fact that both Turkey and Greece were NATO members made the situation all the more distressing for the Western powers.

In the meantime, Archbishop Makarios III had been officially elected president of Cyprus in December of 1959, cementing his role as the leader of the island. Earlier that year, the British had finally come around to the notion of the independence of Cyprus, and they reached an agreement with Cypriot authorities that would establish an autonomous Cypriot republic. These plans came to fruition in 1960 when a republic was officially declared.

Turkey, of course, was not too pleased with these developments, and soon, tensions were on the verge of boiling over. The colonels also had to deal with this problem. In fact, shortly after the colonels' military takeover of Greece, Turkey was threatening to invade the island in the wake of unrest between Greek and Turkish residents.

It was in light of all of this unrest that some began to consider an official union with Greece as a potential means of offsetting Turkish aggression in Cyprus. The colonels also sought to score some political points, thinking that laying claim to Cyprus was a surefire way to stir up Greek patriotism.

In June 1974, Greece's military-controlled government moved to support the union of Cyprus with Greece, thinking that by supporting a popular cause of the people, they would therefore ensure their own grip on power. However, relations with the military junta and the Makarios government on Cyprus were absolutely terrible at the time. Makarios presented himself as a centrist leader, and he had been at odds with the right-wing takeover of Greece from the beginning.

It was not long before Greece's military government began to hatch plots to get Makarios out of the way. These plans unraveled on July 15th, 1974, when Archbishop Makarios narrowly escaped an assassination attempt and ran to a British military base on Cyprus for help before being evacuated by helicopter. After Makarios's departure, Colonel Ioannides had a right-wing journalist by the name of Nikos Sampson installed in his place. Apparently, the Greeks in power hoped that Nikos could work with Greece to unite Cyprus to the motherland, but it was not to be. Before any such thing could happen, neighboring Turkey used the chaos as an excuse to invade Cyprus itself.

Turkey would dig in deep and occupy Northern Cyprus where a large Turkish population was already in place. This invasion would have ramifications that would last to this very day, with Cyprus becoming permanently divided between the so-called "Turkish Republic of Northern Cyprus" and the heavily Greek populated portion of southern Cyprus. The situation soon became so unstable, that Greece's military junta found itself unable to govern Greece—*let alone Cyprus*. And rather than riding on a wave of popular enthusiasm, it soon collapsed under its own weight.

Chapter 17 – Greece at the End of the Millennium

"The tyrant, who in order to hold his power, suppresses every superiority, does away with good men, forbids education and light, controls every movement of the citizens, and, keeping them under a perpetual servitude, wants them to grow accustomed to baseness and cowardice, has his spies everywhere to listen to what is said in the meetings, and spreads dissension and calumny among the citizens and impoverishes them, is obliged to make war in order to keep his subjects occupied and impose on them permanent need of a chief."

-Aristotle

After the military junta failed, the Third Hellenic Republic was declared in 1974, and Greek politician Konstantinos Karamanlis was made the interim prime minister on July 23rd, 1974. Although this was intended to just be a quick fix, Konstantinos was reelected for another two terms, along with his New Democratic Party.

Around this time, another powerful Greek political figure, Andreas Papandreou, made his way back to Greece and established a party known as PASOK. In English, PASOK basically stands for "Panhellenic Socialist Movement." Papandreou's party would continue to gain steam over the next few years, and it would ultimately become the driving force of Greece.

Konstantinos, in the meantime, would be elected once again in 1977, and his party gained 172 seats in the Greek Parliament. But it was Papandreou's party that was the real rising star, as it got a total of 25 percent of the vote that election, making it clearly the next most viable political party in Greece. Although Papandreou had eschewed anything to do with outright communism, he remained the choice for the socialist leftists, a fact that was proven when Papandreou won the presidency in 1981.

With Greek stability finally achieved, Greece entered into the growing European Union. Although Papandreou was a left-leaning socialist, he was at heart a populist since he channeled the popular sentiment of the Greek people at the time. And the most popular sentiment rising in the hearts of most Greeks was the sentiment of self-determination. Greece had been considered an independent state since 1821, but for many, this seemed to have been only an illusion, as Greece was constantly being buffeted by the intrigues of the surrounding great powers.

After all, at the dawning of Greek independence in 1821, European powers had felt that the Greeks were not ready for democracy, so they installed an autocratic king. Through this foreign-installed king, the Europeans continued to meddle in Greek internal affairs. Greece was made to fight in World War One at the behest of its European allies, and it was given the false impression that Greek-speaking regions of the defeated Ottoman Empire would be reincorporated into the Greek homeland.

Yet, when Turkey's Mustafa Kemal unleashed a ferocious onslaught against the Greeks, the Western powers did practically nothing to help. Greece had attempted to stay neutral during

World War Two, but at the behest of Great Britain, it had been forced to allow British troops to enter its land, which led to a German invasion and occupation that the West was either too unprepared or too unwilling to prevent. After surviving the brutality of the Nazis, the Western powers continued to push Greece around, supporting right-wing governments out of fear of a communist takeover.

Many Greeks felt that this interference had led to the military junta and all of the turmoil that it brought. It was for all of this and more that the Greeks were inherently distrustful of the Western powers, even though the nation was a part of NATO and the European Union. It was also for this reason that Papandreou was so popular, as he spoke to the common man and insisted that he would help Greece stand on its own. Andreas Papandreou promised that Greece would determine its own destiny and would not get pushed around by outside forces anymore.

But as beloved as he was at home, his freethinking actions, which were often considered contrary to the Western consensus, caused him problems on the international stage. Papandreou was at odds with his international partners when, for example, he refused to condemn Libya for terrorist actions. This would have seemed like a common thing to do, at least for most of his partners, but Andreas Papandreou was not one who was ready to jump on the bandwagon of condemnation when incidents occurred. Even when Russia infamously shot down a Korean airliner, words of condemnation were not on Papandreou's lips.

And even though Greece was now part of the European Union (EU), rather than letting the EU force Greece into line, Andreas Papandreou turned the tables by thwarting EU objectives unless certain compromises were made to benefit Greece. Papandreou infamously blocked the entry of Portugal and Spain in the EU, and he used the Greek vote needed for their acceptance as a bargaining chip to get what he wanted.

Nevertheless, throughout the 1980s, Greece remained economically depressed. It is true that some living conditions improved. There was better healthcare, and some social safety nets were put in place to help the most unfortunate, but Greece would remain one of the poorest countries in Europe at the time. Papandreou won his reelection in 1985, but his party had lost a significant number of seats in the Greek Parliament. Then, as the economy worsened, Papandreou found himself having to push an "economic austerity package" through parliament.

This effort to curtail some of the excesses run up by the socialists led to fury from former Papandreou supporters, who began to openly riot in the streets in demonstrations in which some activists were killed. In an effort to pacify the growing discontent, PASOK attempted to reform certain areas of the economy and issue changes to the tax code. This led to one of the most controversial of PASOK's social engineering decisions. In April of 1987, the party decided to outright seize land owned by local churches. It was apparently figured that the best way to quiet down the landless peasants rioting in the streets would be to steal land from the church and divvy it up to them.

But none of their schemes worked as they had wanted. In fact, the situation only became worse. Soon, inflation was through the roof, and as currency crashed and grocery store prices skyrocketed, even generous government handouts of drachma meant absolutely nothing when the price of a loaf of bread suddenly cost more than anyone could possibly afford.

Papandreou, in the meantime, took a hit to his own personal popularity when he became embroiled in a scandalous affair with a former flight attendant by the name of Dimitra Liani. Andreas Papandreou left his wife Margaret and married Dimitra that year. It was with this dreadful backdrop that Papandreou ended his second term in the summer of 1989.

Out of this chaos, on November 22nd, 1989, a new coalition came together around perhaps an unlikely figure to lead the nation—an eighty-five-year-old former banker by the name of Xenophon Zolotas. The Zolotas government has been described as a "caretaker" administration, and it was put in place merely as a band-aid to prevent more hemorrhaging during the general political distress of the era. Soon, it became clear to the general public that Zolotas was not going to bring them what they wanted, which was better forms of employment and better economic conditions. Thus, there were once again massive protests in the streets and strikes being waged in the workplace.

Another election was then held in the spring of 1990, which brought forth a new coalition led by the New Democracy Party, which carried 150 seats in the Greek Parliament under the leadership of Constantine Mitsotakis (also known as Konstantinos Mitsotakis). With these staunch conservatives in power, Greece was steered away from its disastrous socialist programs of the past and into the direction of a full embrace of the free market. Soon, efforts were made to create the privatization of businesses, and there was a much more robust sense of competition in the economic sector. Social security programs, while left intact, were drastically curtailed in order to alleviate Greece's inflation, which at that time was the highest in Europe.

In the meantime, world politics were in the midst of a seismic shift due to the collapse of communism in eastern Europe, which was then followed by the end of communism in the Soviet Union itself. This collapse precipitated a massive influx of eastern European migrants passing through the Balkans to seek refuge in Greece. By early 1991, thousands of migrants had crossed into Greece from Albania alone. There was also a great migration of Russian Greeks from southern Russia and Ukraine who flowed into Greece proper, seeking to reunite with what they perceived as being their rightful ancestral homeland.

Waves of massive migration is a challenging issue for any country, especially when a nation is as economically depressed as Greece was at the time. Prime Minister Constantine Mitsotakis used a different tactic than his neutral, independent-minded predecessor and heartily embraced the European Union. He felt that the structures of the EU could do much to aid Greece's internal difficulties. Mitsotakis also slashed government spending and continued the privatization process of the previously state-run industrial sectors in an effort to finally get inflation under control.

Both of these efforts had their critics. There were those who were horrified at the sudden coziness with the EU, feeling that Greece was once again selling itself out to the European powers. And despite the obvious need to curtail inflation, for a public as dependent on socialist-styled programs as the Greeks were, suddenly taking those expensive programs away was not going to be an easy task.

As a result, Greek politics was more polarized than ever before. It was so polarized, in fact, that truth, lies, and even right and wrong all seemed to become secondary to "whose team" the Greeks were on. A perfect case in point of this occurred during the so-called "Bank of Crete scandal." The Bank of Crete was a major banking institution in Greece, which was rocked with a scandal when it was found that the bank had somehow "misplaced" hundreds of millions of dollars.

At the time, the chairman of the Bank of Crete was a rich Greek/American entrepreneur by the name of George Koskotas. Upon coming under investigation, Koskotas ultimately fled the country to escape prosecution. Koskotas was tied to PASOK and had deep links to the former prime minister, Andreas Papandreou. Koskotas, who was apprehended and placed in a Massachusetts prison, would later go on the record to state that bank audits that could have discovered the malfeasance were dismissed by members of PASOK and on at least two occasions by way of a telephone call from Andreas Papandreou himself. Not only that,

Koskotas claimed that Papandreou used the Bank of Crete as his own personal piggy bank to finance political campaigns and events.

In the midst of all of these accusations, Papandreou had charges brought against him in 1992. What should have been a simple, clear-cut case of fraudulent financial activity was increasingly seen through two distinct political lenses by the populace. Rather than focusing on whether or not Papandreou was involved in money laundering, it seemed as if the political motivations behind the defense and prosecution were on trial. Left-wing supporters of Papandreou often agreed that Papandreou was guilty of the crimes with which he was charged but felt that his prosecution was wrong and being done out of sheer political spite. So even though they knew that he was most likely guilty of the crimes with which he was charged, these supporters belligerently clamored for a not guilty verdict.

Those who wished to see Papandreou found guilty were mostly using his financial malfeasance as a club with which to beat a man they found politically displeasing over the head. Not only that, the right wanted to use the indiscretions of Papandreou to castigate basically all who were associated with him. Thus, it was not just Papandreou who was on trial but also his whole political party. Such things are not too pretty, and often the long-term results for society are only increased polarization and discord.

In many ways, Papandreou was the fall guy used by his political opponents to destroy his entire political party. The public saw what was going on, and instead of focusing on simple matters of guilt or innocence, each side dug into their ideological corners and prepared for a long, drawn-out fight.

Papandreou was a rather astute politician, and he must have realized that his political support was his most valuable tool with which to bargain, and he used it. He welcomed the efforts of his political ideologues, and even with damning evidence against him, he steadfastly denied any wrongdoing and declared the whole effort to prosecute him as illegitimate. This must have been music to his base's ears, and they wholeheartedly agreed. Even without the advent of social media such as Facebook and Twitter, Papandreou managed to get the word out that he was fighting the charges, and his supporters rose up to stand by "their guy."

Papandreou, for all his faults, had an excellent political instinct, and as it turns out, his gut feelings were right. He did not think that the prosecution had the stomach to go all the way in their pursuit of justice, and in the spring of 1992, his intuition was confirmed when all charges were dropped. And not only did Papandreou beat the charges against him, he also went on to win the next round of elections, once again becoming prime minister of Greece in 1993.

Shocking their opponents, PASOK garnered roughly half of the vote and achieved a 170-seat majority in the Greek Parliament. And it was without question that the seventy-five-year-old icon of the left, Andreas Papandreou, would be selected to lead this new administration. Part of the reason behind this shocking win was the political and international climate at the time. Conflicts in the Balkan were erupting, and there was a real sense of insecurity among the Greek people.

To keep his base happy, Papandreou restarted some of the social programs that had been so popular in the past. He also curtailed much of the privatization of his predecessor, sticking to certain forms of centralization that Greece had grown accustomed to in the past. But one area in which Papandreou saw a dramatic shift was his change of heart about the European Union and the international community in general.

Faced with growing problems in neighboring regions such as the Balkans, Papandreou saw the EU as a solution rather than a problem. The overarching structure of the EU could help him make sense of the waves of eastern European migrants that had begun pouring across Greece's borders. He also began to believe that signing for a universal European currency could provide an answer to the failing drachma.

With the return of Papandreou, Greek polarization continued. And in what could only be seen as a political tit for tat, the previous prime minister, Constantine Mitsotakis, was suddenly hit with charges for supposedly profiting from illegal archeological excavations. This led to a trial being set for Mitsotakis in 1994, in which he faced these charges, as well as allegations of illegal wire taps and exploiting the privatization of a cement company, among other things. It seemed that there were political points to be made now that the ideological tide had changed. The elder Papandreou's health would give out before his political fortunes gave way, and in November of 1995, he ended up in the hospital with a bad case of pneumonia.

He would be in and out of the hospital, and his condition would only get worse. Finally, in January of 1996, Papandreou resigned, and he would ultimately pass away just months later. PASOK, in the meantime, found a viable successor in the form of one Constantine Simitis (better known as Costas or Kostas Simitis), and the party successfully won a majority in the fall of 1996. PASOK had staved off electoral defeat, but its members would have a wide variety of problems awaiting them as Greece counted down the last few years of the millennium.

First and foremost was the growing threat from the complete collapse of nearby Albania and Yugoslavia. A civil war in Bosnia proved to be the crisis that would draw in the world powers, and it would come dangerously close to provoking a larger regional conflict. The Greeks knew perhaps better than anyone else how much of a powder keg the Balkans really were. After all, one world war had been sparked in the Balkans, and it would not be too hard to imagine another being sparked in this contentious region.

The Greeks did not want to be pulled into a conflict, so they did everything they could to stay neutral while simultaneously attempting to assuage the situation. Greece kept up a dialogue with Belgrade while strategizing with the Russians about the best to way to get the outside powers to go a little easier on the Bosnian Serbs.

In 1995, NATO led bombing campaigns against areas held by the Bosnian Serbs. And as much as Greece wanted to maintain its neutrality, Greek officials went on the record to criticize the bombing.

Fortunately for the Greeks, NATO soon called for a ceasefire, which means that Greece would not be forced to take any action that might threaten its neutrality. Greece did agree to send some Greek troops to the region shortly thereafter, not to fight but as part of a peacekeeping mission. Greece also officially set up diplomatic contact with officials in Bosnia.

However, this would not be the end of the turmoil in the Balkans. In 1998, tensions in the Yugoslavian region of Kosovo erupted in bloodshed. Soon, it seemed that Greece would once again be flooded with countless refugees from the Balkans. NATO then began conducting new rounds of airstrikes in the region, and Greece found itself once again struggling to find its footing.

Many Greeks supported the Christian Serbs and were upset with what they perceived as foreign meddling by NATO. This sentiment was on full display when United States President Bill Clinton came to Athens in 1999. He was thronged by Greek protesters wherever he went. Clinton was there to shore up the support of Greece since it was a fellow NATO member, but he found himself having to become an apologist for all of the previous perceived missteps of NATO in the past.

However, Clinton did manage to gain a few concessions in his discussions with Greek officials. Greece would allow NATO forces to station themselves in Greece, although it was insisted that the Greeks themselves would take no part in any military engagements.

After these international crises in the Balkans had subsided, Greece was able to focus on the even more pressing matters of a failing economy. Knowing that the drachma was beyond redemption, Greece began to pin its hopes on the euro of the European Union. And at the dawning of the new millennium,

Greece had officially made the euro its official form of currency, doing so by 2001.

Chapter 18 – Modern Day Greece (2001-2021)

"Unfortunately, corruption is widespread in government agencies and public enterprises. Our political system promotes nepotism and wasting money. This has undermined our legal system and confidence in the functioning of the state. One of the consequences is that many citizens don't pay their taxes.".."

-George Papandreou

The year 2001 started out as a happy one for the Greeks. The economic situation seemed to be on the mend with the advent of the euro, and Greece's international state of affairs seemed to be at peace. That May, even the visit of Pope John Paul II emerged as a sign of great reconciliation between Greece and the world since it was the first time a Catholic pope had been to Orthodox Greece in around 1,290 years.

During his stop, the pope actually apologized to the Greeks for the historic antagonism of the Catholic Church against the Greek Orthodox faithful. He even apologized for the Catholic Crusaders from the West who had sacked Constantinople in 1204 on their way to fight in the Middle East. The pope spoke in Athens, saying, "Clearly there is a need for a liberating process of purification of memory. For the occasions past and present, when sons and daughters of the Catholic Church have sinned by actions and omission against their Orthodox brothers and sisters, may the Lord grant us the forgiveness we beg of him."

In what seemed to be a repeat of the massive protests against Bill Clinton in 1999, the pope, too, was greeted with throngs of protesters. Some of these shouted a litany of anti-pope slogans in which the pontiff was dubbed an "arch-heretic" and even "the grotesque, two-horned monster of Rome." But despite all of the noise, the pope's trip was deemed to have been an overall success.

Along with apologizing for the past misdeeds of the Catholic Church, the pope spoke of how the Orthodox Church, due to its close proximity to Islamic lands, was situated on the very frontiers of Christianity. Greece had indeed kept a wary eye toward any sign of Muslim extremism rising up among its Middle Eastern neighbors. Cyprus, of course, was still an incredibly contentious issue between Greece and Turkey, and this flashpoint could have created an uncontrollable conflagration.

However, it was not a threat from regional Islamic power players that would gain the attention of Greece's foreign policy advisors in the fall of 2001. Greece, like much of the rest of the world, would be stunned on the morning of September 11th, 2001, to learn of a catastrophic terrorist attack launched against the United States. In one day, a group of radicalized Muslim extremists, working at the behest of terror mastermind Osama bin Laden, had killed nearly three thousand Americans.

In the aftermath of this brazen attack, the United States received an outpouring of both condolences and offers of support from a multitude of heads of state. Among them was Greek Prime Minister Costas Simitis, who proclaimed, "Greece condemns, most categorically, these horrific acts. We hope that the culprits be located and brought to justice immediately." The culprits were the

Saudi-based terror group Al-Qaeda, whose headquarters at the time was in the remote reaches of Afghanistan. The same mountainous and unruly Afghanistan that Alexander the Great had attempted to tame for the Greeks thousands of years before (Alexander founded Kandahar) was now ground zero for the opening stages of the war on terror.

Greece, acting as a NATO member, sent Greek troops to fight alongside Americans in an operation that the United States military termed "Operation Enduring Freedom." The fight was against not only Al-Qaeda but also the Afghan warlords of the Taliban who had sheltered them. The mission was successful in the short term in the sense that it rooted out Al-Qaeda (most fled to the Pakistan border) and severely degraded the Taliban. But the long-term effects are still being debated to this very day.

Overall, the Greek presence was a minimal one, with the first batch of 150 soldiers arriving in January of 2002. The war effort quickly lost popular support among many in Greece, and by 2004, Greek politicians were actively calling for the withdrawal of all Greek forces in the region.

This same year, Greece hosted the Olympics. This was a big deal for Greece. Since the land of Greece was the home of the original Olympics, Athens, of course, wanted to outshine all of the others. As such, Greece spent a lot of money hosting the Olympic Games, far more than it probably should have (in total, it spent nine billion US dollars).

However, just a few years into its entrance into the eurozone (the union of European states that use the euro), Greece was riding high on new economic opportunities and went on a spending spree. All of this spending would come back to haunt them when Greece was hit with the global economic recession of 2007/2008.

The root causes of this global economic downturn, otherwise known as the Great Recession, are fairly complex. A main triggering factor was the bursting of the so-called "housing bubble" in the United States. For many years in the United States, housing prices were steadily rising. It was a sellers' market, but starting in 2007, house prices began to fall dramatically. Many homes were foreclosed upon, and as a result, the banks that backed these properties lost money. When the banks in America began to go bankrupt in rapid numbers, it created a ripple effect that was felt all across the world.

Back in Greece, in the meantime, elections in the fall of 2009 saw the return of PASOK. After PASOK came to power, the Greek minister of finance informed the EU's European Commission that Greece's debt would skyrocket to 12.5 percent of its gross domestic product (GDP), which was over twice of what the prior administration had reported. If this was not alarming enough, further investigation revealed that the situation was even worse than that and that the true figure was closer to 15.4 percent.

The European Union requires all members to produce accurate economic data within the eurozone, and the backlash against Greece was swift and fierce. Other member states of the EU were absolutely appalled at what appeared to be outright falsification of records by corrupt Greek officials. In the aftermath of this loss of trust, Greece's credit rating plummeted, which meant that Greece would now be subject to much higher interest rates. It would later be figured out that Greek politicians had been cooking the books for quite some time and had even given false data to ease its entrance into the eurozone itself.

In the immediate aftermath of Greece's economic collapse, austerity measures were imposed to try and get the Greek economy afloat. This meant that Greece's government would have to scale back spending while funneling more money out of the Greek people through increased taxation. These harsh measures led the International Monetary Fund (IMF) to agree to loan Greece 110 billion euros in 2010. Although not a complete bailout, this money did allow the struggling country to at least pay interest on its current debt so that it could be kept from going into complete default and being forced to leave the eurozone altogether.

The following year, in 2011, the European Financial Stability Facility generously deposited another 190 billion euros to the aid that had already been dished out to Greece. It was also agreed that half of all money Greece owed to private creditors would be blotted out. This made the servicing of Greece's still existing debt much easier to manage.

By 2014, the Greek economy appeared to be on the rebound, with a growth rate of 0.7 percent. That same year, Greece was allowed to come back to the international bond market. But despite these gains, over the next few years, Greece would continue to nearly default while having to borrow additional funds just to stay afloat. Greece had its final bailout in August of 2018, receiving a total of 290 billion euros over the years. As of this writing, Greece is expected to continue to make payments on its debts all the way until August of 2060.

Conclusion: Hellenism at the Crossroads

Greece was a land of many firsts. It was here that democracy, theater, and the Olympics first came to prominence. The ideals of Hellenism quickly spread far and wide. This spark of Greek ingenuity would survive the conquest of foreign powers and even go on to fuel the European Renaissance. Greece then finally gained its national independence in 1821, and the future of the Greek-speaking world seemed promising once again.

Two centuries later, in 2021, Greece was facing some pretty significant challenges. Along with its continuing efforts to get out of debt, Greece, like much the rest of the world, had been rocked by a global pandemic. Greece has been largely credited with doing a good job of handling the pandemic, but the impact of recent events continues to present a challenge.

The fact that tourism was largely shut down in the spring and summer of 2020 was a definite setback for Greece's economy since tourism makes up about 20 percent of Greece's total GDP. However, Greece is a resilient nation, and it seems like when the chips are down, the Greeks tend to be at their best. Greece was among the countries who took a leading role in vaccinations and made sure that all of those who worked in tourism were fully vaccinated.

Greece has fought off ferocious foes in the past, and the pandemic has been viewed as just the latest beast for the Greeks to subdue. The Greeks are willing to overcome this obstacle just like all the others they have faced throughout their long and rich history. Right now, Hellenism may seem to be at the crossroads, but the world can most certainly expect many more new and exciting epochs of Greek culture to come.

Part 2: Classical Greece

A Captivating Guide to an Era in Ancient Greece That Strongly Influenced Western Civilization, Starting from the Persian Wars and Rise of Athens to the Death of Alexander the Great

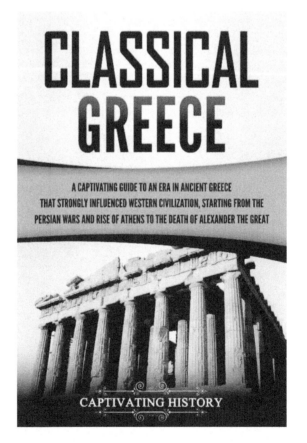

Introduction

The period of Greek history between 478 and 323 is what we now refer to as classical Greece. This was the period when the concept of democracy first appeared. Democracy was the response to the events that occurred during the Archaic period, and it brought new thought to how a state should be governed and how the people should behave. Tyrants were then brought down, and a new structure of polis was promoted, with the people making the majority of the political and social decisions. But this didn't come easily, and various cities developed their own democracies in different ways. Athens rose as the culturally dominant state; thus, most evidence we have on this period comes from Athens. This is why it is easiest to concentrate on the events that involved this particular Greek polis.

After the Persian Wars, Sparta withdrew to the Peloponnese while Athens started an alliance known as the Delian League to continue the struggle against Persia. Through this league, Athens became the most powerful and the richest polis of mainland Greece, and it sought to exploit this advantage. All other cities transformed from being equal members of the Delian League into being subjects of Athens, and the period of the Athenian empire began. It wasn't an empire in the modern sense of the word. In fact, it didn't even consider itself an empire. But in an imperialistic manner, Athens imposed itself on others, and soon enough, it became clear that Athens made all the decisions and collected the revenues of all the other member city-states of the Delian league. Athens had shifted the power balance to its advantage, forcing Sparta to respond. The result was the Peloponnesian War (431–404), in which Sparta tried to break Athens's powerful grip on the Greek world. The result was the decline of Athens's power, but Sparta managed to achieve its goals by bringing Persia back into Greek affairs.

Although utterly defeated, Athens made a remarkable recovery and was able to join Sparta and Thebes in a power struggle that lasted for forty years after the end of the Peloponnesian War. Many alliances were created and broken during this period, and Persia continued to meddle in Greek politics until it finally regained the Anatolian Greek poleis in 387/6 BCE. Sparta was defeated in 371 by Thebes, and although it tried, it never again managed to return to its former glory. The Persians planned to integrate all of Greece into its powerful empire, and they knew very well that there was no Greek military commander able to oppose them.

But in the north, the Kingdom of Macedonia rose to power under the leadership of King Philip II. The Greeks took the opportunity to defend themselves and united again against their common enemy: Persia. By 336, Philip II had managed to create the Corinthian League and drive out the Persians. He planned to continue his efforts by conquering all of his enemy's territories, but his dream was cut short by an assassin. His son, Alexander the Great, continued Philip's plans, and he conquered the whole known world.

The Persians, who wanted Greece to become part of their empire, now found themselves as an extension of the Greek world. But the death of Alexander the Great brought an end to his vast empire, which ended up being divided between four of his most powerful generals. The new kingdoms that sprouted from the territories Alexander controlled transformed the world with new political, cultural, and social ideas. A new era began, one that modern scholars named the Hellenistic age.

Although the events of classical Greece are undoubtedly interesting, this was a period of great social and cultural changes too. The development of the polis, democracy, and citizenship, as well as the rise of tragedy and comedy, gave the people a voice on contemporary issues. In tragedies and comedies, these issues were often voiced by women. This was impossible in reality, as women had no political rights, but it was possible in an imaginary world. Women, the silent foundation of Greek society, transformed into brave heroines who were able to influence events and make their own independent decisions in the plays of great literary men such as Sophocles and Aristophanes.

Plays, like anything else in classical Greece, were interwoven with religion and the worship of the gods on Mount Olympus. Religion dictated the citizens' behavior since one's fortune depended on his actions and whether they pleased or displeased the divine. Religion was one of the many aspects of state life, and priests often took state offices. The temples and the many religious ceremonies and festivals were regulated and financed by the state or by wealthy state officials. But the religion itself wasn't simply a set of correct beliefs. It was more about the rituals and their correct performance, one on which the whole community's future depended. It was through religious festivals that the people pleased the gods, and rituals also included athletic and playwriting competitions. Culture, public life, politics, and religion were all parts that made up a single individual, a citizen of a polis set in classical Greece.

Chapter 1: Prelude to the Classical Period

Map of Greece, drawn in 1791
https://en.wikipedia.org/wiki/Classical_Greece#/media/File:Map_of
_Greece,_Archipelago_and_part_of_Anadoli;_Louis_Stanislas_d'A
rcy_Delarochette_1791.jpg

The Dark Ages

In the period between 1200 and 1000 BCE, the Greek world was suffering the downfall of the Mycenaean civilization. The economic crash, local conflicts, and the movement of the people that followed the Myceneans' fall are staples of what is known as the Greek Dark Ages. Whole kingdoms and independent cities of the Near East were obliterated, which resulted in a weak economy and grinding poverty to the Greek population that depended on trade. But there is a veil of mystery covering this period because not much written evidence survived. And it is the very absence of written sources from the Greek world that testifies to the gruesomeness of the period. It is both the general poverty of the people and the lack of evidence of this period that prompted modern historians to name it the "Dark Ages."

The Near East ended its Dark Ages before Greece. There, the people managed to recover their economy and politics by 900 BCE, while in Greece, the end of the Dark Ages came 150 years later, in the mid-8th century BCE. Although the recovery was slow in Greece, the survivors of the Mycenaean civilization never really lost their contact with the Near East. Trade, technology, religious traditions, and ideas could flow freely. Thus, during this period, the Greeks set the foundations for the values, traditions, and the new forms of social and political systems that would come into full life during the Archaic and Classical periods.

The Greek Dark Ages started with the loss of technology and the ability to write. Although this loss was never complete, it happened due to the economic crisis that came when the Mycenaean economic system fell after prolonged periods of war. The Mycenaean script was extremely difficult to learn, and it remained in use only among court scribes. With the downfall of civilization, the remaining Greek society lost the need for scribes. Since they didn't have an economy, there was no demand for recordings of the flow of goods and money. However, the lack of a written language allowed the oral tradition to survive and prosper.

Storytelling, music, poetry, and other oral performances survived, and they transmitted the cultural ideas of the Greeks as an ethnic group from generation to generation. But as modern history discovered, the Greek oral tradition wasn't always true. For example, tradition says that Dorians invaded mainland Greece and settled there, eventually becoming the Spartans. There are no written records or archaeological findings that can support this claim. It seems that there was never really any Dorian invasion.

The archaeological findings that are dated to 900 BCE show that this was a period when people of mainland Greece started recovering their wealth. They started using luxurious items in burial ceremonies, and many people were buried with expensive goods. But the economic recovery isn't the only thing that is evident from these findings. It seems that a social hierarchy was starting to spread through Greece, as only some people were wealthy while the majority were poor. In the earlier stages of the Greek Dark Ages, most of the findings indicate people could not afford luxurious grave offerings; all that was found in burial sites were clay pots. But after 900 BCE, the trade and the economy started developing, and items such as iron weapons, jewelry, and cutlery could be found in graves. Since they were all made out of iron, it is evident that around 900 BCE, the Greeks imported the technology and knowledge of how to produce it from the Near East.

The use of iron expanded to agriculture. Because it was easier to procure and work with, it also became a cheaper option than bronze. The production of food increased with the introduction of iron tools, and the population started booming. Greek agriculture started recovering by 850 BCE, with the expansion of the grain fields and the livestock herds. The population growth was only natural, and this repopulation created a Greek society ready to invent new political forms and slowly move into democracy.

The elite existed by this time, and they were the wealthiest of the Greeks. However, they were never an aristocracy in the modern Western sense. The term aristocracy comes from the Greek language, and it means "the rule of the best," or what we would know as nobility. But Greeks never had official nobility, such as the aristocrats of western European countries, who inherited their status by being born into an aristocratic family. In the Greek sense, it is better to use the term "elite," as anyone could rise to this social status by acquiring wealth and political power. The Greek elites were still considered the best, and they were the leaders and rulers.

This hierarchical society started developing its own moral values, which later turned into political ideals. Proper behavior within the community became paramount for the ruling elite, as they were expected to assert control over the people. The social values of the Greek Dark Ages are described in the great literary works of the *Iliad* and *Odyssey*, both dated to the middle of the 8th century BCE. The deeds and values of great Greek heroes were described in these lengthy poems, and they were considered to be the ideals to which all members of Greek society should strive. Warriors and family life were cherished, and attributes such as courage, exceptional skills, curiosity, and the tendency to raise children were values the ancient Greeks held in high regard. But the elite members of society also had to strive to achieve *arete*, a Greek word with many meanings, usually translated as "excellence." The shame of failing to achieve excellence in whatever one was doing was a constant threat for the elite. Excellence was also a moral value, and as such, it carried a strong notion of obligation and responsibility.

There was no greater place to exercise Greek values and to display the excellence one achieved than to compete in the Olympic Games. They were founded at the end of the Greek Dark Ages in 776 BCE and were held every four years within a large sanctuary in Olympia, which was dedicated to Zeus. The men who had the time and the ability to reach excellence in athletic disciplines competed in different events, such as running, wrestling, jumping, horse-riding, and many more. There were no teams, and each individual competed for himself, not as a representative of a nation or a city. The winners would receive public recognition as the best of all other male competitors, which in itself was the Greek ideal of masculine identity. Women didn't compete in the Olympic Games, but they had their own competitions in honor of Hera. Unfortunately, little is known about the competition for women, but racing was certainly one of the games.

The Development of the Polis

During the Archaic period, the Greeks developed their city-states, their most influential political entities. But the social development of Greek society started much earlier during the Greek Dark Ages (1100–750 BCE). During the Archaic period (750–500 BCE), it only culminated and developed into the form of city-states (singular: polis; plural: poleis). The population of the poleis consisted of males, females, children, slaves, and resident foreigners. However, only the males who were born in the territory of a given city-state could obtain citizenship, which would give them a set of privileges (such as the right to vote). The polis was a complex social structure with people of different origins, backgrounds, and legal and social statuses. Personal freedom was extremely important, as the poor but free people were eligible to obtain citizenship. They may have been deprived of basic necessities, but poor free men had the right to engage in political life. This was what separated them from slaves and the foreigners and what gave their lives extra meaning.

Polis is a Greek term from which the modern word "politics" is derived. It means "the city," although it is translated as city-state because, unlike modern cities, the poleis were separate political entities. Poleis didn't include only a distinct urban center protected by city walls. The surrounding countryside and the neighboring villages were also a part of the poleis. Thus, the population of one polis could include the inhabitants of the urban environment as well as the farmers and villagers scattered throughout its rural territories. The partnership that developed between various inhabitants of a polis gave the polis its distinct political characteristic. Only adult men, holders of citizenship, were allowed to participate in political life. Women and children still counted as a part of the community, and they had their legal, social, and religious parts to play.

Each polis had a patron god that was considered the city's protector and patron. For example, Athens had the goddess Athena as its city protector. That doesn't mean that each city was obliged to choose a different deity as its patron. Syracuse, for example, had the goddess Athena as their patron as well. Thebes and Delphi shared Apollo as their patron god.

The patron gods were called poliad due to their special connection to the city. However, that doesn't mean a polis didn't worship any other god. They respected and built temples to many gods in the Greek pantheon, but the poliad had a special place, and its temple would be the largest one, occupying the acropolis. The acropolis itself was the nucleus of a polis. It was a citadel, often built on elevated grounds so it could serve as a defensive structure.

Religion played a huge part in the life of ancient Greece. There were many religious festivals organized within the polis, and they were paid for by the citizens. During these festivals, animals would be sacrificed to pay respect to the many Greek gods and goddesses. Dedicated individuals, priests, and priestesses were the religious leaders of the community, and they oversaw and participated in these religious rituals.

A polis maintained relationships with its neighbors, but it was a completely independent and separate political entity. Its urban and rural citizens were tied by political unity. And while Middle Eastern traders brought artistic influences to Greece, it is unlikely they also brought their politics. This is why it is widely believed that Greece is the cradle of its political system. The city-states were organized similarly to Middle Eastern ancient city-kingdoms because the two people had reached a similar level of civilization, not because of political interference.

However, the similarity between city-states ends with the political unity of a polis. A polis's political core was different from one to another. Each city-state developed at its own pace and followed its own natural course. When the Mycenaean politics of the Greek Dark Ages went away, it left a power vacuum behind. This vacuum wasn't filled by the imperial states (like it would in the Middle East). Instead, it allowed each city to develop independently, and the larger ones never displayed a tendency to absorb the smaller cities.

Citizenship was the center of political life in the polis, as it granted the people political autonomy. We already mentioned that only adult males could be the holders of citizenship, and they could pass it to their male offspring. Women had no political autonomy, nor did children or slaves. But that doesn't mean politics didn't concern them. There were sets of laws that regulated the roles of women, children, foreigners, and slaves in society, and they had different levels of freedom attached to them. When it came to women, for instance, some laws regulated their sexual behavior and the control of property.

Citizenship meant equality before the law, and this equality never relied on the wealth of an individual. Social differentiation between the rich and poor was pronounced in the ancient Near East and in Greece during the Dark Ages. But with the development of poleis and citizenship, legal equality emerged. The poor people had a lower quality of life, and they often lacked the basic means of survival, but they were equally involved in making political decisions. Social and economic differences in Greek society still existed, and the people were divided between the elites and the commoners. It is important to make a difference between political and legal equality. Elite families had more political freedoms but were responsible for their deeds as much as any commoner.

The poleis and citizenship weren't the only political forms in place during the eight centuries of its existence (from 750 BCE until the emergence of the Roman Empire). The Greeks also knew political organizations such as federations and leagues. These organizations would politically bind, albeit loosely, a broad territory or multiple poleis into an association. However, the polis remained the nucleus of broader Greek politics.

The development of poleis in Greece wasn't an accident. The ancient Greek philosopher Aristotle observed that the emergence of the polis was only natural, as humans are social beings who tend to group around common interests. However, in Greece, geography also influenced the development of the city-states. The Greek mainland is a very mountainous area, and the cities were separated from each other by a physical barrier. Communication between the cities was hard to maintain, and it is no wonder they started developing political independence, despite the fact that they shared the same language and culture. Some city-states managed to develop independently, even though there was no physical barrier between them, such as the poleis in the plains of Boeotia. Even a single island could hold several city-states that were completely independent of each other (e.g., Lesbos had five poleis). Independence in these cases was possible because no polis controlled more land than it needed to feed its population. This is why the city-states maintained a population from several hundred up to several thousand. Athens was the biggest known polis, amounting to forty thousand people. However, Athens was able to feed its people not because it controlled a large amount of arable land but because it developed a system of food imports from abroad.

As soon as a polis grew above the number of people its arable land could support, the Greeks would migrate. The first migration started as early as the 9th century BCE with the settlement in Ionia. In 750 BCE, the Greeks started spreading from the mainland in all directions. In only two centuries, Greeks started colonies in present-day France, Spain, Sicily, South Italy, North Africa, and along the coast of the Black Sea to western Anatolia and eastern Syria. This is what scholars refer to as the Greek world. By the end of the 4th century BCE, Greece had over 1,100 small states, and it counted over 8 million people. They all shared the Greek culture and language but with localized variations.

The lack of arable land wasn't the only reason Greeks emigrated. They also started developing (or better yet reviving) the international trade in the Mediterranean, and many of them felt compelled to leave their homeland. Commercial interests urged some individuals to take up residency in far-away lands and start their own trading posts. Those who were rich enough to risk their finances would often engage in risky expeditions in search of metals. Sometimes a polis would organize these expeditions and choose one individual who would be a founder (*ktistes*) of a colony. Although the colony would develop independently from the "mother polis" (metropolis; from Greek root meter, meaning "mother"), it was expected to keep close ties. The metropolis and its colony would act as allies in times of war. But there were instances when a colony would break off from its metropolis and side with the enemy. In that case, the colony was regarded as disloyal.

Women's Rights, Marriage, and the Household

Since only adult men had the right to obtain citizenship, equality in ancient Greece was incomplete. There is an ancient Greek feminine term for a citizen, *politis*, but it bears no political significance, unlike its male counterpart, *polites*. The Greeks did refer to women as "female citizens" but only in regards to certain religious roles and to legal guardianship over women. But unlike slaves, women did have their own identity and social status. This alone secured them certain rights that the foreigners (*metics*) and slaves could not have. Free women were legally protected from being kidnapped and sold into slavery. They also had access to courts and could enter property or any other legal dispute, but they could never represent themselves. They needed a male guardian, a representative, who would speak in her name. This requirement of a male guardian speaks of the legal inequality ancient Greek women had to endure.

Every woman had a legal male guardian known as a *kyrios*. It could be her father, brother, husband, or any other man whose duty was to protect her both legally and physically. The interests of a woman were also defined by men, and it was the men who regulated women's everyday lives. Thus, women had no right to participate in politics. They were forbidden from attending political assemblies, voting, and making any political decisions.

But where women excelled was religion. They had their own female cults and could be initiated into the priesthood of certain deities just like men. The female cults were equally respected as the male ones, and they usually centered around the worship of Demeter, a goddess who promised protection from evil and peace in the afterlife. The ancient Greeks were very religious, and the Eleusinian Mysteries, an initiation ceremony of the Demeter/Persephone cult, was a sacred event. It was also a secret event, and its importance is displayed in the fact that those who revealed the rite's secrets were punished by death.

The women's responsibility was the household, which was greatly expanded with the introduction of slavery. Rich women had bigger households and more work since they had more slaves. But when it came to family life, the husband and wife were seen as partners. While men were outside farming, working, and participating in politics, the women's place was inside, managing a household. Roman women held a similar status during the later Roman Empire.

The modern word "economy" comes from the Greek word for household (*oikonomia*). Women were expected to raise children, prepare or supervise food preparation and preservation, keep accounts of the family's finances, make clothing, manage the slaves, and nurse their family members and slaves when they were ill. It was the work of women that allowed families to prosper economically.

Poor women also had to work outside of their homes. They were mostly small-scale merchants in public markets (agora). In Sparta, women had the right to indulge in athletic training just as men, but Sparta was an exception. In the public life of a city, the women had important roles during funerals, religious holidays and rituals, and state festivities. Women who were priestesses enjoyed considerable prestige, which brought them certain benefits, such as a state salary and freedom of movement in public. Some of the religious cults were reserved for women, and they had their own all-women festivals and rites. By the 5th century, Athens alone had around forty such cults.

Upon marriage, a husband would take the role of a woman's legal guardian. This role was previously occupied by her father or another male relative if her father was absent. Marriages were officially arranged by men, but it was no secret that women would often take part in the negotiations. Girls as young as five years would be betrothed by their fathers. The engagement ceremony was an important public event, and it demanded the presence of several witnesses. However, the marriage itself would take place only when the woman reached a certain age, usually her early teens. The groom needed to be at least ten years old for a legal marriage. The marriage procession was similar to more modern marriage celebrations, with the bride going to live in her husband's house. The woman had to bring a dowry as well, which could be money or a part of her father's land. The dowry was her insurance, and the husband had to return it to her in case of a divorce. The divorce law ensured that a woman could leave her husband at her initiative, but the husband had every right to expel his wife from his household too.

Marriage equality ends here. Men were legally able to indulge in sexual intercourse outside of the marriage with prostitutes or slaves, both male or female, while women had no such freedoms.

Adultery was punishable by law and applicable even to men caught in adultery with a married woman. Sparta was an exception here. Childless women were allowed to have multiple sexual partners to produce an heir as long as they had their husband's permission.

The guardianship over women came out of the Greeks' concern for procreation. The Greek men had a paternalistic attitude toward women because of their experience of the Greek Dark Ages when a sudden drop in the population led to an economic crash and poverty. A woman, as a child-bearer, had to endure the blame for what happened during the Dark Ages. She was often described as a necessary evil a man had to endure in order to procreate. This is even reflected in the Greek myth about Pandora, the first woman created by the gods. She was sent to mankind with a box filled with disease and evil. Her mischievous nature led her to open the box and unleash its contents on humanity. Many scholars today believe that the myth of Pandora was altered by later Greeks to justify the existence of a bad wife or to excuse their misogyny. Pandora went from a matriarchal goddess to a human woman and the bringer of evil and misfortune. Some even claim that this change marks the turn from a matriarchal Greek society to a patriarchal one. Nevertheless, to the ancient Greeks, Pandora and women were a necessary evil, as only through them can a man procreate. Having offspring was seen as a man's duty, and being childless was frowned upon.

Chapter 2: Oligarchy, Tyranny, and Democracy

Carved representation of Demos *("population") being crowned by*
Democracy (336 BCE)
https://en.wikipedia.org/wiki/Athenian_democracy#/media/File:De
mos_embodiment_being_crowned_by_Democracy._Ancient_Agor
a_Museum_in_Athens.jpg

The size and the influence of a state could have differed greatly. Among the most influential ones were Athens and Syracuse. Athens's territory was around 2,500 square kilometers (965 square miles), approximately the size of modern-day Luxembourg or California's Orange County. The population of Athens varied greatly during the Classical period, but it can be estimated at around one-quarter of a million people. In comparison, the northern neighbor of Athens was Plataea, a state only 170 square kilometers (66 square miles) large, with a population below 10,000 people. And Plataea wasn't even the smallest Greek state. The smallest known one was on the island of Kea, which occupied only fifteen square kilometers (six square miles).

But no matter the size, the Greek poleis interacted with each other as if they were equal. Diplomatically, economically, and militarily, they were truly equal, but their power, wealth, and influence were different. Each of these state's political life developed independently, but over time, they came to share the most fundamental political institutions and social traditions. They shared the political disadvantage of women, slavery, the concept of citizenship, legal equality of those who held citizenship, and the social predominance of the wealthy elite.

Although the poleis shared political and social concepts, they developed them quite differently. The concept of a monarchy ended with the downfall of the Mycenaean civilization. The only place where a certain form of kingship survived was in Sparta, but even there, it was a unique system of dual kingship that was part of a more complex oligarchic system. In Sparta and some other city-states, meaningful political power was granted only to several individuals. This political system is known as an oligarchy (Greek *oligarkhia*—rule of the few). Other city-states were ruled by a tyrant, an individual who managed to grab all of the political power of a polis. Tyrants could pass their rule to their sons, but this was not a tradition. A tyrant could easily be replaced by another tyrant or a completely different political system.

Another early political system was a democracy, the rule of the people (Greek *demokratia*). Democracy meant giving all male citizens the power to participate in political life. The Greek democracy was an innovation of the late Archaic period that broke the rule of the previous people's assemblies. Even tyrants ruled with the existence of some kind of assembly or council that could influence political decisions. But democracy gave the people full freedom of political decision-making. Democracy came to dominate the political world of Greece during its Classical period, but it developed differently from polis to polis. Athenian democracy is renowned since it gave each citizen immense political power that extended into individual freedoms, something that was unprecedented in the ancient world.

The Political Development of Sparta

Sparta remains famous for its military society even today. But to maintain that defensive readiness, discipline, and military way of life, the Spartans had to come up with a political system that would support it and even strengthen it. Their answer was an oligarchy. Nestled between rugged mountains in the southeastern Peloponnese, the Spartans inhabited the region called Laconia (that is why they are sometimes referred to as Laconians or Lacedaemonians). Spartans had access to the sea, but their harbor, the Gytheion, opened into a very dangerous zone in the Mediterranean, so no one ever dared to sail there. Thus, Sparta was protected by its treacherous sea and the mountains, allowing it to develop perfect defenses.

The earliest Sparta was a commune of four villages that later developed into a polis. The political unification of the small settlements was called synoecism, which was how the polis of Sparta came to be. Synoecism allowed the people to continue living in their village even after unifying into a city-state. However, there were cases in which the people moved to live in one central location after the synoecism.

The unification of the villages that made Sparta allowed this polis to become the dominant one in Laconia. However, since two of the original villages dominated over the others, a dual kingship was formed. The kings were not only the military commanders of the city-state's army but also their supreme religious figures.

Even though they were called kings, they were not alone in governing Sparta. They weren't able to make any political decisions on their own because they weren't despots. Instead, leaders of the oligarchic political system governed the polis through various institutions. Sparta's political group was the "few," twenty-eight men who had to be over sixty years old. The two kings acted as their leaders. Together, the thirty men were called the council of elders (Gerousia), and they drafted Sparta's policies. But they could not do anything more than formulate proposals, as these would be submitted to a vote of an assembly consisting of all free adult males (the citizens). The citizens were expected to approve all the council's proposals, so rejections were rare. However, this was only because the council was able to withdraw the proposal if they concluded that the public did not like it.

The kings and the Gerousia were counterbalanced by a board of five individuals, who were elected annually. Their task was to oversee policy-making. Thus, they were called ephors, the overseers. Ephors had access to all the council and assembly meetings. They also had great judicial power, as it was their duty to exercise judgments and punishments. Not even kings were immune to the ephors' judicial powers. Because the main duty of the ephors was to secure the supremacy of the law, they diluted the oligarchic powers of the Gerousia and the kings. The ephors were obliged to swear an oath each month in the name of the polis and to the king, promising they would preserve his kingship if he obliged by his oath. Thus, the king had to swear an oath to the polis that he would follow the established laws of kingship.

The Spartans didn't write down their laws, but they were very much obedient to them. Tradition says that a leader, known as Lycurgus, reformed the Spartan laws, but there is no written evidence to confirm his existence or to even assign a date to his rule. All that modern history can say about Spartan laws is that they evolved during the period between 800 and 600 BCE. Spartan law was transferred from generation to generation due to Sparta's highly structured way of life and economy. This Spartan way of life was a necessity, as they lived surrounded by the peoples they conquered and enslaved and whom they exploited economically. The Spartans were generally outnumbered by their slaves and servants, so they had to constantly work on maintaining their superiority. This was why the Spartans turned into a society of soldiers, constantly ready for war. To achieve this military society, the Spartans reconstructed and transformed the traditional family and adopted a new set of values and laws to live by.

The enslaved people that the Spartans conquered continued to live in self-governed communities, but they were obliged to serve in the Spartan army and pay taxes to their superior neighbor. What separated them from the Spartans was the lack of citizen's rights. The conquered people were called the *perioikoi* (the neighbors), and it is possible, though never proven, that they never rebelled against Sparta because they were allowed to keep their freedom and their properties. But Sparta also had real slavery, and there was also a layer of society known as *helot* (the captured). It is unclear if the helots were slaves or a new social construction between slaves and free men. It is also unclear if they were an ethnic group or a social layer or maybe even both. Nevertheless, the helots were the most numerous in Laconia. The main concern of the Spartans was keeping them in check, and each fall, the Spartans would declare war on the helots to reduce their numbers. Helots did rebel, and they tried to improve their living conditions and rights, but with no success.

Helots worked the Spartan land and produced food. They also worked in households as servants, allowing the men of Sparta to devote themselves to training for possible warfare. Helots were also employed to carry heavy military equipment during wars. Sometimes they were even armed if the enemy's numbers surpassed those of Spartan soldiers, and they were promised freedom if they fought. But they lacked training, so they were often the first to die on the battlefield, never gaining their promised freedom. However, even those who survived were never allowed full citizenship, meaning they were stuck in political and social limbo.

The Spartan way of life meant keeping the army in tip-top shape. Boys were allowed to live at home with their parents until the age of seven. Then, they were sent to live with other males in communal spaces, similar to military barracks, where they would train, hunt, exercise, and learn Spartan values. They would remain in the communal barracks until the age of thirty. The sons of the royal family were exempted from this harsh training, probably to avoid the social crisis that would ensue if a member of a royal family would fail to survive childhood. And many Spartans did fail. Young boys were often injured or even killed by the harsh environment they had to endure. If they were disobedient, the punishments were so gruesome that many of them preferred death. The boys were also forced to abandon their sentiments for their family to become part of a larger society. This is why they had to call all older men "father" and to emphasize their loyalty to the community, not to their genetic family.

Women in Sparta had more freedom than any other Greek society. They were expected to keep themselves healthy in order to bear healthy children. This is why they were allowed to exercise together with the boys, even wearing minimal clothing while doing so. Women didn't labor in the households, as that was a job for the helots. However, women were the prime educators of young children, and they had to prepare their sons for the rough life that awaited them in the communal barracks. Women were also allowed to own land, and inheritance was always equally divided between brothers and sisters. In fact, women came to hold most of the Spartan land because the male population declined due to the constant wars.

Even though marriages were arranged at a young age, husbands and wives were not allowed to live together, mainly because males had to live in barracks until they were thirty. This is why women had more power and control over the households and why men were expected only to see their wives in short nightly visits to procreate. If a man was incapable of giving a child to his wife, she was free to have intercourse with other men. Producing children was very important because Sparta always had a pressing need for more men, which is why it was obligatory for men to marry.

The Rise of the Tyranny

The opposition to the oligarchy caused the tyrants to rise to power in the Greek states. Sparta was spared from experiencing tyranny during the ancient period. Tyranny first came to be in Corinth in 657 BCE. There, the Bacchiadae family ruled as oligarchs, and they brought prosperity to their polis, making it one of the most prosperous Archaic Greek cities. They were excellent shipbuilders, and other Greek states contracted their naval engineers. This allowed them to be among the first to establish colonies at Syracuse and Corcyra.

But the Bacchiadae were violent rulers, and although Corinth prospered, its citizens were not satisfied. One of the noble individuals, Cypselus, prepared to take over the government. He gained popularity with the population by displaying values such as courage, prudence, and philanthropy. He was the complete opposite of the violent Bacchiadae oligarchs. As he gained popular support, he easily persuaded the Oracle of Delphi to favor his ensuing rebellion. His popularity was such that once he took over power in Corinth, he was able to deal with his rivals easily and could walk the streets without bodyguards. Cypselus continued to reinforce Corinth's economy by starting pottery exports, mainly to Italy. He also founded many new colonies in the western poleis of the Mediterranean, which helped him to promote trade.

Cypselus died in around 625 BCE and was succeeded by Periander, his son. Although he continued his father's economic expansion of Corinth, Periander was a harsh ruler and didn't have the support of the people. Although he managed to stay in power until his death in 585, the hatred among his people was such that his successor, Psammetichus, was overthrown by the people. The tyranny in Corinth was short-lived, and it was swiftly replaced by eight magisters who had the help of a council, which consisted of eighty men.

But there is more to Greek tyranny than what Corinth experienced. What ancient Greeks called tyranny is not at all what a modern Western society would imagine. The ancient tyranny was a political system in which the head of one family would rule with the help of an elite layer of society, one that specialized in government, religion, and/or the military. Ancient tyranny is comparable to the modern-day concept of a monarchy but without hereditary succession (although it did happen). Although the rule was often passed from father to son, all tyrants were easily replaced by their rivals and enemies. When it comes to Greece during the mid-6th century BCE, though, tyrants would rarely be replaced with other tyrants. Instead, the people would rise against their ruler, and once they secured his downfall, they would not bring in another tyrant but would rather establish a citizen-centered government. Tyranny would rarely last for more than two generations, and it was never the same in the Greek cities.

Tyrants came to power by overthrowing their predecessors. But to do this, the Greek tyrants had to cultivate the support of the masses. These masses would make up a tyrant's army, and the ruler needed to keep them satisfied. As soon as he failed to do so, he was under threat of rebellion. To win over a great number of people, the tyrants would extend citizenship to those who were not eligible for it before. They also started public works to benefit the city-state and provide employment for their supporters. The tyrants worked in the interest of the people, and for that, they were rewarded with loyalty and support. But all tyrants had their rivals who wanted to overthrow them and take over the governance. Through the works and machinations of rivals, tyrants would often face a civil war. However, more often than not, the tyrants themselves would rule as oppressors, violently and brutally, which brought the wrath of their people upon themselves.

The Political Development of Athens

As Sparta came to be by synoecism of Laconian villages, so did Athens come to be by synoecism of Attica. Attica had several ports on its shores, and the Athenians were much better seafarers than the Spartans. This allowed them to communicate with other people and establish trade relations. Landlocked Sparta instead turned to conquest.

Tradition says Athens was founded by a hero named Theseus, who was an adventurer who defeated the Minotaur. The labors of Theseus became Athens's foundation myths, as the hero defeated many monsters and criminals to promote the moral institutions of his polis. Thus, Athenians were proud of their superior moral and civilized lives compared to the rest of the Greek world.

Just as the rest of Greece, Athens suffered a sudden population decline during the Greek Dark Ages. But archaeological evidence suggests that it had no trouble recovering from this destructive period of history. As early as 800 BCE, Athens's population started rising, and evidence found in various burial places proves the revival of agriculture.

From 800 to 700 BCE, the fastest-growing population of Attica was the free peasants. They worked the land and produced food, and they insisted on having a say in politics. Some of the peasants became wealthy landowners, gaining enough power to influence the elite families and demand political equality. At the time, these elite families ruled Athens in the form of a broad oligarchy. But the continuous rivalry among them prevented them from forming a united front against the pressure that came from the lower levels of society. The military strength of Athens completely depended on citizen militias, and the elite had to address the political pressure to ensure the survival of its army.

Already at this early stage of its political development, Athens was on the road toward democracy. By the late 7th century, all male citizens, rich or poor, had a share in governance, although not equal. Being this close to democracy, the Athenians had to prevent an individual from rising to the status of a tyrant. His name was Cylon, and in around 632 BCE, he attempted to overthrow the loose Athenian oligarchy and crown himself a tyrant. But the people wouldn't allow it. The population growth of Athens had given the power to the people, and they rallied against Cylon.

During the late 7th century, male freeborn Athenians had the right to attend state meetings. They were ruled by nine archons, who were elected each year. The archons were the oligarchs, and they had the power to render verdicts in disputes and criminal accusations, as well as to head the government. But every free male citizen had the right to be heard. Thus, the elite continued to rule Athens and secure their position as archons, but it was the assembly that elected the archons. The poor even had the right to join the assembly.

In 621, a man named Draco was elected as one of the archons, and he took it upon himself to establish Athens's code of laws (known as the Draconian laws), which would bring stability and equality to the polis. But he wasn't successful at all, as his laws only further destabilized Athens. Draco's laws were harsh, and they brought about the deterioration of the life of free peasants. This further undermined the social peace of Athens and brought forth an economic crisis in which the rich fought the peasants and the poor. Little is known of the Draconian laws except that the death sentence was introduced for all crimes. It is also known that they helped the rich accumulate even more riches and land, and the poor were forced to abandon farming and work for the rich so they could support their families. This led to lower production of food and an economic crash.

Soon, conditions became so bad that civil war threatened to engulf Athens. Desperate, Solon, the archon elected in 594, revised the Draconian laws and introduced a series of economic changes. He attempted to balance the political power between the rich and the poor by introducing four classes in which all male citizens were ranked. The classes were divided according to wealth into *pentakosiomedimnoi* (five-hundred-measure landowners), whose wealth brought much agricultural produce, *hippeis* (horsemen, or three-hundred-measure landowners), *zeugitai* (yoked-men, or two-hundred-measure landowners), and the *thetes* (the laborers, less than two-hundred-measure landowners). The higher the rank one had, the higher governmental offices he could occupy. The laborers were barred from all offices, although they were still eligible to participate in the assembly. Solon also gave the assembly legislative responsibilities, giving the laborers a foundation on which they would later build their political activities.

On an economic level, Solon canceled the income taxes, allowing the entrepreneurs to increase their wealth. Thus, social mobility was introduced, leading Athens one step closer to true democracy. If a man could increase his wealth through production or trade, he could climb the social ladder and increase his eligibility for a governmental office. Archaeologists found a statue erected to honor Anthemion, son of Diphilus. Anthemion was a man who climbed from the fourth to the second social rank. Originally a laborer, he became a horseman, gaining more political and social rights as time passed.

The poor were even more empowered by Solon, who gave every male citizen, regardless of his social rank, the power to accuse others and appeal cases. No longer was justice in the hands of the elite; rather, it belonged to all the people of Athens. Thus, Athens had one of the most developed political systems during the 6th century. All male citizens were able to participate meaningfully in the making of laws as well as in the administration of justice. Athens was so close to democracy, but fate would not allow it just yet.

From Tyranny to Democracy in Athens

Although Solon's reforms managed to elevate Athens above the ensuing civil war, the peace didn't last for long. A new conflict started because of the rivalries for offices and social status. The elites were fighting among themselves, and the poor continued to be dissatisfied. The outcome of the unrest that followed was Athens's tyranny. Pisistratus first rose as Athens's tyrant. He championed the interests of the poor while securing the support of his wealthy friends, ensuring his victory. But it took him three tries to establish himself as the ruler of Athens, doing so in 546 BCE. As soon as he started his rule, he modeled his tyranny on Corinth. He started promoting the economic, cultural, and architectural development of the polis, and he started exporting Athenian goods, mainly pottery.

Pisistratus was succeeded by his eldest son, Hippias, after his death in 527 BCE. Hippias introduced nepotism in Athens by making sure that his family members occupied the most important government roles. But to appease his rivals, he would sometimes allow them to serve as archons, keeping the jealousy among the elites in control, at least to a degree. The wealthy Alcmaeonid family proved to be a harder nut to crack. They were the tyrant's rivals, and they secured Sparta's help in their attempt to overthrow Hippias. The Alcmaeonids were able to do so because of a scandal that happened in Athens that resulted in the exile of many elite families.

In 514 BCE, Hipparchus, a younger brother of Hippias, was killed during the Panathenaic festival. The Greeks often portrayed this murder of the tyrant's brother as the "liberation act," a moment when Athens decided to overthrow its tyrant. But in reality, the murder was of a much more personal nature. It was committed by two Athenians, Harmodius and Aristogeiton, who were lovers. Harmodius had refused the amorous advances of Hipparchus. To retaliate, Hipparchus publicly insulted Harmodius's sister, and the young man felt obliged to defend his sister's honor. He killed the tyrant's brother but was immediately cut down by his bodyguards. It is unclear if Aristogeiton had anything to do with the actual killing, but as Harmodius's lover, he was interrogated and killed. Hippias responded to his brother's murder by hardening his autocratic rule. He started ruling as a sole despot, relying on mercenaries to quell any resistance and exiling his political opponents.

The exiled Alcmaeonids heavily invested in the repair of Apollo's temple at Delphi. It was there that the Spartans first heard of Athens's troubles, for whenever they asked for divine guidance in their domestic affairs, the temple's answer would be "first free Athens." The Spartans didn't hesitate because acquiring Athens for their league would be a substantial addition. Besides, Hippias was at his most vulnerable. Nevertheless, it took Sparta two invasions of Attica and a siege of the Acropolis before Athens finally fell in 510 BCE. Hippias had to flee his city, and he sought refuge in Persia.

The Spartans were aware they wouldn't be able to directly control Athens as the city-state was equal in power to their own. Instead, the soldiers left the city immediately after overthrowing the tyrant, and the Spartans hoped the Athenian elite would see the benefits in harboring good relations. Unfortunately, the Athenian elite was deeply fragmented, and the Spartan king, Cleomenes I, put his man, Isagoras, as the head of Athens's pro-Sparta oligarchy. The leader of the aristocratic Alcmaeonid family, Cleisthenes, found himself representing the political opposition. He started his own coalition of elite families and even expanded it to include the common citizens of Athens. As Cleisthenes's coalition grew, Isagoras realized the threat it posed, and in 508 BCE, he called the Spartans. Cleisthenes was forced into exile, and according to Herodotus (a 5th-century Greek scholar), seven hundred families followed him. But when the Spartans came and Isagoras tried to disband the Athenian council, the Athenians took up arms. Isagoras and his Spartans suddenly found themselves on the defensive, and they were forced to retreat to the Acropolis. After a three-day-long siege, the Spartans surrendered and left Athens, with Isagoras in tow.

This Athenian revolt sparked major changes in state politics, and Cleisthenes managed to recognize the right moment to include ordinary citizens in politics. If it wasn't for his inclusion of the commoners in the coalition, Isagoras and the Spartans would have easily taken over the rule and gathered the Athenian elite into a dominant coalition. But the commoners changed the game. They found out that they were willing to bring about changes that would be in their favor. They were ready to take up arms and revolt.

After the expulsion of Isagoras and the Spartans, the Athenians were unwilling to go back to the old political system of the elite coalitions. Cleisthenes was recalled from his exile, and the people expected him to make good on his earlier promises of the expansion of citizens' rights. He also had to deal with the likelihood of Sparta's return to Attica. As emergency measures, Cleisthenes brought forth a series of reforms that were built on the civic identity of the Athenians. In essence, Cleisthenes invented democratic federalism, granting citizenship to all towns in the region of Attica. In the aftermath of the revolution, this political system proved to be a more successful political model than its inventor could have ever hoped. Thus, Cleisthenes started building a larger and stronger state in a territory that could have easily supported several independent poleis.

Furthermore, Cleisthenes issued a reformed constitution that expanded on the 139 villages and towns of Attica, by which the neighborhood of the region was divided into demes. This term is an Anglicized form of the original Greek *Demos*, which means the people. Therefore, the neighborhoods were divided based on how many people belonged to them. The Athenians were the *Demos* (people) of Athens, and other neighborhoods had *Demos* of their own. Demes were different in size, but on average, they consisted of 15 to 250 male citizens, as only men could hold citizenship. Each citizen was treated on different levels: as a citizen of his deme and as a citizen of Athens. Acquiring citizenship was a complicated process because each male above eighteen years old had to be formally recognized by the assembly of his local deme as having been born by a father who held Athenian citizenship.

Apart from demes, Cleisthenes introduced a division of citizens by artificially created tribes. Each tribe consisted of roughly one-tenth of Attica's citizens, and the tribe's people were drawn from three different regions. That way, one deme would consist of only a third of one given tribe. That means that the tribes were regionally diverse, and these mixed-region tribes were the basis of Athens's civic affairs, such as the army, festivals, and public life.

The Council of 500 consisted of five hundred members, and they conducted Athens's day-to-day public affairs. The members were recruited from the described deme/tribe system. There is no evidence of the council's regulations in its early days, but later, each member was paid for his service, and he had to be at least thirty years old. Each year, the ten tribes would provide fifty counselors, chosen by a lot, amounting to five hundred altogether. The fifty chancellors were chosen from different demes, with each deme sending a different number depending on the size of its population.

The councilors were not the representatives of their demes or their tribe's interests. They were expected to serve all citizens of Attica equally and represent the collective knowledge of Athens's population. The councilors' service was limited to only two non-consecutive years, making it a common experience for all Athenian men. Socrates, a philosopher who often emphasized his uninterest in public life, served as the councilor of Alopece, although only at the advanced age of sixty-three.

Athens's also had a second council, the Areopagus, named after the hill where the council would meet. Its members were chosen among the ex-magistrates, and they played a significant role in domestic politics after the revolution. However, the Areopagus survived only one generation after Cleisthenes's reforms, as the Council of 500 became dominant and, in time, the only Athenian body of government. But the legislative power continued to lay with the citizen assembly, which, together with the Council of 500, represented the earliest forms of Athens's democracy.

Chapter 3: The Persian Wars (499–449 BCE)

Persian king killing a Greek soldier, relief dated to 475 BCE
https://en.wikipedia.org/wiki/Battle_of_Thermopylae#/media/File:
Achaemenid_king_killing_a_Greek_hoplite.jpg

The Athenians were worried that the Spartans would come back to defend the oligarchy they had installed. In 507 BCE, they asked King Darius I of Persia for help in the form of a protective alliance. At this point in history, the Persian Empire was the largest, most powerful, and richest state in the ancient world. Herodotus claims that when the Athenian delegates asked for the alliance, the Persian representatives mockingly asked them who they were and where they came from, symbolizing Athens's insignificance in Persia. Nevertheless, in just two generations, Athens would come to control vast lands, known today as the Athenian empire. This transformation from an insignificant power to one of the world's leading powers was swift, and it marks the beginning of the Classical period, an age in Greek history that modern scholars believe started around 500 BCE and ended after the death of Alexander the Great in 323 BCE.

Previously, Persia extended its borders westward and took over the whole of Anatolia and many Greek poleis on its shores. The people of mainland Greece had every right to fear the expanding Persian Empire, as its intention was unclear. The Persians didn't know much about the Greeks, and the Greeks knew very little about the Persians. This mutual ignorance proved to be the reason behind many explosive misunderstandings that would lead to some of the most famous conflicts in world history.

The Athenian delegation to Sardis, where they met the Persian representatives, knew that they needed to recognize Darius I's superiority. But what they couldn't understand, or probably didn't know, was that Persia would never accept a Greek model of alliance where both sides were equal partners. Darius I expected Athens to bow to him. The Athenian delegation, having no other options, accepted the humiliating terms of the alliance, but the Athenian assembly was outraged. They refused the alliance but failed to send another delegation to Persia to inform them of the breaking of the pact. This diplomatic failure led Athens to continue believing in its independence, while Persia already counted on its loyalty and deference. This misunderstanding started a series of misfortunate events that would end in the Persian invasion of mainland Greece. The wars that ensued forced some of the mainland Greek city-states to work together, even though they saw each other as hostile or even enemies.

The heartland of the Persian Empire was in today's southeast Iran. By the time of Darius I (550–486 BCE), it covered a vast territory from modern-day Afghanistan to Turkey and north-south from the border of Russia to Egypt and the Indian Ocean. Its population was heterogeneous, and it counted millions. The administration of such a vast empire was based on satraps, who ruled smaller territories without the direct influence of the king. The satraps' duties were to raise an army when needed, keep order in their lands, and send annual taxes and revenues to the royal treasury. The taxes were paid in money, food, raw materials, valuable commodities, etc., and all of it greatly increased the wealth and prestige of the Persian rulers. Thus, the Persian monarch was probably the richest individual in the known world. Even the Greeks were awed by the wealth and lavishness of the Persian court, and they referred to the Persian monarchs as the "Great Kings."

The Outbreak of the War

The Persian Wars were a series of conflicts between Persia and Greece during the early Classical period. They took place during the 490s, as well as from 480 to 479 BCE.

The conflicts first started with the revolt of the Ionian (a region in western Anatolia, not to be confused with the Ionian Sea) Greek city-states against the Persian rule. The Ionian Greeks had lost their freedom to the Kingdom of Lydia, which overpowered them during the reign of its King Croesus (560–546 BCE). The Lydians then wanted to claim the rest of Anatolia, which was already under Persian rule. Croesus attacked Persia in 546 BCE, but he was defeated, and he lost all of his territories, including Ionia, to King Cyrus of Persia. The Persians installed tyrants in Ionia, who provoked the Greeks to revolt. The Ionians sent a delegation to mainland Greece asking for help in their effort to overthrow Persian rule. Sparta refused to help because its king, Cleomenes, saw no reason to fight against an empire whose capital was so far away that it would take his army at least three months to reach it. But unlike Sparta, Athens agreed to help, sending military aid first to neighboring Eretria on the island of Euboea and then to Ionia. The Athenian army reached Sardis and burned it to the ground. They roused the Persians' wrath, and they hurried home, but the Persian counterattack in Ionia made the Greek allies lose their coordination. By 494 BCE, the Ionian revolt had been completely crushed.

To prevent Ionia from rising against his rule again, Darius I sent his officer, Mardonius, to reorganize its administration. The result was the admission of democracy in some of the Ionian Greek city-states where tyrannies had previously been in place. But when Darius I learned about Athens's involvement in the burning of Sardis, he was outraged and wanted revenge. The Greeks were insignificant in his opinion, and he had no grand scheme of conquering the Greek mainland, but he desired to punish those who dared attack his territory. If it is to be believed, the historian Herodotus says that Darius ordered one of his slaves to say to him "Remember the Athenians" three times before a meal every day.

To punish the Greeks, Darius sent a flotilla of ships in 490 BCE. Eretria was burned before the Persian troops disembarked on the northeastern coast of Attica. Among the Persians was Hippias, who was now old but still hopeful he would be reinstalled as an Athenian tyrant. The Athenian army was greatly outnumbered, and the men were forced to ask Sparta and other Greek city-states for help. The courier who was dispatched to Sparta became famous, as he ran 140 miles (225 kilometers) from Athens to Sparta in less than two days. He then ran back to Marathon, where a battle between Athens and Persia was taking place, and then ran back to Athens to declare the Athenian victory.

After doing so, he collapsed from exhaustion and died. It is incredibly likely that none of this happened or that events have been blended together. Regardless, the runner was the inspiration for the marathon in the modern-day Olympic Games, which is twenty-five miles (forty kilometers) long, the approximate distance from Marathon to Athens.

In the Battle of Marathon, Athens had the help of a small contingent sent by neighboring Plataea. Against all odds, the Greek army managed to defeat the Persians and marched quickly back to Athens to stop the Persian fleet from attacking their city from the sea. The march was another impossible task, but the Athenians managed to complete it, despite being exhausted by the battle and carrying heavy gear. Their march, in combination with the runner to Sparta, is today celebrated as a marathon race, with major cities around the world organizing similar events every year.

The Persians were forced to return home without taking Athens. But the Greek victory barely affected Persia's might. Back home, Darius had more than enough manpower and resources to crush the whole of Greece. Nevertheless, the Athenians celebrated their victory, as they had proved they were able to fight and defeat a much superior enemy. The symbolism of the victory at Marathon outweighed its military significance. Darius I was outraged, not because the Greeks threatened his empire but because his prestige was suffering. The ordinary men of Athens had managed to take up arms and defend their freedom. The unexpected victory boosted the self-esteem of the Athenians, and they celebrated their victory at Marathon for decades to come.

The Persian Invasion

With their newly gained confidence, the Athenians decided to join the resistance against the Persian invasion of Greece that came in 480 BCE. Darius vowed he would conquer Greece as revenge for the insult to his prestige. However, it took so much time to gather the Persian forces from all the corners of the vast empire that by the time the army was ready, Darius had died. However, the invasion plans weren't abandoned. His son, Xerxes I (518–465 BCE), led the invasion of the Greek mainland. His army was huge, and it consisted of infantry and ships. In fact, Xerxes expected that the Greeks would surrender once they saw the might of his armies. The city-states of northern and central Greece did just that. They were in the direct line of the Persian advance, and they were aware they stood no chance in an open fight. Some of the cities, such as Thebes (in Boeotia, not to be confused with Thebes in Egypt), openly supported the Persian invasion, hoping to gain political and economic advantages once the fighting was over and Xerxes had secured his victory.

The remaining thirty-one Greek poleis, mostly in the southern regions, organized an alliance to defend themselves from Persian attacks. Because Sparta was a military state, it was chosen as the leader of the new military coalition. Syracuse was supposed to join the coalition, but its tyrant, Gelon, demanded the command of all the Greek forces, but both the Spartans and Athenians had refused him.

The first encounter between the coalition and the Persian army became one of the most famous battles in the history of the world. It occurred at Thermopylae, a narrow mountain pass on the eastern coast of central Greece. There, seven thousand Greek soldiers met a Persian army that numbered, according to Herodotus, a million. Modern scholars believe that the numbers were greatly exaggerated by contemporary historians and that it is more likely there were around 150,000 Persians. Nevertheless, the Greeks were once again greatly outnumbered, but they managed to hold the pass and block the Persian invasion for seven days. In the end, they were betrayed by one Greek soldier, Ephialtes, who hoped the Persians would reward him for showing them a secret path that would bring their army behind the Greek ranks. Upon hearing about the betrayal, King Leonidas I of Sparta took three hundred of his soldiers and guarded the Greek army's flank, allowing it to retreat to safety and fight another day. The legend of the 300 has its origin in this episode of the Battle of Thermopylae, but the truth is that the Spartans were joined by 700 Thespians, 900 helots, and 400 Thebans in this defense. Still, they were outnumbered, and they fought until all of them were killed, after which the Persians took over Thermopylae.

The Battle of Thermopylae is famous, but it's not the only battle that was fought at that time. It was a part of a two-front conflict, and it played out together with the naval battle at Artemisium. The alliance of Greek poleis gathered their fleets, although they had a much smaller number of ships than the Persians. The Persian naval force had started at 1,200 ships, but one-third of them were lost at sea early on. Another two hundred shipwrecked when they departed to sail around the Greek fleet and trap it. The naval battle lasted for three days, and both sides lost an equal number of ships. However, the Greek alliance couldn't afford such losses because they had a smaller fleet to begin with. The overall tactics to fend off the Persian invasion involved holding both positions at Thermopylae and the sea. Once the news of the defeat at Thermopylae reached the allied navy, the Greeks decided to retreat to Salamis, located in the Saronic Gulf (sixteen kilometers, or ten miles, away from Athens). The Persians finally had an open passage to Attica, and they quickly captured Athens. But the city had already been evacuated, with women, children, and non-combatants retreating to the northeastern coast of the Peloponnese.

The Persians pursued the Greeks, and another battle occurred in 481 BCE: the Battle of Salamis. Just as at Thermopylae, the Greek allies decided to use their country's geography to defend themselves. The channel at Salamis was too narrow for the Persians to use all of their ships at once, and it greatly restricted their maneuverability. The heavy Greek ships were able to use their underwater rams to sink the smaller Persian ones. Of all of Xerxes's army, only Artemisia I of Caria, Queen of Halicarnassus and general of her fleet of five ships, was against a Persian attack on Salamis. She was wise enough to see the trap the Greeks were preparing, but Xerxes listened to his other advisors, who urged him to attack the Greeks while the victory of Artemisium was still fresh. Artemisia was a great commander, and she fought well during the Battle of Salamis, so much so that Xerxes praised her, saying how his men became women and women became men. In truth, Artemisia was clever, and it seems she fought only for the survival of her ships. She was famous for carrying two flags, and she would pursue Greek ships under the Persian flag. But if she was pursued by the enemy, she would display a Greek flag so the pursuer would abandon his chase. These tactics allowed her to survive, and after the Battle of Salamis, Xerxes recognized her as his best naval officer and awarded her with Greek armor. According to Herodotus, it was Artemisia who advised Xerxes to retreat to Asia Minor and leave his general, Mardonius, with the Persian army to fight the Greeks another day. Xerxes listened to her advice. Following the Greek victory at Salamis, he retreated.

Mardonius remained with 300,000 Persian soldiers, and he told the Athenians that if they capitulated, they could become Persian satraps and rule over the other Greeks. The Athenians refused, and their city was sacked once more. The next year, in 479 BCE, the Greek army, led by a Spartan commander and prince named Pausanias (520–470 BCE), fought the Persians at the Battle of Plataea in Boeotia. At the same time, the Greek fleet fought at Mycale in Ionia. The Greek alliance was successful on both fronts this time and managed to defend its homeland against the invading Persians. They fought the richest and most powerful empire in the world and were able to defeat it. The Greeks had superior weapons and armor, and their use of the topography helped them achieve these victories against an enemy that easily outnumbered them. Thirty-one Greek city-states fought as if they belonged to the same political entity. The rich, the poor, and even some of the women showed remarkable courage when facing the mighty enemy of Persia. Their willingness to fight and preserve their independence came from the new ideals of political freedom that sprouted at the end of the Archaic period.

Chapter 4: The Rise of Athens and the Delian League

The Parthenon as seen today
https://en.wikipedia.org/wiki/Acropolis_of_Athens#/media/File:Th
e_Parthenon_in_Athens.jpg

The Greek alliance managed to preserve the freedom of mainland Greece, but it also achieved something unimaginable. Athens and Sparta left their old rivalries behind and joined the alliance together with the other Greek city-states. Athens and Sparta also managed to share the leadership of the alliance without any internal conflicts. Athens provided most of the fleet and funds, as Attica had a huge source of silver at the time, while Sparta gave its infantry, as well as many capable generals and officers.

But once the Persians were gone, the Greek leaders found themselves unable to maintain their cooperation. There were many Athenians who believed that the two poleis should work together for the mutual good. They started pro-Sparta lobbying during the Athenian assembly, but it wasn't enough. Instead, Athens came to rule the alliance of the city-states that took part in the defense against the Persians. This was the start of the Athenian empire, one of the most fascinating of paradoxes. The Greek city-states defended their ideals of freedom when they were fighting the Persians only to allow Athens to rise to power. Other city-states willingly subjected themselves to Athens and gave it the means to start oppressing them.

But to understand how this happened, one must understand the circumstances in mainland Greece that ensued right after the Persian Wars. The Greeks were afraid the Persians would be back and attempt another conquest of their homeland. They were also afraid that another conflict such as the Persian Wars would lead to the economic downfall of the whole of Greece. The Greeks of the Aegean Islands had even more reason to fear. They were in close proximity to the Persian Empire, and if Xerxes decided to retaliate for the loss, they would be the first to receive the blow.

The conflict continued in 478, but this time, the Greek alliance set sail to liberate the coastal cities of Ionia, as well as in Cyprus. They even laid siege to Byzantium, a Greek colony at the time. But these efforts weren't as productive as the defense of the Greek mainland, mostly because the Spartan commander Pausanias behaved offensively toward the Ionians in the alliance. He was quickly recalled back to Sparta to answer the charges against him. The Ionians asked the Athenians to take over the command, and a new military alliance started, known as the Delian League. The name is a modern invention; modern scholars believed the treasury of the league was on the island of Delos, hence the name.

The Spartans thought of the Athenians as friendly allies, and they were more than glad to let Athens take over the leadership, mostly because they wanted to retreat from the conflict with Persia but also because they were afraid that any Spartan commander they would send would end up being as corrupt as Pausanias. Spartan leaders often displayed behavioral issues when in command of the armies of other poleis. This was probably due to the oppression they experienced during their training days in boyhood. Spartan life and the sense of authority were not mirrored in other city-state's armies, and Sparta was well aware of that. Anyway, Sparta had an ongoing need to keep its army at home and keep the helot revolts under control.

The member states of the Delian League took an oath never to leave the coalition. The islands of the Aegean Sea were the majority in the league, but the members also included the poleis of central Greece, as well as western Anatolia. The city-states of the Peloponnese remained in an alliance with Sparta. They were in an alliance long before the Persian Wars, and they wanted to maintain their loyalty. Athens and Sparta once again found themselves opposing each other, and each was a leader of a different military alliance. The Spartan alliance was named the Peloponnesian League by modern historians, and they shared an assembly that was tasked with setting the league's policies. But no action could be taken without the approval of the Spartan kings. The Delian League also had an assembly, and the idea was to reach decisions together. But in practice, Athens had the final word.

Athens wasn't offered the leadership of the Delian League because it was thought to have advanced leadership skills compared to other city-states but rather because it could provide the most resources, men, and ships. The Delian League's economy was structured in such a way that bigger poleis would provide whole ships with crews and more resources and money than the smaller city-states. The smaller poleis were allowed to group their resources to be able to provide ships and crews.

The Delian League was a naval alliance, so they needed warships. At the time, Greek warships were narrow vessels built for speed. Crews numbered up to 200 men, out of which 170 were rowers. The rest were officers, hoplite warriors, and archers who would engage the enemy's crew if needed. Over time, most of the member cities of the Delian League preferred to pay their dues in money instead of building ships. They had no capacity to build and equip warships, and it was easier to pay money. Only Athens, which was far larger than any of the other members of the Delian League, had engineers, crews, and shipyards, and it had the capacity of supplying the alliance with warships. The poorest of the Athenians served as rowers, but this servitude brought them money, as well as increased political influence, allowing them to elevate socially.

It was because of the superiority of Athens and its huge contribution to the Delian League that the smaller members lost their influence in decision-making. Even if they disagreed with Athens's proposals, they had no option but to accept them. If they proved to be stubborn, Athens would simply dispatch its fleet and attack them to persuade them to remain within the league and pay their dues. The Athenian men found themselves wielding enormous power, and soon enough, the dues became compulsory, more relatable to a tribute from vassal states than a membership fee. But once Athens subdued the rebellious members of the league, it became unpopular, as it would take away the political freedoms of other city-states. In 465 BCE, Thasos, an island in the northern Aegean Sea, withdrew from the Delian League. They did so because of the ongoing dispute with Athens over the control of gold mines in the mainland. To make them stay within the league, Athens led the alliance into a long siege of Thasos, ending it only in 463 BCE. The island was compelled to surrender to avoid the starvation of its populace. The punishment was harsh, as Athens made Thasos give up its whole fleet and pay enormous tribute to the league.

But the main goals of the Delian League were to expel the Persians from the city-states along the northeastern coast of the Aegean Sea. In just twenty years after the Battle of Salamis, the Delian League achieved this, and it even expelled the Persian fleet from the Aegean, ending its threat to Greece, at least for the next fifty years. Athens grew stronger and richer due to the many spoils that came from Persian defeats. By the middle of the 5th century BCE, all the members of the league together paid an equivalent of $200 million (in contemporary terms) annually. Athens had only around thirty thousand to forty thousand adult male citizens at the time, and this amount of income meant the general prosperity of the Athenian population. The expenditure was decided by the male citizens who attended the assembly, and most of the money was spent on maintaining the fleet. Both rich and poor citizens understood the value of the fleet, as it made them the mightiest polis. But the income was also spent on repairing the city's walls, roads, and public buildings.

Democracy in the Empire

The empire and democracy coexisted. Remember, the Athenian empire wasn't an actual empire. It was named that by modern scholars to mark the period of Athens's predominance in Greece. Athens did rule over the other members of the Delian League but never officially. This is why democracy was allowed to develop in certain parts of Greece, even though they were under Athens's control. Greek democracy had a gradual development, and it was based on a very simple principle: those who were able to provide an army should have political rights and power. But in Athens, the men who were in the army were not the elites. They were hoplites who fought on land and the *thetes* who rowed the boats during the naval battles. After the Persian Wars, these men were granted political power, and they were the majority of the adult citizens. They were called the *demos*, the commoners, and they gained sovereignty for the assembly. The political offices that had once held great power and prestige were now diminished in importance.

Due to the proposal of one individual, Pericles (495-429 BCE), the offices that were now open to the *demos* received a daily stipend financed by the state. This was the first time in the history of Greece that government representatives received state-funded salaries. This was because the majority of the *demos* were poor, and they were unable to leave their regular jobs to attend government meetings. They had to take care of their livelihoods and their families. In contrast, the board of military generals (ten members), who were also the most influential public officials, were elected annually and received no state-funded stipend. The stipend that the *demos* received for their participation in government was not lavish. It was equal to what a laborer could earn in one day. Nevertheless, it allowed the commoners to assume the political power that belonged to them. Pericles himself was a member of the elite, and he had no personal gain with the reform he introduced. But like Cleisthenes before him (who was Pericles's ancestor), Pericles worked to strengthen the egalitarian tendencies of Athenian democracy.

Pericles became extremely popular due to his introduction of the stipend for the *demos*. This is why he was able to push for other reforms, both in foreign and domestic policies, starting around 450 BCE. In 451 BCE, he introduced a new law of citizenship, making it available only to the individuals whose mother and father were born Athenians. Previously, citizenship was granted to those of Athenian fathers and non-Athenian mothers.

Pericles did this to emphasize the importance and prestige of Athenian citizenship but also to elevate the status of Athenian women. Suddenly, the citizenship of women became important, and although they still had no political power, it brought a new level of prestige to females. After the introduction of the new law, a review of all-male citizenship had to be done to expel those who claimed it without grounds. This significantly reduced the number of people eligible to involve themselves in Athenian politics.

In foreign policy, Pericles's influence is less clear. During the 450s, Athens offered support to Egypt's rebellion, in which they tried to get rid of Persian rule. Athens raised a large army that was sent to Egypt, but the expedition proved to be an utter failure. More than two hundred ships were lost, together with their crews. Some of the lost rowers and soldiers were not Athenian but members of the Delian League. Nevertheless, the loss of manpower prompted Athens to be more careful, and it moved the league's treasury from Delos to Athens. This way, if the Persians decided to retaliate, the treasury would be safe. And it also gave Athens direct control over the Delian League's funds.

While Pericles's influences on foreign politics involving Persia are not known, he did support foreign policy against Spartan interests in Greece. In 457 BCE, at the Battle of Tanagra in Boeotia, the Athenian forces were defeated by the Peloponnesian League. However, in the following years, Athens took control of the region, as well as of neighboring Phocis. Victories were also achieved against Corinth and some of the island poleis of the Aegean Sea. But there was no enduring victory over Sparta and its allies, and by 447, Athens had lost control over Boeotia and Phocis. The next winter, Pericles agreed to a peace with Sparta, and a treaty was signed that froze the conflict between the two city-states for the next thirty years. Pericles had to do this because his political rivals in Athens started gaining momentum, and he needed to concentrate on dealing with them.

In 443, Pericles secured his political power in Athens by removing his main rival, a man named Thucydides. Pericles was elected as the general for the fifteenth year in a row, and no one could dispute his political influence. He was directly responsible for a war against one of the member states of the Delian League in 441 BCE when he rashly took a side in the political crisis of Samos. The conflict lasted until 439 BCE, and its main cause was that Samos wanted to leave the league as there was no longer a need to defend Greece from Persia. Athens wanted to retain its dominion over the allies, claiming that Persia was dormant only because of the league's existence. Samos wasn't the only city-state that rebelled against Athens at the time. Many poleis wanted to break off from the alliance, but Athens wouldn't let them. After all, Athens came to depend on the money the member states were sending as their part to the league.

Athens's Prosperity

Athens reached its golden age in the decades before the Peloponnesian War (431–404 BCE). During these years, Athens was at the height of its power and prosperity, and its communal abundance was shared by all of its citizens. However, the Athenians remained relatively modest, which can be seen in the unchanged house and farmhouse sizes. The villages were still tightly inhabited, and the urban center of Athens continued to have houses wedged against each other, occupying small spaces. The elite residences followed a similar design, with grouped bedrooms, dining rooms, a kitchen, and workrooms all gathered around an open courtyard in the center of the household. At this period, paintings and art were not yet displayed in the houses, not even in the residences of the richest Athenians. Furnishings were sparse and simple, without much difference between different social classes.

The rich were the benefactors of the public works, and Athens started landscaping its urban environment. The heart of the city had planted trees that would provide shade. Stoas were built at the edges of markets and the urban center. The stoas were decorated shelters that protected people from storms, rain, or the sun. The most famous one is the Painted Stoa, located at the central public square known as the Agora. There, people would gather to discuss local affairs and politics. The paintings on the walls of this stoa displayed some of the most famous scenes in Greek history, such as the Battle of Marathon.

Athens's wealth wasn't only due to the accumulation of the dues from the member states of the Delian League. The city received substantial revenues from harbor fees and sales taxes as well. Nevertheless, Athenians kept to their small-scale buildings, as they saw no need for lavish and monumental public works. The assembly gathered under the open sky, and they needed no building. Only a small raised speaker's platform was installed for the assembly. The first great project of the Classical period started in 447 BCE at Pericles's initiative—the buildings of Athens's Acropolis. There, he built two temples dedicated to Athena: the Parthenon and the Temple of Athena Nike. He also built a monumental gateway to the Acropolis known as the Propylaea and yet another temple dedicated to both Athena and Poseidon, known as the Erechtheion. But Pericles didn't use his own money to fund this project; rather, he used public funds. The cost of these enormous buildings was massive, and many of his political enemies scolded him for spending so much of the public funds.

The Athenians saw the building of the Acropolis as a symbol of their victory over the Persians, who had destroyed the previous temple to Athena that stood there. The old temple had an olive tree in its center, which symbolized Athena as the protector of agriculture, thus Athens. But after the Persian Wars, Athena gained new symbolism. She transformed into a warrior goddess of victory (Nike in ancient Greek). That is why the Parthenon used to house a large gold and ivory statue of Athena in body armor holding a statue of Nike. The Greek temples were not gathering places for worshipers but rather the houses for the divine. That is why Parthenon's design represents the standard Greek architecture of the period—a box with columns and various entrances. The columns were of Doric style, with simple carvings, not as elaborate as the Ionic style, which is often imitated in modern architecture. The temple was open only to priests and priestesses, but on occasion, it would open its doors for public religious ceremonies. The Parthenon alone was constructed of twenty thousand tons of Attica's marble, and it had sixty-five columns in total supporting it. True to the classical Greek style, the Parthenon has no straight lines or right angles.

Athens was the only city-state of classical Greece to build such a lavish temple. Greeks, in general, preferred to keep their public buildings designed for their purposes, not for their looks. But Athens wanted to emphasize its relationship with its patron goddess, and this can also be observed on the carvings that run along the walls of the Parthenon right under its roof. Here, the citizens of Athens were depicted in the company of the gods, even though it was clear there was no interaction between them. After all, the citizens of Athens were only humans, and the mighty gods were invisible and mysterious. But the sheer presence of citizens in the carvings of the Parthenon represents the special relationship the city had with the Greek gods, who always favored Athens. This is why the Athenians believed they were able to repel the Persians in the first place because the gods loved them above all else. Their success against the Persians was proof enough that the gods were on their side.

Chapter 5: Culture and Society of Classical Athens

An ancient Greek relief depicting all twelve Olympian gods
*https://en.wikipedia.org/wiki/Twelve_Olympians#/media/File:Gree
k_-_Procession_of_Twelve_Gods_and_Goddesses_-
_Walters_2340.jpg*

The whole history of classical Greece in the 5th century BCE revolves around Athens. The city wasn't only the dominant political entity of Greece but also the most prestigious and developed, both culturally and socially. The mid-5th century was the Athenian golden age, and not a single other city-state has a similar amount of archaeological or written sources. This is why modern history mainly focuses on Athens when it comes to the discussion of classical Greece. But the archaeological findings of Athens and the focus put on this city by various scholars mustn't be taken as a substitution for the whole of Greece. Athens doesn't equal Greece when talking about this period. Athens was a part of the Greek world, albeit the most developed and prominent one.

The Athenian dominance of the Greek world was no accident. It came as a result of many social and cultural changes of the mid-5th century. But while going through these changes, Athenian life remained unchanged. What came out of it was a sense of continuity in social matters, but there were also cultural innovations and ensuing tensions, which proved to be both destructive and creative. Publicly-supported arts gave birth to the tragic drama, which explored many serious, ethical issues of the period. The new form of education in classical Greece came into existence, but it found opposition among the traditionalists. For rich women, public life remained closed or at least limited by the old traditions of modesty and exclusion from political life. However, poor women gained access to public life simply because they had to work to support their families. The interplay of new and traditional was tolerated until the conflict with Sparta was renewed. This conflict pushed Athens into the Peloponnesian War, allowing the Athenian society to reach its breaking point. But behind everything that was happening in the cultural and social life of Athens lay religion.

Religion in Classical Greece

The main postulate of ancient Greek religion was that the humans, as a group but also as individuals, praised the gods and thanked them for the blessings they received. As seen in the previous chapter, the Athenians thought they had a special relationship with the gods, and they believed they were their favorites. Because of this, they were willing to spend huge amounts of money and goods to honor the gods through monuments or public religious ceremonies. The ceremonies often included sacrifices, gifts to the sanctuaries and temples, prayers, dances, songs, and processions. The individuals gifted the temples and sanctuaries, expecting the gods to repay them—a service for a service. The Greek understanding of the divine is underlain by the idea of mutual benefit between gods and humans. The gods didn't love humans as modern religions often teach. They only rewarded those who respected and honored them. The humans who offended the gods were punished as individuals (disease, death, suffering, etc.) or as a community (quakes, famine, loss in a war, etc.).

The gods' expectations were codified as rules of proper behavior for humans. Thus, humans didn't have to question what would offend the gods and what would please them. For example, the most cherished value that humanity possessed was hospitality toward guests. This value pleased the gods, but arrogance and violence displeased them. The Greeks believed that through dreams, oracles, and divinations, the gods communicated their displeasure to humans. The most common offenses were forgetting an offering for the gods or violating a sanctuary in enemy territory. It was believed that the gods didn't care much about common crimes and would leave humans to police themselves. But breaking an oath made toward fellow humans was a very serious religious offense, and it angered the gods. Homicide was considered the only common crime that offended the gods, and the gods would pollute the whole society to punish the murderer. Society could cleanse itself only by punishing the murderer.

The Greek gods were seen as carefree and immortal. They had easy lives, although they did know pain, usually produced from the dealings they had with the other gods or with humans. The Greek pantheon had the twelve most important gods, with Zeus as their leader. They would gather on the top of Mount Olympus to enjoy lavish banquets. The main thing that concerned the gods was their honor, and just like humans, the gods had to go to lengths to preserve it.

In order to communicate with the gods, the people had to sing hymns, praise them, offer sacrifices, or pray to them. Individuals worshiped gods and laid offerings for them at their homes in the company of the whole family and even the household. Temples were reserved for group ceremonies, which were headed by priests and priestesses. The clergy was chosen from the main citizen's body, meaning they led civil lives too. However, they rarely sought to engage in the political and social matters of the city-state. The special knowledge they possessed involved the performance of the ceremonies according to tradition, but they were never seen as guardians of a doctrine (as modern Christian priests and monks are often seen) because there wasn't any.

Not all the people joined every ceremony, nor were they obliged to. There were ceremonies specific to men and women, joint ceremonies, or those reserved only to married women or virgins. Laborers had a specific number of free days that they could use to attend religious ceremonies and offer sacrifices. Sacrifice was seen as one of the highest honors to the gods, but it wasn't a human sacrifice. The Greeks offered anything from grain, milk, and cakes to slaughtered animals. The sacrificed animals were symbolically given to the gods, and the humans would enjoy the meat on special occasions. Cattle were rare in ancient Greece; therefore, animal sacrifices usually occurred only during a time of great need or during large public ceremonies.

Ancient Greeks also enjoyed religious activities outside of the cults. They celebrated births and weddings and mourned the dead. Both rich and poor started giving offerings to their ancestors during the Classical period. Before this, rituals were mainly practiced by the rich. Everyone was allowed to consult the seers to decipher the meaning behind dreams or to ask for a magical spell that would help them with their love life or lift a curse. Hero cults were also widespread because the Greeks believed that the remains of prominent persons, usually from the distant past, retained special powers. But unlike the gods' powers, a hero's power was local, influencing only the polis in which he was buried. This is why bringing back the remains of heroes who died far away from their polis was important. In 475 BCE, Cimon (an Athenian general and statesman) brought what was believed to be the remains of Theseus to Athens. He was the founder of Athens and the hero who fought the Minotaur. The arrival of his remains to Athens was celebrated as a major event, and a new special shrine was erected for him in the city's center.

The most revered international cult was that of Demeter and Persephone, Demeter's daughter. The rite of the cult, in which its members had to take part, was the Mysteries, and everyone had the right to be initiated in the cult, no matter his or her origin. Even some slaves were granted the right of initiation through their service to Demeter's temple. The importance of the Eleusinian Mysteries was so great that an agreement between poleis was set to withhold from any conflict during a period of five days before the ceremonies. This way, everyone was guaranteed safe passage to join the festivities and ceremonies, which were held in Eleusis (hence Eleusinian Mysteries) in west Attica. The central event of the Mysteries was the revelation of Demeter's secret. Although the rite itself was described in detail, and we know what it involved, no one ever revealed what Demeter's secret was. The knowledge of it remains lost, and the only thing we can say with certainty is that it involved something the cult members had to do, say, and see. But this secrecy only serves as proof of how serious the cult of Demeter was taken and how dedicated the Greeks were to it.

The Eleusinian Mysteries were not the only initiation rites, nor was the cult of Demeter the most prominent one. There were many others, but this one perfectly depicts the ancient Greeks' devotion to their religion and rites. The Demeter and Persephone cult was an agrarian cult that symbolized the death and rebirth of nature. Other cults placed emphasis on the protection of people from disease, war, ghosts, poverty, or anything that could bring about individual or group suffering. The Greek gods were good and evil at the same time, just as humans were (and still are). In many ways, they were mirroring human behavior, so they shared human nature. This is why ancient Greeks didn't have a concept of a paradise or utopia that would rise on earth once the evil forces were banished. The people could only hope the gods would be favorable to them during life and the afterlife as a reward for good religious conduct.

Public Life Seen Through the Eyes of Tragedy

The relationship humans had with the gods further developed into artistic expression. The first tragedies were performed during an annual three-day-long festival dedicated to the god Dionysus. Although they had a religious connotation, some of these plays are still performed in theaters around the world. Comedy was of equal importance, and both comedies and tragedies reached their peak during the 5th century BCE. Just as in the Olympic Games, the drama festivities were competitive, and the writers were rewarded for the winning plays. Three tragedies and one comedy were chosen to be performed during the festival of Dionysus. The main stories tragedies told were the consequences humans had to endure for their malevolent interactions with the gods. After much bloodshed and suffering, a tragedy ended with a resolution to the trouble. The competition was also set for the best actor, and this is why, even today, the leading roles are called "protagonist," which means "first competitors."

Playwrights were usually men of the elite social class, but the actors and other performers were not. The playwrights not only wrote the tragedies but also composed the music, produced, directed, and often played as actors in their own plays. Some of the best classical Greece playwrights were Sophocles, Aeschylus, and Euripides. Their fame wasn't only due to their skills in drama. Aeschylus, for example, fought in the Battles of Marathon and Salamis. The rest held high offices and were elected as generals.

Aeschylus was praised for his military service, and the epitaph on his grave doesn't even mention his success as a playwright. But his own pride in his service to his homeland is expressed in his tragedies. Athenian tragedies were based on the writer's personal pride to be part of the greatest polis. Nevertheless, they often touched upon the ethical themes that sprouted between the humans and gods in the setting of the polis. This is because those themes turned out to be burning ethical questions at the time.

Some plays were mythological in character, and they seemingly took place in distant lands (Troy, for example). Nevertheless, the moral topics always illuminated society and the obligations of contemporary citizens in a polis. This is probably best displayed in Sophocles's play *Antigone*, with the conclusion that there is no easy resolution to the conflict between the divine moral traditions and the political rule of the state. Antigone, the protagonist, wants to bury her brother, who was proclaimed a traitor, while her uncle, the king, forbids it. The burial is a moral demand the humans owe to the gods. But the king needs to make a point about the treasonous act, so he denies the afterlife to him. The tragedy ends in the death of Antigone, as well as in the suicide of the king's wife and son. The king sees the suicide of his family as punishment of the gods, and he finally realizes the importance of tradition and burial rituals. Antigone was written nearly 2,500 years ago, but its moral message is relevant even for our times. The play is still produced in theaters around the world, though sometimes in a new modernized setting.

Many protagonists of Greek tragedies were female characters, although they were played by male actors. Women were not allowed to act, and they did not write plays. All characterizations of women were, therefore, left to the men. Heroines, such as Antigone, Clytemnestra, and Medea, are representations of what men thought Greek women were like. Perhaps the playwrights tried to give women a voice through their plays, but it seems this was not always true, mainly because ancient Greek women had strictly prescribed social behaviors and values, while the women who were the heroines of tragedies mainly spoke with a male voice. Although they were female in name and representation, they behaved and voiced their opinions as male citizens of Greek poleis. Only Medea perhaps represents a true woman. The play named after this heroine insists on a reevaluation of the role of women as wives and mothers. Medea keeps saying that women who bear children deserve the same respect as the hoplite warriors.

The audience and their reactions determined the popularity of plays. Women and men sat in the audience and were touched by the tragic messages the plays conveyed. But they were also greatly influenced by the issues raised by the plays, especially when it concerned gender relations, both in the family and in the polis. The Greek tragedy, just as its mythology, displays humans not as the ultimate villains but as common people susceptible to errors. They would fall out of divine favor due to moral mistakes they committed knowingly or even unknowingly. Thus, in a sense, the tragedies also served as warnings to the audience to mind their behavior at all times, or a similar fate could come upon them or on Athens itself. When the Greek tragedy was at its height, with audiences consuming the popular plays of Sophocles, Athens enjoyed immense power as it asserted full control over the Delian League. Through plays, the citizens were also reminded that the good fortune of Athens lay in the hands of the gods, and although the Athenians were the favorites of the divine, that could easily change.

Training and Education

Athenians didn't have a formal education in a modern sense, and public schools didn't exist. The norms of respectable behavior for both men and women were taught at home and through various events that occurred in their everyday lives. Private teachers existed, but only well-to-do families could afford them. Children's education consisted of learning how to write, read, and learn to play a musical instrument or to sing. For men, physical fitness was extremely important, and special attention was given to physical exercise. Military service demanded all men be in excellent form; after all, boys as young as eighteen and as old as sixty could be mobilized. This is why city-states provided men with open-air exercise facilities where they could work out on a daily basis. These facilities were named gymnasiums, which uses the ancient Greek term *gymnos*, which means "naked." Physical exercises were performed completely nude as both a tribute to the gods and as a promotion of male aesthetics. Some gymnasiums had a space dedicated to wrestling and boxing called a palaestra. But these spaces could exist independently, too, without being attached to gymnasiums. Other than spaces for exercising, gymnasiums also served as gathering spots where people could socialize, exchange political and intellectual ideas, or simply tell the news.

The daughters of wealthy men were given extensive education in writing, reading, and arithmetic, as they would need these skills to manage households successfully once they got married. Poor girls and boys had to learn some trade to help support their families. Usually, they learned the trade by helping their parents in their daily work. If they were fortunate enough, they could become apprentices to skilled craftsmen and artisans. The poor had little use of skills like reading and writing, and the general literacy rate in Athens was low. The poorest people knew only how to sign their names, but some individuals learned more than that. Communication was predominantly oral in classical Greece, and there was little reason for the commoners to learn how to read. If a legal dispute required them to read documents, they would simply find someone to read it to them.

The sons of prosperous families needed to acquire certain skills that would help them join the political life of Athens once they came of age. But there were no special schools that would prepare them for public life. Instead, they learned by observing their fathers, uncles, and other adult males. The most important skill a wealthy young man could acquire was the ability to persuade people during public speeches. Most older men would invite boys to be their students and would even have several such followers to teach. This form of education is today known as mentorship. The students were expected to help their mentors perform their daily duties in public office, but they were also their mentor's workout partners in gymnasiums. They were sometimes allowed to join drinking parties or symposiums where men exchanged political ideas. The relationship between a mentor and a student was often sexual; back then, though, it was seen as an expression of the bond that the pair shared and their dedication to each other.

For Greeks of the Classical period, it was normal for an older man to be attracted to both boys and girls. But that attraction was never seen as purely sexual. The relationship between lovers was more than just a desire; it was even seen as divinely inspired. But same-sex relations outside of the mentor-student relationship were frowned upon, and it brought disgrace to the people who practiced it. Even the relationships between mentor and student were heavily regulated. The older men were allowed to pursue their students, but the students were able to decline their proposals. Also, a mentor always needed to have a young man's education in mind, and one's sexual desire was to be satisfied only if it wouldn't influence the boy's education. Great Greek philosophers, such as Plato, believed that same-sex relationships between older men and young boys only helped society as a whole. That special bond was a motivating force behind one's education, values, and even war.

The overwhelming importance of persuasive speech resulted in the appearance of a new kind of teacher: the Sophists. They offered organized instruction to young men on how to develop public-speaking abilities. Their popularity grew immensely in the second half of the 5th century, but their popularity threatened to ruin the traditional relationship between mentors and students, and they were detested. Nevertheless, young men preferred Sophists because they were able to teach them precisely what they needed— the ability to persuade the masses or their opponents. Even those who failed to learn this oratory skill found ways to use the Sophists. They commissioned the Sophists and paid good money to have personalized speeches written especially for them. Then, they could present the speech as their own during public assemblies. The Sophists expected their pupils to pay for the classes, and unlike mentors, they didn't pursue sexual relationships. Wealthy young men flocked to the dazzling demonstrations these new teachers performed in public squares. But the teachings of many Sophists also brought new ideas to Athens, and many considered them dangerous to the city's political and social traditions.

Chapter 6: The Peloponnesian War

Battle of Syracuse
*https://en.wikipedia.org/wiki/Peloponnesian_War#/media/File:Des
truction_of_the_Athenian_army_at_Syracuse.jpg*

By the middle of the 5ᵗʰ century, the relations between Athens and Sparta had deteriorated greatly. Open hostilities erupted during the 430s, which means the peace signed in 445 failed to last the specified thirty years. The result was the Peloponnesian War (431–404 BCE), which engulfed most of the Greek world. This was one of the lengthiest ancient Greek conflicts, and it wreaked havoc on the social and political integrity of Athens, as it cut off its economic predominance and reduced its population. The war exposed the sharp division of the Athenian public, and the bitterness that ensued between political rivals brought a tragic end to some of the greatest individuals of the Classical period. The execution of the great Athenian philosopher Socrates proved that this political bitterness even survived the war.

The war itself was a result of Athens's stubbornness to negotiate a peace treaty. As the mightiest city-state, Athens believed it had the right to dictate the peace terms. However, what we know today about the Peloponnesian War comes mostly from the writings of Athenian historian Thucydides (460–400 BCE). He was a contemporary to the events, and he even served as a military general in the Athenian army. Eventually, he was exiled for the loss of one of Athens's outposts, and he took this time to interview and write down what other participants of the war had to say. His writing is analytical and direct, but it is impossible to say how much of the thoughts are his personal observations and exaggerations.

The Strategies of the War

The origin of the Peloponnesian War, like so many other wars, is complex. The immediate causes centered around the dispute between Sparta and Athens in the 430s. Athens wanted a free hand when dealing with Sparta's allies. However, the Spartans saw it as the Athenians trying to separate them from their allies. The first violent disputes occurred when Athens aided Corcyra, which was in conflict with Corinth (Sparta's greatest ally). At the same time, Athens militarily blocked Sparta's other ally, Potidaea. Megara, a former Athens ally, rebelled, and seeking to break Athens's yolk, it sought help from Corinth. In return, Athens introduced the economic blockade of Megara, a city whose economy completely depended on seaborne trade. But underlying the immediate causes of the Peloponnesian War was the constant power play between Athens and Sparta. They feared each other's might and influence on the surrounding regions.

Sparta finally sent an ultimatum to Athens, but under the influence of Pericles, the Athenian assembly rejected it. In the ultimatum, the Spartans threatened war if the economic blockades of Megara and Potidaea weren't lifted. Corinth then put pressure on Sparta by threatening they would leave the Peloponnesian League if Sparta didn't react. Thus, it was the lesser powers that used their influence to nudge the two great city-states into a conflict.

Athens reminded Sparta of the obligations it had since it did sign a peace treaty in 445 BCE, but Sparta couldn't risk losing Corinth as an ally because it completely depended on its naval power, which could rival that of Athens. This is why the Spartans started blaming Athens for not even being willing to negotiate the terms and for refusing all concessions Sparta made after the ultimatum was rejected. Although the Spartans believed they were right, they still feared the punishment of the gods if they broke the peace treaty. Athens, on the other hand, was completely confident in achieving a victory in the ensuing war because they still considered themselves to be the gods' favorites; also, they were not the ones breaking the treaty.

Athens's urban center was safe from any direct attack due to the fortifications that surrounded it and the Athenian fleet resting in the harbor. After the Persian Wars, the Athenians encircled their polis with a high wall, leaving a fortified corridor that led to the main harbor at Piraeus. The technology of the mid-5th century wasn't sufficient enough to breach the walls of Athens. The result was a strongly defended city that had access to food supplies by importing grain from overseas. Even if the Spartans took all the agricultural land outside of Athens's city walls, the citizens would not starve.

Athens was rich, and it could always pay for food reserves by using the funds of the Delian League. Sparta was famous for its infantry and would surely attack from the land. Athens planned to send its fleet to attack Spartan territory by the sea or by landing its troops behind enemy lines. Pericles devised this two-pronged strategy to avoid open battle against the Spartan infantry in front of Athens's city walls. He was confident that Athens's wealth and manpower would be sufficient enough to win the war.

But the fault in Pericles's strategy was that it demanded many Athenians abandon their land and come to the urban center. Most Athenians lived in the countryside, and they proved to be unwilling to abandon their livelihood and move inside the city walls. The Spartans attacked Attica annually, and the people were required to move and abandon their everyday lives every so often. In 431 BCE, the first time Sparta attacked Attica during the war, the countryside-born and bred Athenians were forced to watch smoke rise from their destroyed homes and fields. They were angry, and Pericles had to do all that was in his power to stop the people from rushing outside to meet the Spartan infantry. The assembly wanted to ratify a new war strategy, but Pericles managed to persuade them to be patient. Unfortunately, Thucydides doesn't reveal how Pericles avoided the normal democratic procedures and blocked the assembly's meeting.

The Spartans spent one month ravaging Attica's countryside before they returned home. They didn't have the means to supply their army over a prolonged period, and they needed to rush home to avoid another helot uprising. Even though Sparta attacked Attica every year, the invasion never lasted more than forty days. Nevertheless, the Spartan army managed to inflict heavy losses on Athens and its countryside by burning and pillaging the whole region. Although the Athenians remained safe behind their walls and had enough supplies to last them through the war, they could not simply stand and watch the ravaging of their homeland.

The Unpredicted Disaster

Pericles's strategy was smart, and it produced results during the first years of the Peloponnesian War. However, an epidemic started ravaging the population of Athens in 430 BCE, and it took its greatest toll several years later. The consequences for Athens were disastrous. The polis was overpopulated with many people from the countryside. They stayed in cramped, narrow, and unsanitary dwellings, sharing them with the people who were already living in the urban center. Adequate housing and sanitation were missing, as the city leaders had failed to provide it for the people they invited to settle inside Athens. Pericles could only watch how his people disappeared. Thucydides described the symptoms of the disease, but modern scholars cannot determine what it was. The symptoms included painful sores, vomiting, diarrhea, and fever. Thucydides also describes how the disease made people extremely thirsty and how many of them jumped in water cisterns, contaminating the whole city's supply of drinking water. The mortality rate was so high that Athens had no power to man the fleet anymore. The failure of Pericles's strategy was imminent.

Pericles died of the same disease from which his people were suffering in 429 BCE, and the loss of his leadership damaged Athens the most. The Athenian confidence, a product of the belief that the gods favored them, started to wane. And so, the epidemic hurt Athens both physically and morally. The population was devastated, their political leader had been removed, and their self-confidence was crushed. The social and religious norms of the Athenians corroded since their faith in the divine was no longer important. But they continued their fight, and despite great losses, Athens's army managed to inflict damage on the Spartans. Potidaea was forced to surrender as early as 430 BCE, and in 429 BCE, the Athenian fleet won a major victory at Naupactus against Corinth. The city-states of Lesbos mounted a revolt, but the Athenians managed to suppress it in 427 BCE.

However, due to the division of the population started, many city-states in the Delian League started experiencing factional struggles. One such struggle led to a civil war in Corcyra in 427 BCE. The factional struggles in Athens prevented the Delian League from sending annual campaigns against Sparta in enough numbers for Pericles's strategy to work. The military campaigns of the early 420s brought horrible defeats to both sides, and it looked as if both Sparta and Athens were unable to gain the upper hand. But then, in 425 BCE, Athens's general, Cleon, captured 120 Spartan equals (citizens) and 170 infantry troops of the Peloponnesian League at Pylos, giving Athens a unique opportunity to press for peace.

In the previous history of Sparta, not a single man had ever surrendered. Their honor code wouldn't allow it. They preferred to die than to return home as losers. But at this point, the population of Spartan equals was extremely low, and it would be disastrous if the captured group perished. For the first time since the dawn of Sparta, the men chose to surrender. The Spartan leaders offered favorable peace terms to Athens in exchange for their equals. Cleon's victory brought him enormous popularity, and he used it to influence the Athenian assembly. He was a violent man, and he advocated a hard line toward Sparta. The Athenian assembly listened to his advice and refused the peace offer, believing they could win if they only continued fighting.

However, the next development in the war only served to prove that the Athenians lacked wisdom. The Spartans decided to abandon the traditional policy that prevented them from waging extended military expeditions outside of their territory. In 424, under the leadership of general Brasidas, the Spartan army embarked on a long campaign against Athens's many strongholds in the far north of Greece. They were hundreds of miles away from home, and there was no turning back. For Sparta, it was all or nothing. Such determination brought them their first major victory when they conquered Amphipolis, a colony essential to Athens's strategy. Amphipolis was Athens's gateway to silver and gold mines, as well as to timber for shipbuilding. Although the contemporary historian Thucydides didn't fight in this battle, he was the commander of the region where Amphipolis was. The blame for the loss was put on him, and this was when he was exiled.

The Nonexistent Peace and the Sicilian Expedition

After the victory at Pylos in 425 BCE, Cleon became the most influential Athenian. He was dispatched to northern Greece in 422 to stop Spartan commander Brasidas. But both Cleon and Brasidas were killed before the Battle of Amphipolis, the battle the Spartan army won. Both Athens and Sparta had lost their most energetic military leaders, and their deaths opened the way to negotiations. Both sides decided to return to the power balance that was in place before 431, and the Peace of Nicias came in 421 BCE. The peace was named after an Athenian general, Nicias, who convinced the assembly to agree to the peace terms. Sparta signed the peace, but it caused a divide within the Peloponnesian League, as Corinth and Boeotia refused to sign it.

Factions appeared in both the Delian League and the Peloponnesian League that wanted to push the war and reach a decisive victory. The peace was unable to silence them. Among the Athenians was Alcibiades (450–404 BCE), who was one of the loudest people advocating against this uneasy peace. He was a member of the elite, and he was rich, brash, and fairly young. Alcibiades was also raised in Pericles's household after his father died (he was killed in a battle against the Spartans in 447), and this is probably what influenced his political views. Although he was young, he managed to gather a number of people who supported his advocacy against Spartan influence in the Peloponnese. In just a few years, Alcibiades started a new alliance made out of his Athenian followers, the like-minded people of Argos, and some of the city-states of the Peloponnese that were against Sparta. They believed that only through weakening Sparta could they achieve prosperity and political influence in the region. The geographical position of Argos was Sparta's biggest threat. Due to its location in the north of the Peloponnese, an attack launched from there could pin Sparta, rendering it out of options for a retreat. This is why the Spartans quickly raised their army and met the allied forces in the Battle of Mantinea in 418 BCE. They hoped for a quick victory that would eliminate the threat of Argos. However, the Peace of Nicias was still in effect, though it turned into a dead letter, as the violence started manifesting again.

In 416 BCE, Athens attacked Melos, an island city-state southeast of the Peloponnese. Melos was sympathetic toward Sparta, but it took no active part in the war against Athens, so it is unclear what Athens wanted to achieve with this aggression. Although greatly outnumbered, the inhabitants of Melos refused to surrender, hoping Athens would give up since the island was not a strategically important location, nor did it have some great treasure to be plundered. Once they were forced to surrender, the Athenians slaughtered all the Melos men and sold the women and children into slavery. Thucydides wrote about this conflict, but even he remains silent about the true motives behind Athens's attack. He puts the blame on Athens, describing its desire to dominate smaller poleis, and claims Melos only wanted to govern the relations between the states with justice. Thucydides described the conflict as a dialogue between the leaders of Melos and Athens (known as the Melian Dialogue), and it paints a perfect picture of the clash between ethics and power in international relations.

In 415 BCE, Alcibiades convinced the Athenian assembly to launch a campaign against Syracuse, an ally of Sparta. Syracuse might have been Sparta's political ally, but the main reason behind the attack was the fact that the island polis was very rich. But technically speaking, the Athenians attacked Syracuse only because another Sicilian city-state, Egesta (Segesta), was Athens's ally due to the treaty signed more than thirty years before. The Egestans supported Athens's willingness to conquer Syracuse, and they even encouraged it by falsely promising resources and military help that, in reality, they couldn't afford.

Before embarking with a fleet to Syracuse, Alcibiades was accused by his political enemies of taking part in the desecration of some Athenian monuments, as well as for mocking the Eleusinian Mysteries. He tried to have a trial while the army was still in Athens since he was popular among the soldiers. But his enemies managed to postpone the trial until the fleet was on its way to Sicily. Alcibiades went with the fleet, but a messenger was sent, demanding his immediate return to Athens alone. Instead of going back for the trial, Alcibiades defected to Sparta. The Athenian army lost a strong leader who could have kept motivating the army in the attack on Sicily. Nevertheless, they managed to win some initial victories due to the sheer size of the Athenian fleet. But their success was soon undermined by the indecisiveness of their leaders. To deal with the setbacks, the Athenian assembly decided to send reinforcements under the leadership of general Demosthenes. The new forces weren't enough. Athens failed to defeat Syracuse because, due to the persuasion of Alcibiades, Sparta sent help to its Sicilian ally. The decisive battle was fought in 413 BCE. The Athenian fleet became trapped in the Syracusan harbor and was ultimately crushed. Athens's only source of military might was completely destroyed.

The Final Ten Years of the War

Alcibiades's defection to Sparta continued to cause trouble for Athens even after the defeat in Sicily. Under his advice, Sparta established a permanent military base in Attica's countryside. They took advantage of Athens's weakness after the loss of its fleet at Syracuse to make a base of operations in Decelea, located in northeastern Athens. This was a perfect strategic position since Decelea overlooked the walls of Athens itself. The constant Spartan presence made working in the fields of Attica very dangerous, so Athens had to rely on food imported by the sea. This quickly drained the money reserves of the city-state, especially when twenty thousand slaves of Athens's silver mines escaped to Sparta. The flow of revenue from the mines came to a halt, forcing the government of Athens to change its policy. A new board of ten officials was installed to deal with the city's affairs. It was their task to supply the Council of 500.

After seeing Athens's misery that came due to the defeat in Sicily, Persia took an interest in Greek affairs once again. Persia quickly took control of western Anatolia and started financing a fleet to be used by Sparta and its allies. Some of the Ionian allies of the Delian League even took the opportunity to rebel against Athens. They were urged by Alcibiades, who was sent by the Spartans in 412 BCE to instigate unrest among the Ionian members of the Delian League. These riots disrupted the shipping lanes Athens used to import grain from Egypt and the shores of the Black Sea.

A great hardship started for Athens, but its citizens displayed only loyalty, devotion, and communal spirit when dealing with these problems. The excessive rebuilding of the fleet started immediately, and there was no lack of people willing to train how to serve on the ships. To finance the building of a new fleet, Athens had to tap into its emergency reserves that were stored at the Acropolis at the beginning of the Peloponnesian War. By 411, the Athenian naval force had been revived, and it successfully prevented the Corinthian fleet from sailing to Chios. It also managed to win some smaller battles along the coast of western Anatolia.

Despite these successes, political unity did not exist in Athens. Some influential individuals used the financial crisis to overthrow the democracy of the city-state and install a new oligarchic system. They insisted that the city should be led by a small group of elite-born individuals. Alcibiades made it known he would support such an oligarchic system in Athens and even acquire a Persian alliance for the city if democracy was removed. He hoped this would make it possible for him to return to Athens, but before he could persuade the Persian satraps of Anatolia to help him, the Spartans learned of his intentions. It didn't help that Alcibiades seduced the wife of one of Sparta's kings. In 411, the Athenian assembly turned the power over to a group of four hundred men in the hopes that a smaller governmental body would make wiser decisions and provide the city with better guidance in times of war. These four hundred men were tasked with electing the 500 who would represent Athens's main governmental body. In reality, the four hundred kept all the power of decision-making between themselves.

The four hundred elite men soon managed to destroy their unity because of power. Each one wanted to be the leader and assert his dominance over the others. The newly installed oligarchic system was doomed from the start, and it soon fell apart, as the Athenian fleet, which was stationed at the friendly city-state of Samos, threatened they would come back to Athens to reinstall democracy. The four hundred stepped aside but not before they invented a new system that mixed democracy and oligarchy. It was called the Constitution of the Five Thousand, and Thucydides praised it as the best form of government Athens ever had. The newly installed government then voted to recall Alcibiades and some other exiled military leaders in the hopes they could improve the Athenian army.

In 410 BCE, under the leadership of Alcibiades, the Athenian fleet won a great victory over Sparta at Cyzicus, a very important polis that controlled the connection of the trade routes between the Aegean Sea and the Black Sea. Despite the victory, the fleet continued to demand the full reinstalment of democracy in Athens, and the city leaders agreed to do so. However, this resulted in a return to the old politics, and when Sparta offered peace, Athens refused, just as before. Before dealing with Sparta's main base, the Athenian fleet went on to secure the grain routes and to persuade some of the defected members of the Delian League to return.

Sparta didn't offer peace because it could no longer fight. Instead, it wanted Athens to negotiate. At the time, a new leader arose in Sparta, the aggressive commander Lysander, who managed to doom Athens's hopes in winning the war by convincing Persia to finance the Spartan fleet. The first defeat he inflicted on Athens came in 406 BCE at Notion near Ephesus. Alcibiades wasn't personally present, but he was deemed responsible for the loss, and he was forced into exile, this time never to return. Later that same year, Athens won a victory at the islands of Arginusae (south of Lesbos), but it also lost a great number of ships and men due to a storm. In a mass trial that followed, the fleet commanders were sentenced to death for their negligence. Sparta again sent a peace offer, and yet again, Athens refused. Lysander secured more Persian funds, and in 405, he decisively eliminated the Athenian fleet in the Battle of Aegospotami (Anatolia). To prevent Athens from recovering, he installed an economic blockade, forcing the city to surrender in 404 BCE. After twenty-seven years of war, Athens found itself at the mercy of Sparta.

The Corinthians demanded the total destruction of Athens since they were bitter enemies, but Sparta refused. Without the Athenian presence in Attica, the Corinthian fleet would be strong enough to block the access of trade ships to the Peloponnese. Instead, Sparta installed an anti-democratic regime in Athens known as the Thirty Tyrants. They were the members of the wealthy elite who had always despised democracy and favored oligarchy. They ruled for only eight months, but they terrorized the citizens by shamelessly stealing all the property they deemed to be desirable. It was common to see many wealthy men executed under false accusations just so the tyrants could take over his family possessions and valuables. They ruled so violently that even Sparta didn't react when pro-democracy individuals mounted a resistance and took over the city in 403 BCE. Athens once again had a functioning democratic government, but its financial and military powers were destroyed. The Athenian society continued to harbor the memories of the war and the defeat that had brought such bitter political divisiveness.

Athens after the War

The Peloponnesian War drained Athens's treasury and decimated its army. But it was the people who felt the most hardship after the war. Women who lost their husbands and male relatives in the war and who had no personal possessions were forced to seek work outside of Athens to survive. The worst situation was with the people who lived outside of Athens's urban center. They lost their homes to the Spartan attacks, and their fields were damaged. It would take some time before they were able to produce food again. The war forced many men and women to drastically change their way of making a living. The wealthy who had savings were the only ones safe from the economic crisis that followed the war. But most Athenians didn't have any valuables or money stored, and some of them even lost their businesses. The people couldn't afford to spend money, and many artisans and craftsmen had to close their shops. Those who were farmers had their livestock and harvest destroyed, and they had to search for work within the city as common laborers.

The wealthy women who lost their husbands had to completely start their lives over. They were used to weaving clothes at home and managing their households since the men earned money by serving in the army, farming, or engaging in trade. Without their husbands to provide for them, women had to accept low-paying jobs in vineyards or as wetnurses or weavers. More women joined the public life of Athens, although they were pushed there by the poverty caused by the war. However, no women's rights movement ever came to be, and women remained ousted from the political life of the polis.

Because Athens lost its silver mines due to the Spartan base at Decelea remaining in place, the city was no longer able to finance public building projects. Still, the will to carry on had to be maintained, and the city leaders continued investing in the building of the Erechtheum, a temple on the Acropolis. But other than that, the city funds had been drained in the attempt to revive its army, and many public events had to be canceled. To pay the war expenses, the city took the gold and silver items stored in Athens's temples, which they used to mint new coins. All citizens were required to exchange their silver and gold coins for cheaper ones made out of thin bronze.

The hardship of city life within Athens, both during and after the war, was somewhat elevated by the many comedies that were written and performed during this period. They were one of the main means of dramatic expression, together with tragedies. They, too, touched on current topics, but they also consisted of light humor, involving stories of bodily functions, sex, and imaginative profanity. However, the popular comedies were the ones that dealt with social issues. Aristophanes wrote one named *The Birds*. The protagonists of this comedy try to escape the poverty caused by the Peloponnesian War by leaving Athens for a new world called Cloud Cuckooland, which is inhabited by talking birds. Comedies in which women were portrayed as smart and witty were also popular. Through cleverly written dialogue, playwrights voiced female thoughts on the war, although they were written and performed by men. One of the most popular comedies that featured strong women was *Lysistrata*, written again by Aristophanes. In it, the heroine Lysistrata and other women of Athens refuse to have sex with their husbands to compel them to end the Peloponnesian War. They are even joined in this sex strike by the Spartan women. In the end, the sex, or lack of it, and the women's wits stop the gruesome war.

And so Athens entered the 4th century BCE in poverty and disgrace. But the end of the Peloponnesian War didn't mean the end of all conflict in Greece. Athens, Sparta, Thebes, Corinth, and many other city-states continued to fight for political dominance in the region. Fifty years after the Peloponnesian War, the poleis of ancient Greece still fought each other, but the only thing they achieved was to weaken each other. They created a power vacuum on an international scale, a void soon to be filled by the unexpected military and political rise of Macedonia, ruled by King Philip II (382-336 BCE).

Chapter 7: The Rise of Macedon

Philip II of Macedon

https://en.wikipedia.org/wiki/Philip_II_of_Macedon#/media/File:P hillip_II,_king_of_Macedonia,_Roman_copy_of_Greek_original,_ Ny_Carlsberg_Glyptotek,_Copenhagen_(36420294055).jpg

King Philip II had to reorganize his army to avoid an invasion from the north, but the changes he implemented gave him the power to extend his influence to the east and south, where Greek territory lay. In 338 BCE, at Chaeronea, he defeated the alliance of Greek city-states and formed the League of Corinth. He intended to use the combined Greek and Macedonian armies to start a vengeful war against Persia. Before he could do so, he was murdered, and his great kingdom was inherited by his son, the famous Alexander the Great (356–323 BCE), who followed in his father's footsteps and conquered the Persian Empire.

Alexander's conquests reached from Greece to the Near East, all the way to India. Although his wars were bloody and expensive, the result was a much better connection between Greece and the Near East, as well as the exchange of material goods and intellectual and cultural ideas. Alexander died unexpectedly before his son reached a mature age. He could not succeed Alexander as the king of Macedonia, and Alexander also didn't lay down a political arrangement for the conquered lands after his death. The new conditions of the late 4th century dictated events, and the structure of international power that Alexander had built collapsed.

Corinthian War (395–387)

Athens never recovered the might it once had in the 5th century. Even though the silver mine production started once again, it never produced at the same level as before. Nevertheless, the return of democracy did bring progress, and soon, Athens became a major power of the Greek world again. Sparta, on the other hand, tried to expand its influence immediately after the Peloponnesian War, but it only managed to provoke Athens and other Greek city-states. New diplomatic and military approaches were installed, and the first half of the 4th century BCE saw many shifting alliances. The weaker city-states would group together to resist the power play of the strong poleis, but the political disunity doomed those alliances, and they were short-lived.

In 401 BCE, Persian satrap Cyrus tried to unseat King Artaxerxes II of Persia (r. 404–358 BCE) with a mercenary army. It so happened that there were many Greek soldiers in Cyrus's army who supported his rebellion. They were disastrously defeated at Cunaxa near Babylon. The Spartans openly supported Cyrus, which enraged Artaxerxes. He was also provoked by the diplomatic and military efforts of King Agesilaus of Sparta and the Spartan commander Lysander, who tried to assert their control over western Anatolian regions and in northern Greece. Other prominent Spartan leaders meddled in the affairs of Greek poleis, and as a response to them, Sicily, Thebes, Athens, Corinth, and Argos allied. Persia offered its support to the alliance, and in 395, the Corinthian War started. Persia moved first.

In 397, Artaxerxes II started building a fleet, and he hired an Athenian named Konon (also spelled Conon) as its commander. The Spartans heard of the new Persian fleet, and they reacted by sending a large expedition against Persia in 396 under the leadership of King Agesilaus. He intended to establish a zone of rebel satraps in western Anatolia that would rise against Artaxerxes's rule, but the Spartans also helped Egypt keep its independence from Persia, which it managed to do until 340. The Greeks had an uneasy peace ever since the Peloponnesian War. Although Sparta asserted its dominance over Greece, it was never really safe, not even in its own territory of Laconia. The Spartans still struggled to control the helots, and the uprising of the slave-like helots recurred in 399.

Thebes was one of the most powerful enemies of Sparta. After the Peloponnesian War, Thebes emerged as a strong power, and it took control of Plataea in 427 BCE. Another reason for Thebes's power was that the federalization of Boeotia was reorganized after the war, allowing the Thebans to now control the federal magistrates. When Agesilaus prepared to leave for Anatolia, he wanted to perform a sacrifice ritual just like the legendary king Agamemnon did before the Trojan War. However, he was stopped by the Boeotian magistrates, who were directly influenced by Thebes.

But Thebes didn't react this way for no reason. In fact, the city-state was reacting to the events in central Greece. There, Lysander was in command, and his actions threatened to encircle Thebes and Corinth, with the territories falling under Spartan influence. Sparta also interfered in the affairs of Corinth's colony of Syracuse, drawing even more anger toward itself. Unlike Thebes, Corinth didn't emerge as a powerful polis after the Peloponnesian War. Due to its weakness, Corinth agreed to merge itself with democratic Argos in a unique though short-lived political union. By 395 BCE, all of Sparta's enemies had a reason to start a war.

The opportunity to start the conflict presented itself when a quarrel between Locris and Phocis started. The Phocians appealed to Sparta to intervene, and Lysander responded by invading Boeotia. The Battle of Haliartus ensued, in which the Spartan general Lysander lost his life. That was a huge military loss for Sparta, which prompted Agesilaus to return from Asia and win two major battles against the allied enemies. His main opponent was Athenian general Iphicrates, who stationed his troops in Corinth. Although Agesilaus was victorious, he was unable to provoke the Athenians to accept an open battle.

At sea, the allies made more progress against Sparta. In August 394, Konon and Pharnabazus (the satrap of Phrygia) won the Battle of Cnidus in southern Anatolia. At this point, Sparta had to deal with another helot uprising back home, and a total victory was almost achieved by the allies. However, the violence continued for two more years. Finally, in 392, Sparta offered peace, abandoning its claims in Anatolia. But Artaxerxes was not ready to stop fighting. He couldn't forgive the Spartans for the support they gave to Cyrus. The war continued.

Although Persia and Athens were in an alliance against Sparta, in 392 BCE, under the leadership of Thrasybulus, the Athenians started their democratic institutions in the Anatolian cities. Persia finally realized that Athens was working against the interests of the empire, and it concluded a peace treaty with Sparta. With Persia's help, Sparta was able to block the Hellespont (Dardanelles), Athens's main trade route, starving Attica once again. Athens surrendered, and the peace was signed in 386 BCE, known as the King's Peace (or Peace of Antalcidas, who was the king of Sparta). It granted Cyprus and Clazomenae to Persia, but the majority of the Greek islands and city-states in the Aegean were given autonomy. However, Athens gained control over Lemnos, Imbros, and Scyros.

Any additional clauses to the peace remain unknown, and modern scholars still discuss various possibilities that could have been part of the treaty. However, they all agree that there was little change in Anatolia after the Corinthian War. Some evidence suggests that the Ionian cities remained autonomous after Sparta abandoned them. Anatolia as a whole became the political property of Persia, and this generalization was never seriously disrupted, even though the Greeks occasionally attacked. The political line dividing Greek and Persian interests became very clear after the King's Peace of 386, and it remained so even though many of the mercenaries Persia used were, in fact, Greek.

Philip II

The last decades of Artaxerxes's rule were marked by many uprisings in the western territories of the Persian Empire. They started as early as the 370s BCE when Datames, the governor of Cappadocia, proclaimed himself independent. By the middle of the decade, Hellespontine Phrygia had revolted with the joint help of Athens and Sparta. The last and greatest revolt was mounted in Mysia by its satrap Orontes. But at the same time, rebellions in Lydia and Caria began, each with different aims. All of these uprisings came to an end by the time of Artaxerxes's death in 359. They were not quelled by his army; rather, they simply fell apart due to the rivalries between the rebel leaders. The successor to the Persian throne was Artaxerxes III, and he immediately ordered the dispersion of all the satraps' mercenary armies to prevent any possibility of future rebellions. This order was an early sign of the new vigor with which Persia was to be ruled.

At the same time, in Macedon, King Perdiccas III was killed in 359 or 360 in a battle against the Illyrians in the north. He was succeeded by his younger brother, Philip II, whose achievements would overshadow those of his predecessors. But Philip's achievements would later be diminished by the successes of his son, Alexander the Great. This is why there is a lack of evidence for Philip's early rule and the consolidation of power. As tradition explains, the Macedonians inhabited the region of Macedonia or Macedon (today's northern Greece and North Macedonia) after migrating from the area known as Thessalian Perrhaibia and from the regions surrounding Mount Olympus. They brought their Greek religion with them, although local variations sprouted. The language of Macedon was Greek in its base, and all of the personal names are of Greek origin. But this cultural Hellenization is strongly contradicted by the social and military structure of Macedon. Instead of resembling the Greeks, it strongly resembled the structures of later European feudal societies. The Macedonian kings of the 4th century BCE granted land in exchange for military service, and this system was similar to the one present in Persia.

King Philip II was known for his preference for diplomacy rather than military intervention. When dealing with his enemies, he always tried to calm the situation first, if only to buy some time and prepare his armies. In his early years on the throne, he had to deal with the Illyrians and Thracians, who saw the opportunity to invade Macedonia upon the death of Philip's older brother, Perdiccas. But Philip managed to thwart this invasion by promising his enemies a yearly tribute. In reality, he was buying time to prepare his army for a greater conquest. Philip wanted to expand his kingdom and take over parts of central Greece. Sparta was busy trying to conquer Messenia, Persia was fighting its wars in Egypt, and Thebes diluted its power by overextending. The only serious threat would come from Athens, but Athens relied on its fleet to attack, and Philip was aware that Macedon couldn't be approached by the sea during a certain time of the year due to the etesian winds of the Aegean Basin. He needed to perfectly time his invasion of central Greece. Thasos controlled the silver mines of the Pangaion region, but it had no military power to defend them, and Philip was certain he could easily deal with Thasos.

To reorganize his army, Philip introduced extensive training and started hiring mercenaries. He tested his new army against the Illyrians and other northern enemies, and he was victorious, expanding his territory to the north as far as Lake Ohrid. In 358, he visited Thessaly to prepare an attack on Amphipolis, which was launched the next year. He kept Athens away from meddling by promising he would give Amphipolis to them, but he never did. Instead, he continued his conquest and took Pydna and Crenides, mining cities. The Olynthians became alarmed by Philip's conquest, and they rushed to ally with him. Philip accepted it, as he preferred diplomacy over war. Athens tried to stop Philip when he launched a conquest of Thrace, but it didn't have much success. At the time, Athens had troubles of its own with the outbreak of the Social War in 357, which led to the break of the Second Athenian League, which included the great poleis of Chios, Byzantium, and Methymna. But the war went badly for Athens, and in 355, it had to accept a very disadvantageous peace because Artaxerxes III threatened a Persian intervention.

In Thessaly, Philip used his diplomatic skills to convince the Greek leaders to install him as the commander of the armies of the Thessalian League. With this, he became the leader of Greece, as, at that moment, Thessaly was one of the most prosperous regions. Macedonia was never part of Thessaly, but it was its neighbor, just over the mountains of southern Macedonia. Since Philip claimed that the great Greek hero Heracles was his ancestor, the Thessaly leaders saw him as their kin. In their eyes, he was perfectly qualified to become a Greek leader. But in reality, the league needed the king of Macedon to form an alliance with Thebes and to defeat a tyrant that ruled in Thessaly. It took two defeats before Philip was able to expel the tyrant Lycophron, but the league was amazed by his success and named him the leader of their armies.

Due to the alliance between Thebes and the Thessalian League, Philip II became involved in the Third Sacred War (355-346 BCE), helping Thebes to take Phocis. Athens was an ally of Phocis, which was the cause of the eruption of hostilities between Macedon and Athens. However, Philip was defeated by the Phocians, something nobody could have predicted. But Philip managed to recover by 352, and he reversed the defeat at the Battle of Crocus Field. This victory brought Philip enormous prestige, which he used to take over the leadership of Thessaly in a fuller sense. He acquired its ports, trade, and mine revenues, which he used at his will. Southern Thessaly was also a gateway to central Greece, and at the end of 352, Philip tried to invade using the same pass of Thermopylae the Persians had previously tried to use to enter the Greek mainland. Athens stood up to defend it. Philip then laid a siege on Heraeum Teichos (in Thrace) in 351, prompting Athenian statesmen Demosthenes to denounce Macedonian imperialism and promise Athens would move to counter Philip. But it was too late, and Athens couldn't do much in defending Thrace.

The conflict between Athens and Macedonia continued in 349 when Philip decided to attack Olynthus, even though they had been in alliance since 356. Olynthus asked Athens for help, and even though Athens responded, the city fell in 348. Its citizens were sold into slavery, and their poor treatment prompted Euboea to revolt, as Athens proved incapable of protecting its allies. By the end of the 340s, King Philip II managed to unite the northern and significant parts of central Greece and impose his international plans on them. He was preparing to launch the conquest of the Persian Empire, but he was aware of the Persian might. He knew that he needed to add the army of southern Greece to his own to be able to launch his grandiose invasion.

However, Athens continued to resist him. In 338, Athens and Thebes entered a coalition, intending to block Philip's plans and military actions. That same year, they fought the Battle of Chaeronea in Boeotia, in which Philip defeated the Athens-Thebes coalition. The peace they signed stated that the defeated Greek city-states would keep their independence as long as they joined Philip's alliance. Modern scholars call this alliance the League of Corinth, although Corinth as a polis lost its influence in Greece a long time ago.

The Battle of Chaeronea marks the beginning of a period in which Greek city-states stopped making foreign political decisions for themselves and followed a stronger, outside power. They were no longer independent to make foreign policies, but they continued to be the backbone of Greek economic and social structures. Throughout the reign of Philip, his son Alexander, and the Hellenistic kingdoms that followed the death of Alexander the Great, Greek city-states remained an important factor, as the great new monarchs needed their loyalty and the taxes they paid. The many poleis of Greece continued to be an important political element of the ancient world, but they would never again be independent entities completely able to guide their destiny.

Back home, in Macedonia, some individuals didn't understand Philip's motives in creating the Corinthian League. They preferred straightforward conquest that would allow them to loot rich Greek city-states such as Thebes or Athens. To appease his people and to consolidate his power, Philip depicted himself as the thirteenth god of Olympus. He would never risk showing the Greeks such representations of himself, but in Macedonia, he thought it would install fear and respect. He might have even received a cult in Philippi, previously known as Crenides; it was renamed to Philippi after it fell to Philip's army. However, it is not known if he was worshiped as a god anywhere else in Macedonia. Scholars believe he had no time to spread his cult through the lands he ruled because he was suddenly assassinated in 336. The perpetrator remains unknown and so do his motives.

Chapter 8: Alexander the Great

Roman bust of Alexander the Great
https://en.wikipedia.org/wiki/Alexander_the_Great#/media/File:Ale
xander_the_Great,_from_Alexandria,_Egypt,_3rd_cent._BCE,_Ny
_Carlsberg_Glyptotek,_Copenhagen_(5)_(36375553176).jpg

Philip II was in the prime of his life when he was assassinated. His successor, Alexander III of Macedon (better known now as Alexander the Great), reacted swiftly and with a cool head to his father's death. Many contemporaries and modern historians believe that Alexander was actually behind his father's assassination. Some believed Philip was killed by Olympias, his wife and the mother of his successor. Nevertheless, the young prince quickly arrested and killed the highly suspected individuals, most of whom were his rivals. Then again, Alexander's succession was never in question since he was Philip's oldest legitimate son. He also enjoyed the support of the people compared to the son of Philip's predecessor, who was still alive at the time and was a possible pretender to the throne.

Alexander was barely twenty years old when he became the king of Macedonia. Although his succession was smooth, he was forced to deal with Macedonia's northern enemies as soon as he came to the throne. Their traditional enemies, the Illyrians and Thracians, thought to use Philip's death to break free of Macedonian dominion. But in a couple of swift campaigns, Alexander was able to subdue them without any losses of territory or his army. Alexander then took the opportunity to conquer even more territory in the north, and the expeditions there led him across the Danube. In the meantime, the Thebans believed Alexander had been killed somewhere in Illyria, and they tried to break off from the Corinthian League. It took Alexander only seven days to reach Thessaly and five more to enter Boeotia. He not only subdued Thebes but also destroyed the city as an example to all the other Greek poleis that considered abandoning the league.

Alexander in Anatolia and Egypt

With the succession of the Macedonian throne, Alexander also succeeded the leadership of the Persian conquest. Once he dealt with the rebellious city-states, he started the campaign in Asia, doing so in 334. He installed his general Antipater as the governor of Greece, leaving 12,000 infantry and 1,500 cavalry units in his charge. Alexander took forty thousand foot soldiers and over six thousand cavalrymen with him to Asia. He had inherited this army, as well as the plans of the conquest, from his father, and it remains unknown if he had to make any changes and reorganize the army before he launched the campaign. But as time passed, and during the conquest itself, he often changed plans, adapting them to new circumstances. He also rethought the supply of his army and started using wagons to haul equipment and provisions. This was his addition to his father's army, as Philip's soldiers had to carry their weapons, armor, and provisions.

The core of Alexander's infantry was the Macedonian phalanx, a rectangular military formation in which the soldiers stood very close to each other to make an impregnable wall. They were armed with long spears or any kind of long weapon, which they used to keep the enemy at a distance. The main body of the cavalry was called the Companions, which was led by Alexander himself, positioned on the head of the right wing. The left one was led by Philip's favorite general, Parmenio, the commander of the Thessalian part of the cavalry. The army also had additional troops such as scouts, slingers, and other irregulars. They all had light armor and any weapons they could muster. Alexander also made use of war machines, such as siege engines, that could be easily assembled on the spot. They were cared for by the Thessalian siege engineers previously employed by Philip. These machines were probably the reason for his swift victories in Anatolia. When Alexander crossed the Hellespont with his army, he threw his spear into the ground and laid claim to the whole of Asia. First, he visited Troy, where he paid his respect to the heroes of old, Ajax and Achilles.

Artaxerxes III died in 338, leaving behind a power vacuum. His death also made the conquest of Asia (in a sense, the Persian Empire) much easier than it had been during his life and those of his predecessors. The next in line was Darius III, a much weaker king, who assumed the throne only in 336. Darius managed to convince the Anatolian satraps to gather an army and oppose Alexander's conquest. The first conflict occurred in the general region of Xanthus (in modern-day Turkey), and the combined Greco-Macedonian army found itself facing a large Persian force. This was not the main Persian army, but it was sizable, and the conflict was bloody. Alexander the Great won, though, opting for a daylight battle and the personal leadership of his cavalry. If anything, Alexander contributed to history with his heroic generalship, as he would always personally lead his army and shout a battle cry dedicated to the Greek gods. After the battle, Alexander immediately reorganized the satraps in Anatolia, giving leadership to his own men. In a sense, he declared that he wouldn't change the organization of the Persian Empire. He only planned to succeed it. However, he did install democracy, restored the laws, and ended the tradition of the Ionian cities of sending tribute to the Persian king.

Alexander proved to be very rewarding toward the Ionian city-states that rebelled against the Persians during his father's rule. For instance, on the island city-state of Chios, Alexander left a monument to testify to the beginning of democracy. Many cities bear his name, but it is unknown if he founded them or merely renamed them. He certainly rebuilt the poleis that had been destroyed during combat. One such example is Priene, a very old city of Ionia. The city was crumbling, and it is unknown if Alexander renewed it with building projects or if he re-founded it, bringing new people to settle in the place where old Priene used to be. Whatever was the case, the city was physically reconstructed during Alexander's time, and so were many other Anatolian Greek cities, e.g., Heraclea and Smyrna.

The next encounter with the Persians was in 334 BCE at Halicarnassus, and this was where Alexander met the strongest resistance. The Persians brought their fleet to the city in order to make a new defense line. However, the political events before Alexander's conquest determined Halicarnassus's fate. Its former queen, Ada of Caria, was overthrown by her brother. He soon died, and Darius III installed a Persian satrap to rule Caria. Alexander met Ada at the fortress of Alinda, which was still in her possession, and the two developed a mother-son relationship. She used her influence to get Alexander's army near the city, and after some fighting, the city fell. However, the retreating Persians burned it, leaving only ruins for Alexander and Ada. Nevertheless, Ada was restored as the rightful queen of Caria, and in turn, she officially adopted Alexander as her son.

After Halicarnassus, in 333 BCE, Alexander moved his army to the east. In the Battle of Issus, he had the first opportunity to meet Darius III, who came to personally lead his army. Alexander used his characteristically bold tactic of leading his cavalry in the attack on the right side of the Persian lines. A flanking maneuver against Darius's position, who was in the center of his army, followed, and the Persian king was forced to flee for his life. By tradition, Darius was accompanied by his wives and daughters, and he decided to leave them behind while he escaped. Alexander's chivalrous treatment of the captured Persian royal women became legendary. But at the time, it served to boost his support among the local people of Anatolia.

In 332 BCE, Tyre, a city on the coast of Lebanon, refused to surrender, forcing Alexander to use the siege engines he inherited from his father. The walls of Tyre cracked, and the city fell after a lengthy siege, losing its reputation of being an impregnable city (this was the first time in its history that it had fallen). However, the siege engines weren't typically successful. It was still almost impossible to wreck the walls of fortified cities, and it seems that Tyre was just luck. Nevertheless, the citizens of walled Anatolian cities never again felt safe behind their defenses. The unity of the people often broke under the psychological pressure they felt when they saw the siege engines and catapults.

With the conquest of Anatolia finished, Alexander turned toward Egypt, which he took without a struggle. Archaeologists found hieroglyphic inscriptions that seem to describe how Alexander presented himself as the successor to the Persian Empire. In 331, he founded Alexandria, a city on the west shore of the Nile River. This was the first of many cities we know for sure was founded by Alexander. Alexandria was founded by the joining of several villages, but the main intention of Alexander the Great was to Hellenize Egypt through public building projects. He also introduced Greek-style athletic games and tragic and comedic plays. During his time in Egypt, Alexander visited the oracle of Ammon, a counterpart of the Greek Zeus. The oracle was settled far in the western Egyptian desert in the oasis of Siwah (Siwa). Alexander never revealed what was told to him by the oracle. However, the news got out that he was told that he was the son of a god and that he accepted it as the truth.

From Egypt, Alexander crossed Phoenicia. In the open field of Gaugamela (northern Mesopotamia), he met Darius III once more. The battle started in October 331 BCE, and Alexander managed to crush the king's army and proclaim himself the king of Asia. The Persian Empire was extremely heterogeneous, and the fact that the new king was Macedonia did not alarm them. There was no change to the lives of the empire's population anyway. They continued to pay taxes, sending them to a distant king they would never know or see. As in Egypt, the local Persian administrative system was left in place, but only some of the Persian governors were replaced with Macedonians and Greeks. This was probably done because Alexander had a long-term plan to make the Macedonians, Greeks, and Persians work together for them all to assimilate into one single empire under his rule.

To India and the Death of Alexander

Conquering the Persian Empire wasn't enough for Alexander's megalomaniac personality. He decided to lead his army eastward, probably in search of the farthest point and the edge of the world, although Aristotle, his teacher from his younger days, believed the earth was round. But going east, through lands the Macedonians and Greeks had never even heard of, meant many hardships had to be overcome. The supply of the army was the biggest problem, as the land they passed was arid. Hoplites were used to carrying their own provisions but never for this long and this far away from home. The army marching through the hostile lands was also followed by a large number of non-combatants, such as entertainers, merchants, wives and children of soldiers, and prostitutes. The army commanders weren't responsible for feeding the non-combatants, but their numbers meant less food could be foraged or hunted for the soldiers. The merchants would go in front of the army and buy whatever they could from the locals, only to sell it to the army's provisional officers at much higher prices. The local population consisted of farmers, but they often had no surplus to sell.

Since Alexander marched his army through what he considered to be friendly land, he expected the locals to provide for his soldiers. They needed to donate the food for the passing army or to sell it for money, which they had no use for. The remote villages sustained themselves, and they had nowhere to go to buy the food they now lacked. Starvation often came after Alexander's Greco-Macedonian army passed by.

In 329, from the heartland of Persia, Alexander marched his army toward the steppes of Bactria and Sogdiana (in modern-day Afghanistan and Uzbekistan). There, he fought highly mobile locals, but he was unable to defeat them. His army was used to open battlefields, while the locals preferred guerilla-style tactics. In the end, Alexander satisfied himself by negotiating an alliance with the local tribes. The alliance was sealed with the marriage of Alexander and a local princess named Roxane (Roxana) in 327 BCE. Alexander took the opportunity of peace to deal with his opposition. Those who resisted his plans to keep going east were accused of treachery and disloyalty, and they were executed on the spot. Among them were some of the leading commanders of

Alexander's army. Alexander was known for using terror to discourage rebellions.

From Bactria, Alexander pushed his armies through monsoon rains for seventy days toward India. The soldiers' resolution finally shattered, and in the spring of 326 BCE, they raised a mutiny against Alexander, even though the army had just achieved a great victory against King Porus in what is today Punjab. Alexander wanted to proceed toward the Bengal region, and his soldiers were not in the mood to face another great army. They had already been away from home for so long, something that Macedonian and Greek armies had never practiced before. All of the expeditions were kept short so that the soldiers could go back home and contribute to the public and political life of their poleis. Whenever his troops showed a lack of morale, Alexander was always able to inspire them or at least shame them into action. But this time, he could do nothing to persuade them to proceed, and he had to agree to take them home. However, he wouldn't allow them a simple march home. Instead, he ordered attacks on local tribes who resisted accepting his dominance. Alexander personally fought, often risking his life. Perhaps he did it to inspire his troops, but more often than not, he horrified his generals, who had to save him on a couple of occasions. Once, he climbed the walls of a town practically alone and was dangerously wounded before his troops were able to rescue him.

Once he reached the mouth of the Indus River, Alexander decided to divide his army in three. One part of his army was sent on the eastern route inland. Under the command of general Craterus, the largest portion of the army marched to Carmania (today in Iran). Alexander sent the second part of the army, under the leadership of admiral Nearchus, westward along the coast of the Persian Gulf to explore possible spots for founding new cities. Alexander personally led the last part of his army toward Persia through the dangerous deserts of Gedrosia and Makran. He planned to surpass the prestige of previous Persian kings by achieving what they considered to be impossible; marching through the desert. Most of the non-combatants who followed the army were lost, but hunger, thirst, and exhaustion also took the lives of many soldiers. In the Gedrosian desert, scientists frequently measure temperatures up to 127°F (52.7°C) in the shade. Alexander shared the hardships with his men, and it is said he often refused water, choosing to suffer just like his army did. Finally, they reached safety in Susa, in the Persian heartland, in 324 BCE.

Alexander wasn't finished with the war, and upon his arrival in Susa, he immediately started planning an invasion of the Arabian Peninsula, which he would then follow up with the North African territories west of Egypt. By the time he was back from his Indian campaign, Alexander had stopped pretending he ruled Greece as anything less than an absolute monarch. Earlier, he promised internal freedom to loyal Greek cities, but he sent a decree in which he demanded they restore citizenship to all who were exiled before. He did so because the increased number of exiled influential men created tension in the Greek world. These men belonged nowhere, but they still asserted political influence, turning cities against each other. Alexander also demanded some Greek cities recognize his divinity, and the poleis sent delegations to honor him as one of the Olympian gods. Previously, many modern scholars believed Alexander wished divinity because the city-states would be obliged to follow all of his commands, as they would be the commands of a god. But this theory is considered wrong, as it seems that he convinced himself that he was actually Zeus's son. Because of his successful conquests of the known world, Alexander also believed he surpassed the deeds of many famous Greek heroes and that he was no longer merely a mortal. In ancient terms, Alexander's divinity emerged as a consequence of his power, and it was natural and righteous.

Alexander's conquests benefited humankind on many levels. He united the known world into a single political entity, but he also allowed many geographical units to stay administratively independent. He also recognized the experience local leaders had, and he didn't always replace them with Greek generals. The new cities Alexander founded along the way served as royal outposts that made sure the whole region would stay loyal to him. They also served to open new trade possibilities between the regions, making the exchange of goods and ideas easier. He pushed for not only conquest but also exploration, and he would always have scientifically minded individuals with him. His explorations revealed more information on geography, botany, mathematics, and medicine to Greek scholars, who later passed their knowledge to the Western world.

Alexander's plans to conquest Arabia and North Africa ended with his premature death. The great conqueror and leader died on June 10th, 323 BCE, in Babylon. He was only thirty-two years old, and there are two different accounts of his death. Plutarch, a Greek philosopher and historian, claimed Alexander entertained his generals and spent day and night drinking with his friends. This caused him to develop a fever that lasted for fourteen days, rendering him incapable of speech until he finally died. Diodorus, another ancient Greek historian, wrote that Alexander experienced a sudden great pain after he drank undiluted wine. He was very ill for the next eleven days, after which he died. According to Diodorus, there was never any fever. But many contemporary historians seem to agree that foul play was involved in Alexander's death. In ancient times, poisoning was a common way of getting rid of one's political enemies. Only Plutarch dismissed the theory of poisoning, but modern historians still can't agree on what was the real cause of Alexander's death. Some suggest that poison with such a long action wasn't known in antiquity. After all, Alexander the Great died between eleven and fourteen days after he initially got sick. Some propose he contracted typhoid fever or malaria and that he died due to illness, not poison.

Alexander had made no plans about what should be done with his great empire after his death. He had no children yet, although his wife Roxane was pregnant at the time of his death and would give birth several months later. Alexander's closest friends asked him on his deathbed about who should inherit his kingdom. He only answered, "to the most powerful" (Arrian, Anabasis of Alexander 7.26.3). But since some ancient writers claimed Alexander lost the ability to speak during his illness, this story may be apocryphal.

The plan was to take Alexander's body back to Macedon for burial, but Ptolemy II of Egypt confiscated the sarcophagus with his remains and took it to Alexandria, where it remained until the end of antiquity. But its later fate is unknown, and it remains yet to be discovered.

Because Alexander had no successor, his vast empire was ravaged by the succession war. Finally, it was divided into four: Ptolemaic Egypt, Antigonid Macedon, Attalid Anatolia, and the Seleucid Empire, which controlled Mesopotamia and Central Asia.

Conclusion

Nineteenth-century scholars invented the term Hellenistic to mark the period that started with the death of Alexander the Great in 323 BCE. The break-up of his vast empire meant many political, cultural, and social changes, not only in Greece but also throughout the whole known world. The earliest Hellenistic period saw the emergence of new kingdoms and a new form of kingship, as Alexander's successors were his generals who had no blood relations to any of the royal families that previously existed. They also didn't have a historical claim to the land they governed, yet they were accepted as the successors of the great leader. Still, acceptance didn't come easily. It was forced by military power, prestige, and the ambition of Alexander's generals-turned-monarchs.

The end of Alexander's Persian Empire thus came at the same time as the end of the Classical period. The beginning of the Classical period began with Greece recognizing Persia as its national enemy, a Greece that never could have comprehended being a part of Persia, let alone being the driving force behind that unity. The unity of the ancient Greeks had started with recognizing

Persia as their enemy, with Sparta, the strongest polis, being the original leader. But for a variety of reasons, Sparta could no longer continue the war against Persia, and the leadership of the struggle passed to Athens and the Delian League. The conflict continued until 449 BCE, and Athens managed to drive Persia away from Ionia and the western Anatolian coast.

With no enemy to fight, the Delian League transformed into the Athenian empire, in which many Greek city-states became subordinate to Athens. In turn, Athens became the richest and most powerful political entity in Greece, and although it promoted democracy in itself, it discovered how easy it was to oppress other poleis. But even Athens's democracy was designed so it could exclude certain people. Women, foreigners, slaves, and those who could not prove their Athenian lineage could not make any state decisions. Citizenship was a privilege only for those who could prove both his parents were born Athenians. But soon, it became obvious that not everyone agreed with the democracy in the Greek world, as some still preferred the oligarchy. So, a conflict between Athens, a champion of democracy, and Sparta, a champion of the oligarchy, began, a conflict known as the Peloponnesian War. Athens had the advantage of being the economic and intellectual center of Greece. In this period of uncertainty and war, some of the best art was produced in Athens in the form of both architecture and literature.

The Peloponnesian War came to a halt with the Thirty Years' Peace in 445, but many revolts in Athens reversed its role as the economic center. The conflict resumed in 431 when the balance of power between Athens and Sparta was overturned. Athens's ambitions became far too great and unchecked, and the polis provoked Sparta into another war. In 404, the fighting was over, thanks to Persia meddling in Greek affairs. It sided with Sparta and helped bring Athens to its knees.

But soon, a new conflict arose, this time between Sparta and Persia when Sparta saw fit to liberate Greek cities in Anatolia from Persian rule. The new war is remembered as the Corinthian War, and this time Athens joined the Persian side. The end came in 386 with the King's Peace or Peace of Antalcidas. Sparta agreed to leave the Anatolian Greek cities as Persian possessions but proclaimed all other Greek cities and islands as autonomous.

However, Sparta couldn't forget about Ionia, and it proceeded to interpret the peace treaty as it saw fit. The Spartans escalated the situation with their attempt to occupy Thebes, and Athens responded to the aggression by starting the Second Athenian League to fight Spartan imperialistic tendencies. Many alliances were switched during this period, and in the mainland conflict, Athens saw fit to help Sparta against Thebes when Thebes started grabbing power for itself.

While the Greek poleis quarreled over dominance, in the far north, Macedon was on the rise. Shielded by a mountain range and the unpredictable waters of the Aegean Sea, Macedon started looking at southern Greece as a possible source of revenues. But the intentions to exploit the south turned into an ambition to unite the whole of Greece when Macedon's King Philip II came to rule. Philip was able to exploit the sentiment of Persia being a national enemy to gain full control over Greece. He even started planning a conquest of Persia as retaliation for all the evils it had committed upon Greece, but he was assassinated before any action was taken.

His son and successor, Alexander the Great, took his father's dream upon himself. The great leader that he was, he not only conquered Persia but also went on to further explore the east, intending to reach the end of the world, which was, in his mind, just east of India. Instead of discovering the world's edge, Alexander brought the end of the Classical period by failing to name a successor before his untimely death. But the world didn't end with Alexander the Great, as many contemporaries certainly believed. It continued into a new era, one that brought the foundation of many

Greek cities in Asia with Greek and Macedonian rulers. This new period lasted through the rise of Rome until, finally, Rome became powerful enough to dare venture and take over the Hellenistic world.

Part 3: Modern Greece

A Captivating Guide to the History of Greece, Starting from the Greek War of Independence Through the Balkan Wars, World War I and II, to the Present

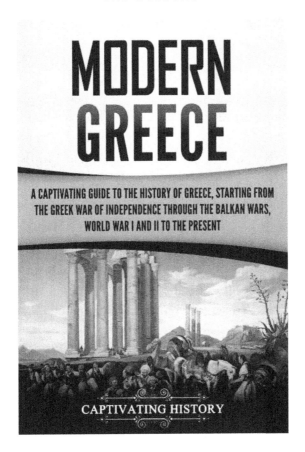

Introduction

You may think you know Greece, but I'll wager that most of your knowledge ends at about the 2nd century BCE (Before Common Era) with the Roman conquest of the Greeks in 146 BCE.

You're not alone. For most people, including a lot of Greeks (especially in the Greek emigrant community worldwide, "the Greek diaspora"), Greek history is filled with stories of the gods, of Zeus, Apollo, Athena, Aphrodite, Poseidon, and many more. Then there are the heroes of Greek myth: Achilles, Ajax, Jason and his Argonauts—the list goes on. Then there are the thinkers: Socrates, Plato, Pythagoras, Hippocrates, Aristotle...and again, the list goes on and on.

Perhaps you are one of the relative few that are aware that in the early 19th century, British and other European writers, thinkers, and politicians fell in love with the idea of a renewed and glorious Greece based on the ideals of ancient times. You can see this idea in the following, which was written by George Gordon, better known as Lord Byron:

The Isles of Greece

The isles of Greece, the isles of Greece!
Where burning Sappho loved and sung,
Where grew the arts of war and peace,
Where Delos rose, and Phoebus sprung!
Eternal summer gilds them yet,
But all, except their sun, is set...

The mountains look on Marathon—
And Marathon looks on the sea;
And musing there an hour alone,
I dreamed that Greece might still be free;
For standing on the Persians' grave,
I could not deem myself a slave.

A king sat on the rocky brow
Which looks o'er sea-born Salamis;
And ships, by thousands, lay below,
And men in nations--all were his!
He counted them at break of day—
And when the sun set, where were they?

And where are they? And where art thou?
My country? On thy voiceless shore
The heroic lay is tuneless now—
The heroic bosom beats no more!
And must thy lyre, so long divine,
Degenerate into hands like mine?

'Tis something, in the dearth of fame,
Though linked among a fettered race,
To feel at least a patriot's shame,

Even as I sing, suffuse my face;

For what is left the poet here?

For Greeks a blush–for Greece a tear...

Fill high the bowl with Samian wine!

Our virgins dance beneath the shade—

I see their glorious black eyes shine;

But gazing on each glowing maid,

My own the burning teardrop laves,

To think such breasts must suckle slaves.

Place me on Sunium's marbled steep,

Where nothing, save the waves and I,

May hear our mutual murmurs sweep;

There, swanlike, let me sing and die:

A land of slaves shall ne'er be mine—

Dash down yon cup of Samian wine!

Byron's obvious love of Greece led him to go there in the 1820s to help the Greeks in their war of independence against the Ottoman Turkish Empire. His death there rallied many other Europeans to the Greek cause, though it came by illness, not in battle.

Perhaps you know of Byron, but perhaps not.

Maybe you're a part of the early "Baby Boomer" generation and know a bit of Greece's story in WWII through the book and movie *The Guns of Navarone* (1961), a thoroughly fictional and barely informative "action" movie.

Then, of course, there's *Zorba the Greek* and its soundtrack. Millions of older British and Americans think they know a bit about Greece and Greek culture from this (admittedly outstanding) movie based on the even better book by Nikos Kazantzakis. *Zorba the Greek*, unfortunately, fed into many of the stereotypes Greeks face even today—great lovers of life who will dance for any reason, laugh in the face of tragedy, and drink, eat, and love their lives away.

My Big Fat Greek Wedding (2002), by Greek-American comic Nia Vardalos, told the story of an extended family of Greek immigrants in Chicago. They love to dance, eat, declaim on how everything good in the world, especially language, is a product of Greece and the Greeks. Oh, and the grandmother hates the Turks—can't forget that. The movie was hilarious, and while it includes some serious stereotyping, most Greek immigrants (or descendants of the same) will recognize the many truths held within. No mint jelly on the lamb—remember that.

And that's likely it. Perhaps you, too, are the descendant of Greek immigrants and want to know more about what Greece has done in the roughly two thousand years since the Golden Age of Greece. Or perhaps you're just curious about what happened to Greece. One day, it was at the top of the world, the apex of civilization, and the next?

Captivating History's *History of Modern Greece* is going to try to fill those gaps.

Chapter 1 – 1,453 years in a Short Chapter

One thousand four hundred and fifty-three seems like a really arbitrary number, but it is not. In the year 1453 CE, the Ottoman Turks finally seized the Byzantine Greek city of Constantinople (today's Istanbul). With the Turkish conquest of the city, what was left of Greece's former ancient glory was taken away, never to be returned.

Even during Rome's long rule over Greece, the Greeks supplied educators, writers, tutors to emperors and their families, musicians, architects, and doctors to the Romans. Much, although not all, of later Roman civilization had its roots in Greek antiquity, including its gods, which were mostly rebranded Latin versions of the Greek originals.

Even before the rise of Rome to world power, the people of the Italian Peninsula had had contact with Greece. Greece had colonies in southern Italy, Sicily, and along the Adriatic coast. Greek colonies even existed for a time in southern France.

To Julius Caesar and the Romans before and after him, Alexander the Great was *the* model of everything they wanted to be, and some Roman emperors would even claim they were descended from Alexander or were even Alexander reincarnated.

However, in history, glory is fleeting, and while the Romans' awesome military abilities allowed them to gain an empire far greater in size, strength, and duration than Alexander, they, too, were subject to the shifting sands of history. By 324 CE, the Roman Empire was in decline, battered by corruption and much else from within, as well as the "barbarian" attacks of the many different tribes of northern and central Europe.

By the late 5th century, Rome, as it had been known, had fallen prey to the many Gothic tribes that had assailed her for over a hundred years. However, the spirit of Rome and also of ancient Greece lived on in the Eastern Roman Empire, which began upon the declaration of Emperor Constantine ("the Great"), the first Christian Roman emperor, that the "new Rome" would be located at the crossroads of Europe and Asia in the new city of Constantinople, which the emperor dedicated on May 11th, 330.

The size of the Byzantine Empire (also known as the Eastern Roman Empire) waxed and waned for many years. It mostly waned, but at its height, under Justinian I (b. 482–d. 565; r. 527–565), it included parts of the old Roman Empire.

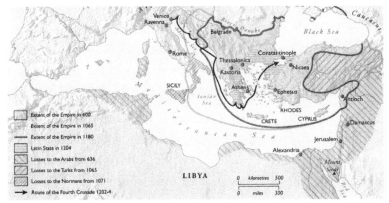

Illustration 1: The Byzantine Empire through the 11th century.

As you can see from the map above, the empire was assaulted by a variety of people for centuries, but it managed to survive until the mid-15ᵗʰ century, which was when the Ottomans finally captured Constantinople.

Various Turkish tribes had migrated westward from the steppes of central Asia, entering Asia Minor and the Caucasus areas in the early 7ᵗʰ century. Soon after their arrival, they were exposed to the spreading religion of Islam, which was carried by Arab tribes into the region after the death of Muhammad the Prophet in 632. From the 7ᵗʰ century to the 13ᵗʰ century, the armies of Byzantium (another name for the Byzantine Empire) and the Turks clashed with regularity, with one side temporarily gaining the advantage for a time only to lose it. In between wars, trade did go on with the Turks, who supplied raw materials and food items to the Byzantines (who, by this time, were almost exclusively ruled by emperors of Greco-Roman or pure Greek heritage) in exchange for gold and beautiful finished works of jewelry and much else that was, at that time, beyond their abilities.

In 1280, a powerful Turkish tribal leader named Osman united the various Turkic tribes of the area into a new entity—the Ottoman Empire, with "Ottoman" being an English term for "Osman." Osman is known to history as Osman I or, in Turkish, Osman Ghazi ("Osman the Conqueror"—sometimes the word "ghazi" referred to "raider" and sometimes "Conqueror of Christians" or "Infidels"). With the ascension of Osman and his uniting of the Turks under one banner, the war against the Byzantines became a war for not only power but also domination of the Turks (for they took over many Arab lands as well) and the religion of Islam.

By the beginning of the 13ᵗʰ century, the Byzantine Empire was a shadow of itself. It consisted of the still rich city of Constantinople. a small part of European Thrace, the Peloponnese (the southernmost part of Greece), and some islands. In 1453, the siege of Constantinople began.

The siege lasted for fifty-three days, from April 6th to May 29th. The Ottoman army numbered close to 200,000 men and perhaps 60 cannons. The Byzantines could only put together an army of about eight thousand, and most of those were foreign mercenaries. The emperor had sent out a call for men throughout Europe to defend his capital, which had been regarded by many as the successor to the glory of ancient Rome, but his call for help went unheeded.

The battle was won before it was over. Aside from their great numerical advantage, the Ottomans possessed the most and best of new technology. One of their largest guns weighed tons—four hundred men and sixty oxen had to pull it. The barrel of this "bombard" ("siege gun") was thirty inches in diameter and fired huge solid marble balls at the walls of the city. Initially, the guns caused panic more than anything else, but as more and more of the huge cannonballs struck Constantinople's walls, which were not in the best of shape to begin with, they began to collapse in huge chunks. Eventually, the Turks and their allies swept into the city, and over one thousand years of Byzantine history came to an end.

When Constantinople fell, much of Europe panicked, though many of its leaders had had the chance to aid the city. The city was not only the last political link to ancient Rome but also the center of Greek (or Eastern) Orthodoxy, one of the two dominant Christian belief systems of the time. From this time until relatively recently, the center of Orthodoxy shifted to Russia.

One of Byzantium's lasting contributions to Greece was its religious iconography (the painting of icons). While the rest of Europe was entering the Renaissance and experimenting with new techniques in painting (especially the use of perspective), the Byzantines continued to create beautiful, often gilt with gold, two-dimensional icons depicting scenes from the Bible, mostly the New Testament. This art form survives today in the nations dominated by the Orthodox Church (Greece, Russia, Serbia, and Bulgaria). Though icons exist in the Catholic Church, in the Orthodox Church, they take on greater meaning and import. Simply put, the idea is that the icon is not just a depiction of a holy scene but creates in the viewer some idea of holiness and is said to be a "window on the Divine."

Illustration 2: This icon of the Annunciation was painted on wood in 1895 and brought to the US in the early 1900s by the source's grandmother. Courtesy Matthew Gaskill.

Chapter 2 – Greece in the Ottoman Empire

It is impossible to tell the story of modern Greece, which essentially begins in 1821 with the Greek War of Independence, without discussing the Ottoman Empire. The Greeks and the Ottomans were intertwined for centuries, and one cannot understand the events of the 1820s without some background. The history of the Ottomans in Greece and the lives of the Greeks as part of the Ottoman Empire is rich and long—almost twice as long as American history.

From 1461, when the majority of Greece (mostly but not completely on the mainland) fell under Turkish rule, until the time of Napoleon Bonaparte in the late 1700s to early 1800s, Greece was controlled by two major powers: the Ottomans and the Venetians (the Italian city-state of Venice). The Italian city-state of Genoa also controlled a number of Greek islands for a time. (Interestingly enough, many of the residents of the Greek island of Chios, which figures large in the history of the War of Independence, believe that explorer Christopher Columbus was actually a Genoese born on Chios. We do know that he visited the island at some point.)

The Venetians and the Ottomans had a strange relationship. At times, they were on good or at least peaceful terms, trading with one another and angering more conservative elements within their respective empires and alliances who felt that war should be taking place between the "True Believers" and the "infidels" (substitute Muslims and Christians interchangeably).

For quite a long time, the Venetians had a distinct advantage at sea and used their economic and naval might to press the Ottomans into trade. On mainland Europe and, of course, in Asia Minor (and eventually the whole Middle East and the coast of North Africa), the Ottomans, with their immense and powerful armies, had the advantage.

Of course, at times, these two powers went to war with one another over the centuries. The unfortunate part, at least from the Greek point of view, is that not only were they powerless spectators in the conflict, but it was also their lands that were being fought over. Their cities were attacked, farmlands were destroyed, and the economy was ruined from time to time. "Luckily," this happened on a relatively local though large scale. However, on top of that, their women were subject to rape and kidnapping, and their men were subject to being put in chains as slaves. Both the Venetians and the Ottomans were perpetrators in this, with the Ottomans likely taking more Greeks as slaves to locations nearby.

Slaves were needed everywhere but perhaps most importantly for the navies of the respective powers. In 1571, the Ottomans fought a collection of Christian powers at sea in the Battle of Lepanto, which brought an end to the "Age of the Galley" and marked the beginning of the "Age of Sail." But until then, both sides needed men to power both their war and merchant ships. Galley slaves were chained to the benches. In most cases, when the ship went down, the slaves did too; they weren't worth saving and risking one's life for.

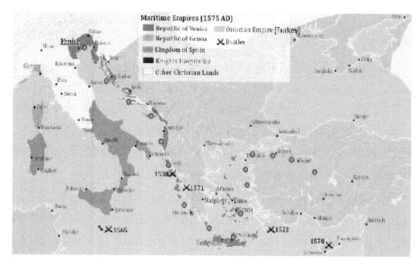

Illustration 3: The various empires in the Eastern Mediterranean in the late 16th century.

For the Venetians, the richest and most important islands were the Ionian Islands on the northwest side of Greece across from the Italian Peninsula. They were not only close by and easier to defend but also provided an important staging area and transfer point for products coming from the area of modern Lebanon and Israel and, to a degree, spices from farther east in Persia and India.

On the map above, you can see the location of the Battle of Lepanto, which will be discussed in more detail later in the chapter, which is on the western side of Greece and marked "1571." This was a vital area, and it was fought over many times, as the Gulf of Corinth leads along the northern Peloponnese toward Athens and the Aegean Sea. The use of the Gulf of Corinth took much time off the travel from the west to the east of Greece and vice versa.

Today's tourist island of Corfu was, at the time, the most important strategic island in the Ionian Islands. The island was heavily fortified by the Venetians, and four fortresses/castles looked out over the north and the south to guard both the approach from the south, the Mediterranean and Aegean Seas, and from the mainland through the Gulf of Corinth.

On the western side of Greece lies the large island of Euboea, which is located immediately offshore north of Athens and is separated from the mainland by approximately 2,300 feet at its narrowest point. Needless to say, this island was fought over many times and was heavily fortified.

In the south, the largest of the Greek islands, Crete, along with another large island farther east, Cyprus (a source of tension between the Greeks and Turks even today), as well as varying numbers of smaller Aegean islands, were fought over for centuries, as they provided both staging points for trade with Asia and the Middle East but also food and other trade goods—and, of course, slaves.

The Ottomans had expanded into Europe decades before their conquest of Constantinople. Naturally, this alarmed the Christian states of Europe, and many large and bloody battles were fought from the late 1300s until the 1600s on the Continent. But from the 12th century until the late 13th century, the Europeans (especially those living and ruling on the coasts) did not have much to fear from the Ottomans at sea. The Turks had been a land power since their expansion from central Asia, and until the dawn of the 16th century, the Europeans expected their domination of the sea, especially the Mediterranean, would continue.

However, in the last decade of the 1400s, the Ottomans began constructing a fleet to compete with the Europeans, especially the Venetians. For decades, the only real competition to the Venetians at sea were the ships of the North African and Middle Eastern corsairs. Corsairs were privateers or pirates, and like most criminals, they preyed on the weak, slow, and isolated. When the Turks began to grow their navy, they slowly but increasingly began capturing Venetian and allied trading vessels and raiding the coasts of Venetian-controlled territories for slaves.

In 1499, a war between the Ottomans and the Venetians broke out at sea, and the Venetians suffered a string of humiliating defeats. One of the key Ottoman victories was the conquest of Lepanto (not to be confused with the later Battle of Lepanto), which allowed them to better control access to the interior of Greece and to move into the Adriatic Sea if they so wished. The Venetians did win a small victory and gained control of a couple of small islands, but that was nothing compared to the loss of Lepanto, which led to mainland Greece being entirely in Turkish hands by 1503.

In 1520, a new Ottoman sultan, Suleiman I (also known as "Suleiman the Magnificent" or "Suleiman the Lawgiver"), who is considered to be the greatest Ottoman ruler, came to power. Under Suleiman, the Ottomans pressed forward into central Europe, completing their conquest of the northern Balkans, after which they pushed into Hungary, arriving at the gates of Vienna in 1529.

Illustration 4: Suleiman the Magnificent.

Luckily for Christian Europe and unluckily for Suleiman, bad weather, sickness, and supply problems, combined with the tenacious defenders (who were outnumbered about ten to one), caused the siege to fail. Despite another failed attack on Vienna in

1683, Suleiman's expansion into Europe was the highwater mark of the Ottoman Empire in Europe.

All of this shows that Greece, whose ancient history was considered by many to be the zenith of civilization, had become a very small piece of a very large and powerful empire. Suleiman was determined to not only advance Ottoman interests and control into southern and central Europe but also conquer all of the Greek islands as well. If large islands such as Crete and Cyprus were in enemy hands, the Turks' supply lines and coastlines would be at risk.

One of the other large islands of concern to Suleiman was Rhodes, which lies just off the coast of southwestern Asia Minor (today's Turkey). The island was the headquarters of the Knights of Saint John (also known as the Knights Hospitaller, the Knights of Malta, or the Knights of Rhodes), which was a devoutly (one might say fanatical) Christian order of knights that had been expelled from their home in the Holy Land in 1306 by Muslim forces. By the time Suleiman came to power, the Knights of Rhodes had become known less for their devoutness and more for their piracy, which cost the sultan large amounts of treasure. Despite the knights' Christian faith, they preyed on both Ottoman and Christian shipping.

Still, when the island fell to an immense and powerful Ottoman siege in 1521, the knights evacuated to Malta, where they would later fight the Turks in an epic siege in 1565. The Ottomans added more land and tens of thousands of more Greek subjects to their realm after the siege of 1521.

From 1521 to 1534, the Venetians and the Ottomans were at peace, but everyone knew it was only a matter of time before war began again. In 1540, the Venetians sued for peace, having lost almost all of their Greek territories to the Turks except for some tiny islands and the large and important island of Cyprus, which is just over 550 miles southeast of Athens in the Mediterranean.

From 1540 until 1570, the Venetians carried out trade with the Ottomans to the dismay of many Europeans, both the powerful and the poverty-stricken. However, in 1570, a new Ottoman sultan, the son of Suleiman, known to history as Selim II "the Sot" (a drunk, despite the Muslim stricture on alcohol), wanted to expand the empire even further and outdo his great father by winning a major victory at one of the oldest Venetian outposts in the Mediterranean and conquer Cyprus.

The Venetians, despite having angered many Europeans, including the pope, by trading extensively with the Ottomans, called upon them to help them save Cyprus when the Turks attacked in the late summer of 1571. The Papal Navy (yes, the pope had a navy) and the Spanish sailed to Cyprus, where they argued amongst themselves and left without engaging the Turks. Without aid, Nicosia, the capital city, fell in September, and the rampaging Ottoman soldiers killed thirty thousand people and took many more into slavery.

The last outpost of Venice on Cyprus was the fortress of Famagusta. The powerful fortress held out throughout the summer, fall, and winter of 1570/71. In the spring, Selim brought 200 ships and 250,000 men to Famagusta. The city held out against a powerful siege, in which over 150,000 cannonballs, some of which were huge, were fired at the fort, but on August 1ˢᵗ, the Venetians and their mercenary allies could hold out no longer. What happened next enraged Christian Europe and marked the beginning of a slow decline of the Ottoman Empire on the Continent and in Greece.

The commander of the Christian forces in Famagusta was Venetian Marcantonio Bragadin (sometimes spelled Bragadino). Bragadin accepted the Ottoman terms of surrender but likely did not envisage his own fate. By the time Bragadin surrendered, the Turks had lost thousands of men in the Cyprus campaign, as well as much treasure, so they decided to use Bragadin as an example to people as to what might happen should they oppose the Ottomans.

First, Bragadin was forced to endure a mock execution (head on the chopping block, etc.). Then, his nose and ears were cut off. After that, he was forced to crawl about the fortress on his hands and knees, kissing the ground. And as if that were not enough, he was tied to a chair and hauled to the top of a galley mast, where he was flayed (skinned) alive. His skin was then stuffed with straw and paraded through the streets, and what remained of him was then cast into a jail cell.

Before Famagusta, it might have been possible for the Venetians and the rest of Europe to make peace with the Turks or at least engage in trade agreements. But once word of Bragadin's fate spread through Western Christendom, a fire was ignited under the Europeans.

Occasionally throughout history, a battle will occur that changes history in an instant and forever. One of those was the Battle of Lepanto on October 7th, 1571.

Illustration 5: The Battle of Lepanto, *attributed to the Italian master Tintoretto.*

At Lepanto, the Europeans of Venice, Spain, Genoa, Savoy, Tuscany, the Papal States, the Knights of Malta, and the Italian city-state of Urbino, as well as some English and French and a number of Christian adventurers, arrived with over 206 galleys, 6 galleasses (smaller but sometimes more heavily armed galleys), and 60,000 men (40,000 sailors and 20,000 soldiers). The Ottomans had 222 galleys with about 60 small galliots, which altogether carried 13,000 sailors, 35,000 men, and nearly 40,000 galley slaves (oarsmen).

In a battle that lasted all day and involved the massive exchange of cannon and musket fire at close range, as well as bloody boarding parties in which no quarter was given or taken, the European navy prevailed, having inflicted much more damage on the Turks than they themselves had sustained. Ironically, some of the commanders and soldiers of the Turkish fleet were Greek, as the Greeks had made their living off the sea since time immemorial. Many of the slaves in the holds of the galleys were Greek; this disparity in treatment will be explained in the next chapter.

The victory at Lepanto was celebrated throughout Europe, and it marked both the end of the "Age of the Galley" and the beginning of the "Age of Sail," as well as the highwater mark (so to speak) of the Turkish expansion in Europe. The last great Turkish conquest over Venice took place when the Ottomans conquered Crete in 1669 after a campaign that took fifteen years.

The Greeks had seen their islands and seas used as a battlefield between the Venetians and other Europeans and the Turks for over two hundred years. From the end of the Battle for Crete in 1669 and the start of the Greek War of Independence in 1821, the Greeks suffered, endured, and sometimes even thrived under Ottoman rule.

Chapter 3 – Greece and the Greeks under the Ottoman Rule

Even today (June 2021), feelings can run quite hot between the Greeks and Turks (the inheritors of the Ottoman Empire, which, though run from Constantinople and founded by the Turks, consists of many nationalities).

The latest tensions are due to the ongoing refugee crisis, with people mainly fleeing from war-torn Syria. As of this writing, the Turks are urging Syrian refugees who have fled to Turkey to continue on to other European nations, which is the goal of most refugees. However, since the avalanche of Syrian refugees in 2015, many of the other European countries have been less than eager to take in more of them. Under an agreement made in Brussels with European Union members in 2016, Turkey had agreed to hold Syrian refugees while they were vetted for admission into Europe. All the countries involved have become overwhelmed by the problem, and in the last year, Turkey has pushed (sometimes literally) refugees over its border with Greece, which has attempted to house refugees in camps among its various islands near the Turkish coast.

Tensions have run so high that tear gas has been shot toward either side, either at one another's troops while refugees are pushed forward or sent back or at the refugees themselves. Naturally, each side blames the other for the problems that exist along their border.

Illustration 6: Syrian refugees in the no-man's land between Turkey and Greece with tear gas in the background. Courtesy Getty Images.

Before the Turks even arrived in Asia Minor, the Greeks and the residents of what is now Turkey were fighting. Geography has played a major role in the hostilities, but so have religion and culture. Then, of course, add in grievance after grievance stemming from those wars and occupations, and you have a recipe for disaster.

However, while many people in Greece and Turkey know of the problems and hatreds of the past, few realize that there have, at times, been cordial relations between the Turks and Greeks. Or rather between some Turks and Greeks, and those were mostly at the top of the socioeconomic scale, with some exceptions.

Like many an empire before and since, the Ottoman Empire depended on a few things in order to survive in the way to which it had become accustomed. For the first two and a half centuries or so of Ottoman rule in Greece, the Ottomans were at war, expanding their empire, or at least attempting to. Through the first part of Ottoman history, the empire and its sultan depended on wars for riches, power, and personal and imperial prestige. Without military conquests, the sultan was not able to reward his followers and demand their loyalty. And like so many other empires before, the Ottomans were subject to the same court intrigue, power struggles, and assassinations that came with leaders that were or seemed to be weak.

Greece was the most important Ottoman possession. From a prestige standpoint, the Turks were able to tell themselves and the world, "We have conquered the people who once ruled the world." Never mind that that was over one thousand years ago, but such was the power of ancient Greece in the popular imagination.

By the 1500s, the Ottoman Empire had become so large that it required more soldiers than were available in the Turkish population alone. Within a very short period of time, the Ottomans were taking in, either by way of volunteers or force, soldiers from other peoples. First, they took in Arabs and other people who had been Muslims since the Age of Muhammad nearly one thousand years before: Arabs, Egyptians, North Africans, Lebanese, Syrians, etc. However, as time went by and larger and larger armies and navies were needed, the Ottomans cast a wider net.

Greeks and other non-Muslim subjects could not serve in the army, except for one important exception. Greeks could become officers, especially in the navy. With increasing regularity and the bending of rules during the later Ottoman period, Greeks also became powerful figures at court and in the empire's administration, and they could often make or break other powerful figures, including the sultan himself.

The Ottomans were (in)famous for raiding the towns and cities of non-Muslims and taking their children to raise as Muslims and soldiers. These were the famous Janissaries (meaning "new army" in Turkish), whose ranks were filled with Serbs, Bosnians, Croats, Bulgarians, and other subject peoples, but they were mostly Greeks.

The Janissaries were fanatically loyal to the sultan, at least at the beginning of their history (they began in the 1300s and were banned in 1826 just after the Greek War of Independence), as long as the sultan was strong and provided them with opportunities for conquest, riches, and power. The Janissaries, the occasional powerful woman, who was usually but not limited to one of the sultan's wives or concubines, the court eunuchs, and others could sometimes play the role of kingmaker or, in this case, "sultan-maker."

The odd thing, as you can see, is that the Janissaries were frequently ordered to war on their own people. Since they had been taken as children and essentially brainwashed, it did not affect the Janissaries themselves to any great degree until later in Ottoman history, but it caused great resentment among the conquered for obvious reasons.

Even though a large part of the Greek population lived in the country's interior and was usually involved in some type of farming, a great many Greeks, then as now, lived near the coasts and have so for centuries. The Greeks, more than any other people in the Ottoman Empire by far, knew the sea. Greeks were some of the highest-ranking officers in the Ottoman navies, and they designed most of their ships and fleets and also captained and ran many of the Turks' merchant ships.

For those Greeks in the Janissaries, the Turkish navy, and the Turkish administration, life could be bearable or even good—sometimes very good. But for the vast majority of Greeks, living under Ottoman rule was sometimes a heavy burden.

The Turks considered their non-Muslim subjects not as people but as rayah, which means "cattle." These "cattle" were made to serve the Turks, mostly under a heavy tax burden. Intermittent and random raids would take slaves away from Greek villages, never to be seen again. As non-Muslims, taxes were high, and non-payment of taxes could bring severe punishment.

However, the Ottomans did not forcibly attempt to convert their subject peoples. As long as the Greeks and others fulfilled their duties to the sultan and obeyed the law, they were generally left in peace. Of course, there were numbers of Europeans who converted to Islam, most notably many of the Slavs of today's Bosnia. This was sometimes done out of genuine religious zeal but also to get ahead. Anyone who had converted could never return to the Christian faith, or they would suffer exceedingly unpleasant treatment under apostasy laws.

The overwhelming majority of Greeks belonged to the Greek Orthodox Church (just as they do today), though there was a significant minority of Jewish people, especially in the north in or near the city of Salonika. To the Turks, these were "People of the Book." Although they were not Muslims, they believed in the same God; they just did not acknowledge the Prophet Muhammad and his teachings. The Bible itself, along with the Jewish Torah and Talmud, were considered to be the revealed words of God through the prophets until the latest word, that of the Holy Quran.

As far as the established Greek Orthodox Church went, the Ottomans left it mainly alone. They knew the level of devotion the Greeks had for their church and realized that the institution could be useful in governing and maintaining control over the Greeks. In 1454, Mehmet the Conqueror confirmed the appointment of the Greek Patriarch Gennadios. From that point until the War of Independence (in which the church played a large part), the Greek Orthodox Church was considered an administrative branch of the Ottoman government.

The Ottomans did not impose Sharia law on their subjects but expected the Greek Church to keep order under their own written and unwritten rules. Though the Ottoman Empire was divided into administrative regions run by a governor or *hodjibashi*, most Greeks dealt with other Greeks when it came to government affairs.

During the time when Greece and the Greek isles were fought over by the Turks and the Venetians, many Greeks preferred to live under Turkish rule than Venetian rule. Part of this was historic. In 1204, the Venetians led a huge expedition of Europeans, ostensibly to the Middle Eastern Holy Land. But along the way, their giant fleet, carrying eighty thousand hungry and greedy western European warriors, stopped at Constantinople. Rather than go onto the Holy Land after being resupplied, they sacked the great Greek city. In Greece and much of the Mediterranean, memories stay for a long time. A very, very long time.

Adding to that, the Venetians treated the Greeks contemptuously, and to the Greeks, it seemed as if they were also attempting to establish the Catholic Church. The Venetians also placed a greater tax burden on them than the Turks, and while the Ottoman administration could be horribly corrupt, the Venetians apparently put them to shame. Very few Greeks were in the Venetian armed forces, either on land or sea, but quite the opposite was true regarding the Ottoman armies and navies.

Still, though many Greeks preferred the rule of the Turks over the Venetians, it was not as if Turkish rule was easy or celebrated by most Greeks; though as time went on, certain Greeks and Greek islands did benefit economically from their proximity to Turkey. Money aside, however, the Turks certainly let the Greeks know exactly what their status within the empire was, especially in the early part of the Turkish occupation.

The status of Greeks vis-à-vis their Turkish masters and their behavior was written in a series of codes and regulations. For instance, the Greeks were not allowed to bear arms or ride horses (though this usually meant dismounting at the approach of a

Turkish official). Occasionally, a rule was enforced that forced Greeks to wear black clothing as a means of identification, as they could not wear Turkish-style clothes. Greek churches could not be built near mosques, and the common Greek (and Christian) practice of bell-ringing from church towers was tightly regulated as not to interfere with Muslim worship or holidays. The houses of Greeks could not be built taller or overlook Turkish homes or buildings nearby.

All of this was irksome but somewhat tolerable, and by the beginning of the 1800s, most of these regulations were honored in the breach and rarely enforced. What really bothered many Greeks was the imposition of heavy taxes, and Greece, especially those towns and cities near the coast, was one of the richest areas in the Turkish world. On top of that, as time went on, Turkish officials, as well as some Greeks, became more and more corrupt and constantly had their hands out for bribes.

However, the most resented aspect of Turkish rule was the devshirme or the "tax of children." This "tax" was enforced stringently at the beginning of the Turkish rule but fell off toward the end. However, the memory of it lingered on even after the Greeks had won their independence. The devshirme meant that Ottoman officials, not just in Greece but throughout the Christian parts of their empire, would tour the areas under their jurisdiction and select who they deemed to be the "most promising" Christian children for training in war and administration or both. These children would then be converted to Islam.

The strongest or most physically gifted among the boys would be sent to the Janissaries. These troops would be the sultan's and other officials' guards throughout the empire, as well as shock troops in battle. In a horribly ironic twist of fate, it was the Janissaries who were most often loosed on the subject populations when a point of discipline had to be made or a rebellion put down. In other words, these young Greek men, who had essentially been brainwashed into fanatical Muslim "holy warriors," would be turned upon their kinsmen.

Young men and boys gifted with intelligence would be trained as administrators and clerks to make sure the wheels of the empire kept turning. As in many warrior cultures, these jobs were "beneath" the Turks, and so they were filled by foreigners. A great many of them were Greek, not only in Greece itself but also in Asia Minor, other parts of the empire, and especially in Constantinople, where many Greeks rose to become quite influential figures by guiding policy, controlling budgets, gaining access to the sultan, and more.

As Muslim culture proscribed the painting or imagery of holy figures and greatly discouraged the image of sultans and other powerful figures, one of the Ottoman Empire's greatest contributions in the field of decorative arts was architecture. The greatest Ottoman architect was not Turkish, however, but Greek. His name was Sinan, and he was taken to Turkey in the devshirme in 1491. When he died in 1588, he was ninety-one and had created two of the most remarkable structures in the Ottoman Empire: the Suleimaniye Mosque in Constantinople and the Selimiye Mosque at Edirne in European Turkey or Eastern Thrace. Even today, eighty-four of his buildings can be seen just in Istanbul alone.

In addition to being important administrators and bureaucrats, the Turkish navy was filled with Greeks, not only as galley-slaves during the age before modern sailing vessels but also as captains, admirals, engineers/ship designers, and shipbuilders. When the Greek War of Independence began, the Turkish navy was at a serious disadvantage in both numbers of vessels and leadership.

During the very early part of the occupation, Turkish soldiers and sailors would raid the Greek coastline and islands for galley slaves. During the period just before the Battle of Lepanto (1571), tens of thousands of slaves were taken to power the sultan's ships. Galley slaves were not the only people forced into a life of slavery. Throughout the Ottoman Empire's history, it was powered to a great degree by slaves, who worked in the mines, fields, and homes of local and imperial officials. Naturally, this was resented by all of the subject people, not just the Greeks.

Of course, one of the most well-known aspects of Turkish rule was that of the harem. The word "harem" has many meanings. It can mean the section of a house (or palace) that is set aside for the women of the household. It can also refer to the women who lived there: wives, concubines, female relatives, and servants. Lastly, and most infamously, it can refer to a group of women kept as the sexual partners of the same man, who was almost always someone who held some power and wealth. (Some of these women were real "partners," married or not, and they often played the role of adviser.) Of course, many of the women and girls of the harem in this last sense were not there by choice. Like they did with the strongest and smartest boys, Ottoman officials and raiding parties would frequently take the most beautiful girls and/or young women to serve as sexual slaves for some powerful official.

In rare cases, concubines in the harem of the sultan or other high officials might wield some influence, as in the case of a Slavic girl from the area of southern Poland/western Ukraine named Roxelana, who is better known in Turkish history as Hurrem Sultan. She rose from being Suleiman I's (r. 1520–1566) favorite concubine into a woman of great influence at the sultan's court. In the middle of the 1600s, a number of these women managed to gain influence within the sultan's court, most famously a Greek girl from the island of Corfu named Kösem. Unlike Roxelana (who bore Suleiman a son who became the sultan himself, Selim II), Kösem and the other powerful women of the 1600s were ultimately put to death by the Ottomans' favorite method of execution—strangulation by bowstring. Of course, most of the kidnapped girls enjoyed no such fate and were destined for a life of sexual slavery and perhaps lived out their old age as a maid, nanny, or cleaning woman.

As you just read and as you likely know already, under a regime such as that of the Ottomans, it was dangerous, especially as a foreigner, to rise too high, too openly, too fast, or all three. One Greek, known to history as Ibrahim, rose from being a slave to a rich woman in Istanbul, ultimately becoming the grand vizier (adviser to the sultan and the chief administrator of the empire). Unfortunately for Ibrahim, he made enemies in high places, which included the sultan's first wife. In the end, he was strangled by a bowstring. Another Greek, Michael Cantacuzenos, became one of the wealthiest and most influential merchants in Istanbul. In 1578, he, too, was strangled. His offense? Being an "over-mighty subject."

As horrible and as onerous as some of the treatment and laws of the Turks might have been, many Greeks lived their lives relatively untouched by them. In mainland Greece, especially away from the coasts, life went on much as it had before. In the cities of coastal Asia Minor and Eastern Thrace (now European Turkey), where the vast majority of people were Greek, not Turkish, the footprint of the Ottomans was relatively light. The Turks needed the economic benefits of these areas and peace in places so near the capital and heart of the empire. In Salonika, a great port and trading city whose population was mostly Jewish, religious rules kept the population in their place, but for the most part, as long as they paid their taxes and necessary bribes, the people of the city were left alone. Salonika was too important and too rich to interfere with on any great scale.

Throughout much of Greece, on the mainland and in the interior of the larger islands, small-holding farms were the economic order of the day. Again, as long as they paid their taxes, didn't complain too much, or rebel, the Ottomans let things be. In the often-mountainous and rugged Greek interior, ordinary Greeks oftentimes had more to fear from other Greeks than the Turks or their minions.

Bands of klephts, which can mean "thief" but is best defined by the word "brigand," roamed the countryside, especially in the remote mountainous areas. Many times, the klephts were organized around families and clans and were similar in many ways to tribal cultures in other parts of the world. Klephtic bands often plundered farms and villages of other clans, so a cycle of vendetta began. During and after the Greek War of Independence, the klephts were romanticized as heroic guerrilla warriors, and they were often just that. However, they often sold their services to the highest bidder and might later turn on them if a higher price was offered. During the War of Independence, bands of klephts were sometimes as feared as Turkish troops, as they would often march into a village, take away or kill the men, rape women, and steal whatever they could carry. Many Europeans and metropolitan Greeks, who had an idealized version of both the Greeks as a people and the klephts in particular, were disillusioned when bands of klephts carried out atrocities on Turkish or other ethnic groups during the war.

Illustration 7: Klepht, circa 1820. Courtesy Getty Images.

Facing the klephts were bands of Greek and Albanian irregulars known as the armatoli. (Many Albanians lived in what is today northwestern Greece.) The almost constant warfare in the mountains and hinterlands of Greece caused an exodus to the coastal cities, such as Thrace and Constantinople, the latter of which may have been the most cosmopolitan of cities from the 1600s until the early 20th century.

By the late 1600s, the Ottoman Empire had started its long slow decline. One of the reasons for this was the rise in power of the western European nations and Russia, which limited Ottoman expansion. For a culture that counted itself among the great "warrior cultures" of the world, the end of expansion meant the end of plunder, and the end of plunder meant both heavier taxation on subject people and many dissatisfied soldiers.

Another problem was that an established system of succession had never existed among the Ottoman Turks. In many cases, by the late 1500s and early 1600s, a sultan came to power through court intrigue, military coup (usually and ironically carried out by the Janissaries, who were foreigners), assassination, or all three. Sultan Murad III killed nineteen of his brothers and seven pregnant royal widows to gain the throne.

This act of assassination was replaced by another equally destabilizing practice, that of "the cage." On the death of the sultan, his recognized heir would be almost literally "caged." He would be limited to the harem and not allowed access to the outside world. This might keep him safe, but it would also keep him ignorant of the world and his empire and what made it function. Many times, the empire was run by the chief eunuch, who was usually a sub-Saharan African, the sultan's chief wife, the grand vizier, who, as we have seen, could sometimes be a foreigner, or the Janissaries.

Mentioned above was the increase in taxation among the subject peoples of the empire. But this alone, while resented to a great degree, was perhaps not enough to push people into rebellion. High taxation rates can many times be overlooked if that money went to pay for the common welfare (land improvement, infrastructure, libraries, public safety, etc.). But by the end of the 1700s and early 1800s, these high taxes simply went into the pockets of the sultan, his court, or his administrators without making life better for the people. And since local officials seldom had enough money to carry out public works, things frequently only got done through bribery or influence. Not only did that mean that not much was improved, what was improved was the lives of those who could afford bribes. In other words, the rich got richer, but even the rich began to resent the high taxes that did nothing to better society.

One of the things taxes are supposed to pay for is public safety. Not only can violence lead to more violence and resentment, but economic progress also begins to grind to a halt. Throughout the empire, particularly in Greece, this is what began to happen.

In 1789, the French Revolution began. Like in other parts of Europe, the news of the progress, troubles, and terror of the French Revolution was followed in Greece. Among the many reasons for the revolution in France were the arbitrary and heavy tax burden and the corruption of the state and its officials.

While the devshirme was naturally resented, and very few people wanted to be ruled by outsiders, it's important to remember that for most Greeks under Turkish rule, life was not that different from people in the rest of Europe. Everywhere—in France, the states of Germany, and especially in eastern Europe and Russia— the lives of most people, who were often poor peasants, were hard. In eastern Europe and Russia, peasants had very few if any rights, including the right to choose what to do with their lives, where they could live, and much more. Even in western Europe, torture was commonplace for heresy and breaking the law, which could include criticism of the government or ruler, even into the 1800s.

People will put up with much if they are secure, but as the Ottoman Empire declined, the security of the people, especially in the countryside, became more and more tenuous. As the number of Ottoman conquests declined, the plunder available to the Janissaries did too. Throughout the empire but particularly in Greece, these elite troops began to prey on their own people. At times, the government representatives became worse raiders than the klephts in the mountains and hinterlands.

Of course, another factor in the rise of Greek resentment was religion. Again, while the population was able to worship relatively freely, and the church hierarchy worked with the Turkish government to keep order, Greeks, at the time and even today, were quite devout and resented not only the rule of the Turks but also their religion. In many cases, Greeks looked to the most powerful Orthodox power, the Empire of Russia, to help or even liberate them from Turkish rule.

In some cases, the tsars and tsarinas of Russia (meaning Catherine the Great, r. 1762–1796) paid lip service to the idea of helping their "little Orthodox brother" Greece, but for the most part, the Russians used this idea and threat as a bargaining chip against the Turks, with whom they frequently went to war.

However, in one case in 1770, Catherine sent two noblemen, the Orlov brothers, to Greece to foment rebellion while Russian troops fought the Turks for control of Crimea, a part of Moldavia, and other smaller territories around the Caspian Sea and Ukraine. Though the Orlov brothers did win one important naval victory, the expedition was a disaster, and they were forced to retreat back to Russia in the winter/spring of 1771. During the Russian expedition, the klephts of the Greek mountains organized, which was a feat in itself due to their constant infighting, and rebelled against the Turks in mainland Greece. In response, the Turkish government ordered hordes of Albanian guerrillas and Janissaries down into the Peloponnese, where they carried out brutal reprisals and atrocities.

The treaty that ended the war between Russia and Turkey (the Treaty of Kuchuk-Kainarji) gave the Russians an ill-defined right to interfere on behalf of Orthodox Christians in the Ottoman Empire and allowed Greek merchant vessels to fly the Russian flag for their protection. This allowed the Greek merchant fleet to grow into one of the largest in the world, but the Russians' "right" to interfere wasn't worth the paper it was written on, as they weren't going to go to war with Turkey over religious issues in Crete (for example). However, these provisions did give the Greeks hope that if they did decide to rebel, the Russians would be there for them. However, they were not.

Over the course of the French Revolutionary period and the rule of Napoleon afterward, Greek nationalism grew. This was partly due to the spread of the French Revolution's ideals and the Greeks' exposure to them in foreign ports. However, under the rule of Napoleon, what was left of the Venetian empire in Greece, as well as the Ionian Islands on the northwest coast, were occupied by France (1797). For a short time, France gave them over to Russia, doing so in 1799, but they were taken back by the French in 1807 under an agreement. During French rule, the French worked with an Albanian official of the Turkish government, Ali of Janina, who had amassed great wealth and a private army and was believed to have imperial aspirations in the Balkans.

All of this came to naught after the defeat of Napoleon. Some Greeks, mostly those living in Europe and among Greek intellectuals in the Ottoman Empire, believed that the Congress of Vienna (the gathering of nations brought together to discuss the maintenance of peace after years of war) would insist that the Turks give Greece at the very least some measure of autonomy, but this was wishful thinking. No one at the Congress of Vienna wanted to upset the status quo. Turkey had not been involved in the wars against Napoleon, except for when he had attacked Egypt, and the dominant statesman of the time, Austrian Count Metternich, along with Tsar Alexander I of Russia, did not want to encourage any more national revolutions.

Despite this, the French Revolution and the spread of representative governments in the rest of Europe had lit a fire under many Greeks. They saw the Ottoman Empire weakening from both within and without, and they began to make plans for the time when action toward independence seemed right.

The Road to Independence

By the start of the 18th century, Greeks within the Ottoman Empire and in the rest of Europe began to feel more "Greek" and less a part of the Ottoman Empire. This was helped by the ideas of the French Revolution but also by the beginning of the Romantic movement in Europe, which, among other things, called for freedom of thought and expression for all men. Romantics yearned for a time in the past when freedom was the "rule of the day." They found this "Golden Age of Freedom" in the history of ancient Greece, particularly that of Athens.

Within Greece, the church began to teach young Greeks about their heritage, and wealthy Greek merchants in Greece, Asia Minor, and the rest of Europe began to establish libraries filled with books about Greece's "heroic" past that were written in Greek. Though this had not been forbidden under the Turks, it was certainly not encouraged, and throughout the time before the Renaissance, Greeks, like many other Europeans, were more concerned with survival than history. This was the situation for many in Greece after the Renaissance and until the time of the French Revolution. It is likely that the average upper- or middle-class Englishman in 1780 knew more about ancient Greece than many Greeks of the same social background.

The Greeks of the diaspora (those Greek living outside of Greece) were key in this revival of Greek identity and national feeling. Large Greek communities, centered around the many ports of Europe and even in Asia, as far as India, had gathered together, and for their own emotional and sometimes physical security, they lived together and valued their history as a way to retain their identity. The largest Greek communities of the time outside the

Ottoman Empire were in Venice, Geneva, Moscow, Marseilles, Nice, and along the northern Black Sea coast.

Like many people throughout history who have been subjugated by another power, there were also secret societies of Greeks within the Ottoman Empire that taught their children and discussed the idea of Greek independence.

One problem facing the men and women thinking about a "free Greece" was they didn't really have an idea of what Greece should be. Outside of what we call Greece today, many Greeks lived in Constantinople and Asia Minor, living with millions of Turks and people of other ethnicities. Even in Greece, especially on the islands near Albania and Turkey, the population was mixed. The population of the coastal mainland, including Athens, which, in 1821, the year the War of Independence began, only contained just less than twenty-four thousand people (today that number is just under eleven million, about one-third of the population), was also a jumble of Greeks, Turks, and others living next to one another to a great degree. The only part of today's Greece that was predominantly Greek was the lower central area and the Peloponnese. The mountainous borderlands contained Greeks, Albanians, Macedonians, Bulgarians, and a small number of Serbs. That left what was readily identifiable as "Greece" as the poorest, most backward part of the country. Hellenism, the idea that the last great Greek civilization existed at the time before Alexander the Great, rose up in Greece and Europe, especially France and England. By looking back to this distant history, Greeks in the 19th century could readily identify areas of the world that had been governed by Greeks, where Greek was spoken as the dominant language, and where Greek culture was dominant. However, looking back to a world that existed nearly two thousand years before did not hold much relevance.

This idea of Hellenism, which contained not only geographic concepts but also ethnic ones, combined with the ideas that had grown with the western European Enlightenment and the French

Revolution, primarily the idea of a nation-state, one over which the people (not a sultan, emperor, or king) would govern.

One of the dominant figures of the Greek nationalist movement at the turn of the 18th and 19th centuries was Rhigas Pheraios (Rigas Feraios), who mapped out where the new "Greek Republic" would exist. Pheraios's idea was for Greece to be modeled on the early French Revolutionary governments and consist of what we call Greece today, as well as Constantinople, the entire Aegean coast of Asia Minor (Turkey), and a large slice of the Balkan Peninsula along the Black Sea. Never mind that this was incredibly impractical since millions of other ethnic groups lived in these areas. Despite the impossibility of Pheraios's ideas, the Ottoman authorities hunted him down. He was betrayed by his fellow Greeks and was strangled and thrown into the Danube River.

Illustration 8: Rhigas Pheraios.

In 1814, a group of expatriate Greeks in Odesa (part of today's Ukraine) banded together to form the Etairia Philike ("Friendly Brotherhood"), which soon gained followers throughout the Greek community abroad, especially in Russia. Many Greeks joined because they believed that the group was backed by members of the Russian government. What truly spurred this belief on, as well as the growing belief that the tsar himself might actually back an independent Greece, was the appointment of a Greek from Corfu as the Russian foreign minister.

His name was Ioannis (Anglicized to "John") Kapodistrias (b.1776–d. 1831). Kapodistrias was from an upper-class family and had absorbed the ideas of the Enlightenment and French Revolution in his travels and thorough education. In 1799, Kapodistrias took his father's place in helping to govern the Ionian Islands, which had been jointly set up by the Russians and Turks in their peace agreement. In the course of his career there, he became acquainted with a Russian diplomat stationed in Italy. Kapodistrias became his student and eventually became an ambassador to Switzerland. Finally, in 1814/15, he became the Russian foreign minister.

Despite holding liberal Enlightenment ideas himself, Kapodistrias worked for the decidedly illiberal Russian tsar. Kapodistrias also did not believe that the Greeks were able to govern themselves at that point in time. The Etairia Philike also believed that Greeks should control a new Byzantine Empire, which put them at odds with both Russia and Russia's allies in the Balkans, such as the Bulgarians and Serbs.

Not only was Kapodistrias against any rebellion, but the leaders of the Greek Orthodox Church in Greece were too, as were many of the wealthy merchants of Greece and the Greek islands. Both groups believed a rebellion would bring a massive Turkish backlash, which would not only cost tens of thousands of lives or more but also destroy the economy and the position of the Greek Orthodox Church and its leadership in Greece and the Ottoman Empire.

However, with Kapodistrias in a position of power in the largest Orthodox country in the world, the Greeks of the Etairia Philike came to believe that the time was right for an armed rebellion against Turkish rule. The Etairia Philike enjoyed the most support in the Peloponnese, where the Ottoman rule was weakest. A powerful klepht warlord named Theodoros Kolokotronis, along with Bishop Germanos of Patras and Governor Petros Mavromichalis of the Mani Peninsula, all threw their support behind the Etairia Philike and the idea of an armed rebellion.

When Kapodistrias told the Etairia Philike in no uncertain terms that he and Russia would not support an armed rebellion, the society approached a Greek from Constantinople who was now in the service of the Russian army, one Alexander Ypsilantis, to lead the rebellion. (Incidentally, Ypsilanti, Michigan, is named in honor of Alexander's brother, Demetrios Ypsilantis, who also took part in the rebellion.)

Unfortunately, Ypsilantis was about as deluded as the members of the Etairia Philike who had fallen in love with their own propaganda of a giant new "Byzantine" Greece. He also believed that the time was right and pushed ahead in an attempt to raise an army in the hinterlands of the Peloponnese and the mountainous regions of Greece. His hope was that he could win the armed support of the Serbs, who had just won their independence from the Turks, and that a few victories would push the Russians and Slavic people of the Balkans to aid the Greeks. None of that would happen. The Serbs had no interest in further warring with the Turks, and the Russians, as has already been shown, were firmly against an armed Greek rebellion.

In the end, however, as has happened so often in history, events outside of the Greeks' control influenced what was to happen in their country next.

In the mountains of southern Albania and northern Epirus (the northeastern part of Greece), a Turkish governor or pasha named Ali had ruled for thirty years. Ali is a common Muslim name, so this man is known to history as Ali of Janina" (in Greek known as Ioannina). Ali's sons ruled the Peloponnese in his name. In essence, Ali was the true ruler of the area, with the sultan being a distant personage who collected taxes.

Ali had proved himself in battle and had proved himself ruthless when faced with rebellion. In 1803, Greeks in the area of Souli in Epirus rose up against Ali's rule. Ali killed virtually all of the men, and many of their widows and children threw themselves off a nearby cliff rather than face capture by Ali's forces. Ali ruled from central Albania south to central-western Greece, and he was powerful and influential enough to summon foreign ministers to his elaborate court.

Illustration 9: Ioannina, Greece, today. It is one of the few Greek cities in which mosques from Ottoman times still stand. Note the minarets near the water and the remnants of the old Ottoman fortifications.

By 1820, however, Ali was growing too strong and independent-minded for the Ottoman government in Constantinople. The sultan, Mahmud II, declared him an outlaw and sent fifty thousand men to remove Ali from power. This took two years, and while the Ottomans were fighting among themselves, the Greeks of the Etairia Philike decided to make their move, believing that the Turks would not be able to stop their revolution.

Taking the lead was Alexander Ypsilantis, who was in the Russian army and stationed in Moldova. Alexander, along with several other Greek officers serving in the Russian forces, moved south into Turkish territory to begin the Greek Revolution. One of Ypsilanti's men, an officer named Soutsos, informed the Turks of Ypsilantis's intentions, and they began to move forces to intercept Ypsilanti, who had moved into Romania, hoping to encourage the ethnic Greeks and Romanians to revolt against the Turks.

Ypsilantis's entire time in Romania was a fiasco of betrayal, miscalculation, disappointment, and bloodshed. Even before the Turkish forces arrived, Ypsilantis and his men had been excommunicated from the Greek Orthodox Church by the archbishop in Romania for bloodthirsty crimes that took place while Ypsilantis's men were searching for supplies (and plunder). Not only did Ypsilantis's actions result in his excommunication, but they also discouraged any of the Balkan people from rising up against the Turks or helping the Greeks. Even the Russians, who Ypsilantis had hoped would support him, allowed Turkish forces to cross their territory to get to him. At Dragastani in present-day Romania, Ypsilantis and his forces were totally wiped out by the Turks.

Ypsilantis's dream that a Balkan-wide revolt against the Turks would never come to fruition, and his defeat was a humiliating one. However, no one likes a heroic death in the face of impossible odds more than the Greeks (remember Thermopylae?).

Word spread of Ypsilantis's uprising and defeat in the south, and it lit a fire in Greece, where open warfare soon broke out. Combat between Turks and Greeks, at this point in time, was rarer than the fighting that took place between Greeks. On the one side, there were regions of Greece that had prospered under the stable Ottoman rule and were not eager for the uncertainty of war or the certainty of Ottoman punishment. On the other side, there were the independence-minded Greeks. And within both camps were various factions. When war did break out, many klephtic bands warred against each other because of their respective stands on war against the Ottomans, personal and historic feuds, and/or plunder. Making things worse, as the war went on, the Ottomans were able to bribe certain chieftains to join their side only to see them counter-bribed later and fighting against them once more.

Chapter 4 – The Greek War of Independence

Illustration 10: The Reception of Lord Byron at Missolonghi *by Theodoros Vryzakis, 1861. Courtesy National Gallery of Greece.*

The Greek War of Independence began two hundred years ago, as of this writing in 2021. Like many important events in the life of a nation, the painting above, which was completed forty years after the Greek Revolution began, portrays a romantic ideal that many Greeks still adhere to today. Here, we have the various factions of Greek independence represented: the Greek Orthodox Church, the klephts, intellectual- and middle-class Greeks in "modern" European clothing, humble yet brave women kneeling at the feet of the archbishop, and Lord Byron, the Englishman who came to epitomize the Greek War of Independence for many Europeans and Americans. In the painting, Byron is welcomed as the representative of England and other western European powers, which many Greeks thought would rush to their aid.

Like the painting of George Washington crossing the Delaware River during the American Revolution, the painting above bears little resemblance to what actually happened. Byron had the support of many intellectuals in Britain, France, and the United States, but he hardly brought welcome news for the Greeks. Western Europe would not send forces to their aid. Byron spent much of his own money, a sizable sum, in fact, to refit many of the ships of the Greek navy. However, much of Byron's time in Greece was spent writing poems and letters, urging his friends and others in the West to send money to help the Greeks; most of his pleas fell on deaf ears. Byron was also greatly disillusioned by many of the Greek leaders, all of whom competed with and against each other for a share of his sizable checkbook.

In Greece today, the monastery of Ayia, southwest of the city of Patras in the Peloponnese, holds the flag that Archbishop Germanos raised to "signal the revolt" among the Greeks. While Germanos was an early supporter of Greek independence, his gesture was more of a symbolic one, for the war had already broken out throughout much of Greece by the time he raised the flag in late March 1821. Monks in the monasteries near Mount Athos rose in rebellion, and the clans of the Mani Peninsula (the westernmost peninsula of the Peloponnese) had already seized some important towns and Turkish outposts.

The war broke out for a number of reasons. Obviously, the first one was occupation by a foreign power. But the Turks had controlled Greece for centuries, so why rise now? The men of the Etairia Philike had roused the people with propaganda and dreams of a greater Greece ruling from Constantinople, and many believed that Russia, an Orthodox country and the traditional enemy of Turkey, would support a Greek uprising. Many Greeks believed this would be especially true if they managed to win a few victories against the Turks themselves.

Many Greek Orthodox officials (from Archbishop Germanos down to local priests and monks) also encouraged the idea of a rebellion. For the most part, Muslims and Greeks (the overwhelming majority of whom were Orthodox) managed to coexist, but discriminatory laws and behavior on the part of the Turks and the Greeks' belief that the Turks were "infidels" who had to be pushed out of their Christian land always had tempers at a slow boil.

By 1821, the Greeks had also recognized that the Turks were no longer the power they once were. The Serbs had recently won their independence, so why couldn't the Greeks? Of course, the Turks were, at least on paper, much stronger than the Greeks, and Serbia was not worth as much to the Ottomans as Greece.

Even today, Greece and Turkey point fingers at one another for any number of atrocities committed by the other. Nationalists on both sides do not hesitate to bring up incidents from hundreds of years ago as if they happened yesterday. Suffice it to say that there was enough bloodshed on both sides in the history between the two people for both sides to be guilty of a number of what today could only be called "war crimes."

In the Peloponnese, the mainland region farthest from Turkey, Greeks from every part of society rose up to remove the forty thousand or so Turkish residents from the area. It's estimated about half of this number were killed in what today would be called "ethnic cleansing," but the Greeks at the time and since would state that they were reclaiming their homeland for themselves.

Throughout the islands in the western part of the country, rebellions also began. The shipping and naval centers on Hydra, Psara, and Spetses fell to the Greeks, and combined with their already strong position within the Turkish navy, the Greeks gained control of the seas, which made it difficult if not impossible for the Ottomans to reinforce and supply their isolated outposts.

In October, in the city and the area around Tripolitsa, located in the center of the Peloponnesian Peninsula, foreign visitors and consular officials, many of whom, like Byron, held idealistic notions of the Greeks based on the Greek "Golden Age" of ancient times, were stunned to see mobs of Greeks led by clan chieftains and klephts involved in the wholesale killing of over ten thousand Turkish men, women, and children. Also caught up in the carnage were about two hundred Jewish residents of the town; they, too, were killed by the Greeks, who began to see themselves as Christian "holy warriors." Some of the methods of execution included burning and crucifixion.

From the spring to the autumn of 1821, the reaction of Sultan Mahmud II was relatively muted, at least in Greece itself, and gave the Greeks a sense of false hope. Mahmud was actually somewhat of a reformer, and he was between attempts to change entrenched and archaic administrative and governmental practices. He also had to contend with tensions with Persia, Russia, and the tribes of the Arabian Peninsula, so he had much more to deal with than the rebellion in Greece.

Not that Mahmud was idle. On Orthodox Easter Sunday, 1821, the Orthodox patriarch of Constantinople, who was responsible for keeping his Christian subjects in line, was hanged outside of his palace and left there for three days. His body was then cut down, and in a sign of how the sultan ruled by the principle of "divide and conquer," it was given to influential Jewish officials, who then dragged the body to the water of the Golden Horn and threw it in. The Greeks and Jews in Constantinople had competed for centuries for influence and power within the Ottoman Empire, and now, they set upon each other once again.

The hanging of the patriarch was a signal to the Greeks of what would happen should they support the rebellion. Throughout Constantinople and the areas of Turkish Thrace and Asia Minor where large numbers of Greeks lived, the sultan and his officials had hundreds of influential and well-to-do Greeks executed. In Anatolia (today's central Turkey), the town of Kydonies (now Ayvalik), which had been mostly Greek for centuries, was destroyed, and its thirty thousand Greek inhabitants were slaughtered. Upon hearing of the Greek atrocities in the Peloponnese, Turkish reprisals spread and grew more savage. On the islands of Rhodes, Cyprus, and Kos (all relatively far from the Greek mainland and none of them fully sold on the idea of rebellion), thousands of Greeks were put to death.

The most infamous Turkish atrocity of them all was on the island of Chios. At the beginning of the rebellion, most Chiotes were either apathetic or against the rebellion. Part of the reason for this was the location of the island, as it was less than four miles from the Turkish mainland. If the sultan wanted to punish Chios, it would not take long. Second, Chios was one of the richest islands in Greece and a prize possession of the sultan. The island was the center of shipping, trade, and mastic (a gummy pine resin that is in various incense, liquor, gum, and wine—definitely an acquired taste!). The merchants on Chios knew that joining the rebellion would be disastrous for them and likely for most of the people on the island.

However, in the early spring of 1822, a few hundred Greek fighters landed on Chios and attacked the Turkish garrison there. They then forced the Turks into the citadel near the capital (also named Chios). By appealing to the islanders' patriotism and making veiled threats, the Greek rebels gained the support of some Chiotes, but the vast majority remained on the sidelines. After all, along the eastern coast of the island, most of the Chiotes could just look out their window and see Turkey.

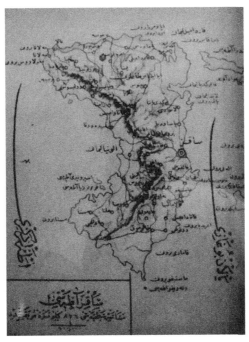

Illustration 11: Ottoman era map of Chios. Courtesy Matthew Gaskill.

On March 22nd, 1822, a large Turkish fleet arrived in the harbor of Chios and seized the city. Eventually, some forty thousand Ottoman troops landed on the island (one for every three inhabitants). On April 12th, orders came for the troops to burn the city of Chios to the ground and to kill all males over twelve, infants, and women over forty. The rest were to be enslaved unless they agreed to convert to Islam. Bags of bones and other remains of the

Chiotes were displayed in parts of Constantinople, both as a warning and a victory symbol.

Over the next few months, about ninety thousand Chiotes were killed, died from disease or malnutrition, or were enslaved. Perhaps twenty thousand escaped the island or hid in its central highlands, and it's estimated only about two thousand to five thousand people remained on the island when the war was over. After Greece had won its independence, many people from the island of Crete were encouraged to settle on Chios to help repopulate the island.

Stories of the massacre on Chios spread throughout Greece and Europe, rallying many more to the Greek cause despite the Greeks committing atrocities such as those described above. In 1824, the famous French painter Eugène Delacroix finished his giant painting, *The Massacre at Chios*, which today takes up almost an entire wall at the Louvre Museum in Paris. The painting, seen below, did much to garner support for the Greeks in France.

Illustration 12: The Massacre at Chios, *Eugène Delacroix, 1824* Chios never recovered its former wealth after the massacre, but the events there did inspire many more Greeks to join the rebellion.

At the start of 1822, the sultan's armies moved into mainland Greece. What they seemed most focused on was putting down Ali Pasha's (Ali of Janina's) rebellion in southern Albania and northwestern Greece, but while they were destroying his forces, they put many of the Greek rebels in northern Greece and the Peloponnese to flight. In Salonika in Thrace and in the city of Naousa in central Greece, Turkish massacres of Greeks occurred, as they did in village after village. In some cases, Greek fighters and civilians threw themselves off cliffs to avoid capture by the Turks. What was left of the rebels on mainland Greece fled to the interior of the southern Peloponnese, as they knew they would be facing even more Ottoman troops once Ali Pasha was defeated, which he was in February. His troops were cornered and besieged, and one among them assassinated Ali and delivered his severed head to the Turkish forces. This was then sent to Constantinople to be put on display to discourage any other ambitious officials.

With Ali Pasha out of the way, the Ottomans could concentrate on the Greeks. They possessed a marked superiority over the Greek forces, who were disorganized, spread out, differed on what path forward to take, and had no real source of income. The Greeks did, however, control the seas, which meant the Turks had to take grueling and narrow coastal roads in order to march on Greek strongholds and to relieve their various fortresses and bases, particularly the one in Athens, which was nearing starvation. Taking to the interior mountains would not have saved much time and would have left the Turks susceptible to the klephts and their guerrilla attacks at which they excelled.

In addition to the Turks' goal of relieving their garrison in Athens, they were also determined to seize Corinth, which made access to the Peloponnese much easier, as well as the town of Missolonghi, which did the same.

The year 1822 started off well for the Turks. Though the garrison in Athens, which was stationed at the Acropolis and had been destroyed by a Venetian barrage in 1687, fell before it could be relieved, the Turks captured the ancient city of Thebes and crossed the Isthmus of Corinth into the Peloponnese, causing a short-lived Greek "government" to flee before them in terror. Many of the klephts fled to the mountains and even debated switching sides.

At the beginning of August, at the citadel of Argos, Alexander Ypsilantis's brother Demetrios (the namesake of Ypsilanti, Michigan, 1793–1832) and a few hundred of his followers held up thousands of Turks under Dramali Pasha before moving out to seek water. Just when the Ottomans could have moved farther into the Peloponnese and perhaps won the war, Dramali Pasha's nerves got the best of him, and he began to move back toward Corinth. Unfortunately for him and the men under his command, he hadn't secured the important and narrow Dervenakia pass leading back to Corinth. There, anywhere between eight and ten thousand klephts and Greek soldiers fell upon the estimated twenty thousand or more Turks, slaughtering most of them. Leading the Greeks were Ypsilantis, and a number of klepht chieftains, the most important and powerful of which was Theodoros Kolokotronis (1770–1843), who later became the head of all the Greek forces in the War of Independence and is a national hero in Greece to this day.

Illustration 13: Kolokotronis and other klepht chieftains at Dervenakia.

The Greek victory at Dervenakia led to the recapture of Corinth, as well as the important Peloponnesian city of Nauplion (also known as Nafplio).

Ypsilantis, Kolokotronis, and many other men were heroes of the Greek War of Independence, but many women fought, gathered, passed intelligence and weapons, and worked as nurses. The most famous woman of the time was Laskarina Pinotsi, better known to Greeks and history as "Bouboulina"—the feminine version of her second husband's name, the rich shipowner and captain Dimitrios Bouboulis, whose fortune she assumed when he was killed in a battle with pirates. Bouboulina was born in a Turkish prison to a woman from the island of Hydra who had been permitted to see her captive husband. Bouboulina, however, lived much of her adult life on the island of Spetses.

When he was killed, Bouboulina took over his affairs and did much business with Russia, for whom her husband had sailed. The Ottomans tried to seize her property, and she fled to the Russian consulate in Constantinople, from where she was then sent to Crimea. She must have been a woman of great charisma because while at the Russian consulate, she actually met Sultan Mahmud II's mother, who convinced her son to leave Bouboulina's property alone.

Bouboulina had a number of ships built before the war with Turkey broke out, including one which she commanded: the *Agamemnon*.

During the war, Bouboulina and other captains prevented Turkish reinforcements from reaching isolated bases and fortresses and raided Turkish-held lands for weapons and resources. Unfortunately, the Greeks in 1824/25 were not only fighting the Ottomans but fighting each other as well.

Illustration 14: Bouboulina in command on her ship, Agamemnon.

In 1824, Bouboulina was arrested by the nominal Greek government for her support of Kolokotronis, who had been jailed both for not following commands (from a government that barely existed) and for seemingly holding ideas about becoming the "Greek Napoleon." She was released back to her home on the island of Spetses in late 1824, but her family became embroiled in a feud over the elopement of Bouboulina's son and his bride. In patriarchal Greece, a young woman did not get married without her father's permission. An armed group from the girl's family marched to Bouboulina's house, and when she went out on the balcony, she was immediately shot in the forehead and died. No one was ever brought to account for her murder.

After her death, Tsar Alexander I of Russia named her an honorary admiral in the Russian Navy, and in 2018, though she had been regarded as a hero in Greece for centuries by then, she was named the rear admiral of the Hellenic (Greek) Navy.

Fortunately for the Greeks, the Ottoman forces faced considerable problems as well. But despite having sustained a number of defeats at the hands of the Greeks and losing control over many Greek islands, the Greek forces really only controlled a large part of the southern portion of the country—the Peloponnese and the rugged mountains in the center and far north of the country.

However, due to the Greeks' control of the sea, the Turks were forced to march long distances for each campaign, and this could only truly be done in the relatively good weather of late spring and summer. This also forced the Ottomans to plan exceedingly well, something they did not always do, and at this point, Sultan Mahmud II had to deal with large-scale corruption in his forces, mainly in the elite Janissaries.

By this time, the Janissaries were made up of not only men who had been taken from their homes as children but also foreign volunteers and the children of Janissaries. They had grown in size to about 100,000 men at the turn of the century, and they could make or break governments. By this time, they also had to be bribed into fighting in Greece, whether it was with money, gold, jewels, lands, and/or positions.

Though the Turkish forces were fraught with troubles, so were the Greeks, and like the Ottomans, the trouble was of their own making.

In Greece, the rebels were divided into four main factions: Western-thinking Greeks, rich landowners, former Greek Ottoman officials, and the klephts (though among the klephts and landowners, there were factions within factions within factions).

In the early 1800s, the ideals of the French Revolution spread throughout Europe. It was brought to foreign lands by French troops and the writings of the Enlightenment and revolutionary authors. Among the educated and more wealthy Greeks of the diaspora in Russia, France, Italy, England, and elsewhere, these ideals were the perfect answer to the problems they faced, and since many of the ideas of the Enlightenment were based on modern thoughts on the ancient Greeks, it seemed a perfect fit for a future Greek state.

The wealthy landowners felt differently. They wanted to hold onto their land and influence. Some of them might have been in favor of an English-style bicameral system where they would be members of the Greek "House of Lords," but most of them believed that they should govern. They saw the Greek people as being uneducated and used to authoritarian government, so they thought the common people were not ready for the kind of "freedom" the "Western Greeks" preached.

The klephts sort of blew with the wind, but all of them (meaning their leaders) wanted a say, and since they had done much of the fighting, as opposed to Western-style soldiers raised by other wealthy Greeks, they expected a say in the country's future. In the interim, the klephts raided one another's territory and took what they needed and wanted from poor villagers throughout the country.

In 1824/25, the war was at a stalemate. The Greeks were fighting among themselves and were not strong enough to defeat the Turks on the mainland. The Ottomans were not able to subdue the Greeks and were confronted by the problems described above. The Greeks had hoped that the people of the Balkans and the Russians would help them, but that was a pipe dream. The only hope the Greeks had was to win a stunning victory and show the foreigners that victory was possible or to sustain more of the horrors inflicted on them by the Turks, such as that on Chios.

The sultan needed more forces to retain and regain his Greek territories, and the only way to do that was for him to ask one of his powerful vassals for help. By the 1800s, the power of the sultan was not what it had been. In the 1500s or 1600s, all the sultan had to do was command a vassal, and it would be done. By the 1800s, however, corruption, the rise of powerful administrators, and the ever-present fear of assassination, on top of long distances and the lack of a treasury, meant that Sultan Mahmud II had to call upon his vassal, the powerful Mehmet (Muhammad or Mehmed) Ali of Egypt, for aid. Mehmet was, like Ali of Janina, an Albanian who had risen through the ranks of the Ottoman government. He had established himself as the governor of Egypt, but in actuality, he was its ruler. In order to secure the help of Mehmet Ali, Mahmud II had to promise him the rule over Crete and his eldest son, Ibrahim, the rule over the Peloponnese when the war was over.

In the spring of 1824, the forces under Ibrahim landed in Crete and began marshaling forces for the invasion of the Peloponnese, which occurred about nine months later in January 1825. Now with a powerful naval force and armies both well equipped and trained in Western tactics, Ibrahim's men began to drive deep into the Peloponnese.

Greek infighting had weakened their forces, and the guerrilla tactics that had been previously used against the Turks did not have much effect on Ibrahim's troops and his experienced commanders. The Greeks even released Theodoros Kolokotronis from prison in the hope that he could rally the Greek forces and defeat Ibrahim's armies but to no avail. Throughout their march north, the Ottoman forces conducted a campaign of terror, capturing thousands of Greeks and opening a huge slave market in the city of Modon (Methoni). Elsewhere, entire villages were destroyed, livestock seized, and fields and orchards burned.

The only "bright" spot was at the Battle of the Lerna Mills, which protected the city of Nauplion (the seat of the Greek government, such as it was). There, Demetrios Ypsilantis, along with two other men whose names are familiar to Greeks today, Yannis Makriyannis and Andreas Metaxas, and three hundred soldiers with two gunboats held off an Egyptian/Ottoman force of five thousand, preventing the seizure of the city and the government.

By 1826, the Greeks held just a small part of the northern Peloponnese around Nauplion, the Isthmus of Corinth, and the town of Missolonghi, and they were besieged and isolated in the Acropolis in Athens. It seemed like nothing could save the Greeks from defeat except foreign intervention.

Foreign intervention would come in two forms, but before nations like England became involved in the conflict, some of their citizens, known collectively today as the "Philhellenes" ("those who love Greece and the Greeks"), volunteered to help the Greek cause.

The rise of the Philhellenic movement in Europe was a boon to the Greeks. However, the fact the War of Independence and the Romantic movement happened all at the same time shouldn't be discounted as they all influenced each other. Throughout western Europe, many young men and quite a few wealthy women were attracted to the Greek cause. The struggle of the Greeks and the desire to aid them fit perfectly with the renaissance of learning the Greek classics and antiquity. It also seemed to fit the ideals of the Enlightenment for men to be free and with the Romantic ideals of individualism, emotion, and adventure.

As you read earlier, the most famous of the Philhellenes was George Gordon, Lord Byron, who was already famous in Great Britain for his poetry and wealth and infamous for his many affairs (one of them with his half-sister, which was the immediate cause of his leaving England). In January 1824, Byron arrived in Greece in style. He brought nine servants, an assortment of military uniforms, a personal doctor, and crates of books. Byron was in Greece (at Missolonghi) for a total of three months before succumbing to fever brought on by malaria. In that short time, he worked to try to bring the various Greek factions together to work as one against the Turks. He was not very successful in this, but his fame, his work, and his death, which came at a time when Philhellenism and Romanticism were at their height in Europe, did much to bring attention to the Greeks' plight. Byron is a hero in Greece today, but to be frank, the poet was shocked by the primitive attitudes and cruelty he met among some of the Greek factions.

Illustration 15: Statue dedicated to Byron in Athens. Here, Byron is in the arms of a loving Greece.

Other Europeans had more of a literal effect on the war. Some of them raised money to buy weapons, ships, and equipment for the Greeks, much of which was sent along with volunteers who came from England, France, and Italy. One of the most famous volunteers was British naval officer Frank Dabney Hastings, who had actually joined the Greek navy at the beginning of the struggle and distinguished himself in many battles at sea. Another was Earl Thomas Cochrane, an adventurer who, among many other things, hijacked much of the Brazilian Navy and fought for many Latin

American countries in their fight for independence from Spain. Unfortunately, the principal plan of these two British expatriates failed. They wanted to build a modern navy powered by steam. Much of the money was lost to corruption and incompetence. Only one ship, which was built in America, was completed. Others blew apart due to faulty steam engines, and others lay half-built on the Thames in England, victims of bankruptcy.

Despite the Philhellenes' seeming failure, their participation and the news coverage that followed them (much of it a glorified half-truth) caused many of the governments, especially in England and France, to take notice. It also helped that the educated public put great pressure on them to come to the aid of "poor Greece."

Even the tsar in Russia, who had not wanted to involve itself in the conflict, preferring the familiar status quo with the Ottomans, came to believe that he had to do something to protect the Orthodox faith in Greece, where the Turks were destroying churches and killing clergymen. In 1825, the Russians announced they would support the idea of three small Greek territories that would be under the sultan's control while remaining largely autonomous. Though this was progress, it was not what the Greeks wanted.

In England, in 1822, a new government under Prime Minister George Canning had come to power. Although England had originally been against the Greek bid for independence for the same reasons as the Russians (upsetting the status quo and possibly the balance of power in Europe), as the years went by, Canning and many Britons began to show support for the Greeks.

In July of 1825, the Greek government asked the British to make Greece a protectorate, which was rejected by the British since they knew the rest of Europe would object. Still, Canning was working toward achieving peace in Greece and had approached King Charles X of France for help. Together with the Russians, the British and French drew up the Treaty of London, which stated that there should be an autonomous Greek state under the sultan.

The borders of this small state would be negotiated when peace came.

Of course, the Ottomans had no interest in this "treaty" that had been written without them; besides that, they were winning. However, that was about to change, for a fleet of English, Russian, and French ships were sent to Greece to prevent the resupply of Ibrahim's army. They were met by a Turkish and Egyptian fleet near Navarino (on the southwest coast of the Peloponnese) on October 20th, 1827. In perhaps the last European battle of sailing ships, the Allied fleet utterly destroyed the Ottoman naval forces.

Over the course of the next two years, a Greek government was slowly put together, and Ioannis Kapodistrias, the former Russian foreign minister, was named president. The war went on, but the outbreak of conflict between Turkey and Russia in 1828 near the Caspian and Black Seas meant that Greece was a lost cause for the Turks. They simply did not have enough manpower to hold off the Greeks, English (Lord Cochrane was one of two English officers that had been put in charge of the Greek war effort, with the agreement of the Greek factions), French, and Russians in Greece and fight a war with Russia in the north at the same time.

Chapter 5 – Small Greece, Big Ideas, and Many Wars

Even as the Greeks were embroiled in their war with the Ottomans, they fought among themselves, sometimes savagely. However, with the increased involvement of the major European powers (England, France, and Russia), the Greeks were forced to come to some kind of solution to their issues, lest the "Great Powers" back out and the Turks take over once again.

In May of 1827, the two Greek assemblies that had formed during the last couple of years managed to put aside their differences long enough to meet, draw up a republican constitution with a president as the chief executive, and name Kapodistrias as president.

Kapodistrias, who had rejected the offer of leading the Greeks in 1820, reluctantly accepted. His experience in government was in Russia, which hardly possessed a representative government, and he personally was authoritarian in style. His first goal was to grow Greece's border as much as possible before the Great Powers imposed a settlement on him and the Ottomans. He wanted to build a unified national army, but he would not have time for that, so he sent bands of klephts to the north and northwest to seize as much territory as possible. None of these offensives was successful.

However, Kapodistrias's ideas about what needed to be done in Greece were spot-on: construct an efficient administrative system and civil service and begin to build a nationwide educational system.

The problem wasn't Kapodistrias's plan; it was Kapodistrias. He had spent the war in Russia and on diplomatic travels. In 1827, he was in Geneva when he got word of his nomination. He was known as a workaholic, but he did not know his native land very well, and he also did not know many of those who had fought in the war. He was perceived as aristocratic, which was not necessarily a bad thing at the time, but his attitude toward many of his countrymen was that of the worst kind of snobbish aristocrat. To him, the major landowners were "Christian Turks." The Phanariots, those Greeks who had been raised in Constantinople and were close to the seat of Ottoman power, were known as the "Children of Satan." The klephts were "robbers," and the "Western Greeks" who prided themselves on being the bearers of Enlightenment and French Revolutionary thoughts and ideals of the French Revolution were "fools." Within a very short time, Kapodistrias alienated virtually all of the factions he needed to complete the war and establish a unified government.

In the end, all of Kapodistrias's efforts came to naught. By 1829, the Great Powers were the ones calling the shots, not the Greek president. Though the powers eventually settled on the idea of a Greek monarchy, which leaned more toward the English model than the Russian, they also began to see Greece as a place to either grow their own power or limit that of the others.

In 1829, the Russians emerged victorious in their war over the Turks, which they felt gave them the right (or at least the power) to dictate much of what went on in Greece. The English, not wishing to see the Russians gain important influence and especially warm-water ports in the Mediterranean, were adamant that the Ionian Islands (those former Venetian islands in the northwest of modern Greece near Albania) would remain under their protection, as well as the coastline opposite them. Knowing a weak Greece would not be able to stop Russian intervention, the British prime minister, the famed Duke of Wellington, who had defeated Napoleon at Waterloo, insisted on making the territory a British protectorate, which it was until 1864.

The Russians exerted pressure on the Turks and had made gains in their war, which had broken out over treaty violations involving the Russians' involvement in the Battle of Navarino. The Russians won territories in the Danube Delta and parts of what is now southern Russian and the Caucasus.

The French hoped that by evacuating Ibrahim's Egyptian army from Greece and taking them home, they would have influence over both the Greeks and the Ottomans.

What all three powers agreed upon was a small Greece that did not threaten the borders of Asia Minor or Constantinople and that Kapodistrias had to go. Kapodistrias had already become highly unpopular because of both his attitude and his prevention of various war leaders to either seize or keep the spoils of war they had gained in the war's last days.

The Great Powers cast about, looking among the royal houses of Europe for a prince who would accept the position of the first "King of Greece." The first royal they offered the position to was Prince Leopold of Saxe-Coburg, who declined on the grounds that the borders of his potential new kingdom were too small (he eventually became King Leopold I of Belgium—hardly a giant country).

The search for a king took on urgency when, at the beginning of October 1831, the klephtic chieftains and brothers Constantine and Georgios Mavromichalis assassinated Kapodistrias on the stairs of a church in Athens. Kapodistrias was shot in the head and stabbed in the heart, and he died instantly. One of the brothers was beaten to death by the nearby crowd, and the other was executed just days later. Despite his unpopularity at the time, Kapodistrias is honored in Greece today, at the very least for his hard work for the newly independent country.

A few months later, the Great Powers, fearing a civil war, made Greece a protectorate until they could find a suitable monarch who was acceptable to both themselves and the Greeks. They eventually settled on Prince Otto, the son of King Ludwig I of Bavaria (Germany was not a united country until 1871 and was divided into many independent states). Otto took the name "Otho" and became Otho I, King of the Greeks.

Unfortunately for Greece, Otho was more of an autocrat than Kapodistrias, and a new constitution created a unicameral legislature over which the king had much power. As king, Otho already had much power, and a popular uprising in 1843 backed by the army left Otho with even more, such as veto power, the power to appoint and fire ministers, and dissolve parliament. However, he was forced by a popular vote of men—women would not get to vote in Greece until 1952—to agree to a bicameral legislature and call elections.

Otho unfortunately also brought in many of his Bavarian subjects and advisers, whose culture and ideas about the role of government differed greatly from those of most Greeks, who, unlike the Germans of the time, valued individual freedoms and rights and were, to say the least, "tax-avoidant." They also resented Otho's place as the head of the Greek Orthodox Church, which put him at odds with not only the people but also the church hierarchy. Making matters worse, Otho placed a large number of Phanariot Greeks in his government. Many saw the Phanariot Greeks as foreigners at best and Turkish stooges at worst.

To be fair, while Otho was not popular, Greek factions, especially the klephts, did not help matters. These bands, meaning their chieftains, were not eager to relinquish their power. Making matters worse, they were often used by politicians and various factions as strongmen to intimidate others, including voters.

Corruption, which had been endemic to the later Ottoman occupation, simply carried over into the newly independent country. The army, in particular, was rife with it, and bribery was almost a necessity for a promotion of any kind, which meant the rich and/or influential and oftentimes the incompetent moved up the ranks.

Corruption, tax evasion, inexperience, and much else prevented Greece from advancing into the 19th century, which was already moving into the Industrial Revolution, especially in Great Britain and the German states. There were no railroads in Greece for quite some time. There were no modern roads, and there was only one real source of export: currants. And that depended on horse and donkey transportation and a shipping fleet that was rapidly declining with the advent of the steam engine. Just to keep itself running, the Greek government went into massive debt, which eventually meant that paying off the interest on that debt consumed money that would have been better spent on infrastructure.

To expect a newly independent nation to move from a relatively primitive (economically speaking) former colony nearly five hundred years old into a modern one in a decade or two was unrealistic. On top of that, the problems mentioned above actually caused many Greeks to move into the prosperous areas of the Ottoman Empire. Constantinople, the coast of Asia Minor, and Egypt had significant and relatively well-off populations of ethnic Greeks within them. Many of the islands that are today part of Greece were, for a considerable time after its independence, still part of the Ottoman Empire. These included the large islands of Crete, Cyprus, and Rhodes, as well as many of the islands in the eastern Aegean, of which the aforementioned Chios is one.

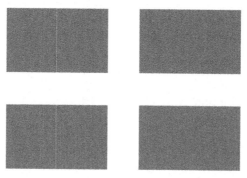

Illustration 16: Greek flag: 1822–1978.

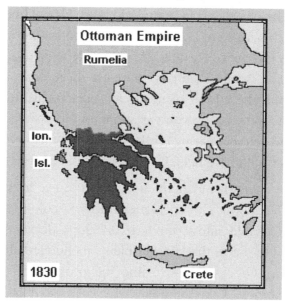

Illustration 17: Greece in 1830. "Rumelia" is the Ottoman term used at the time to describe that part of the Balkan Peninsula.

The "Megali Idea" (pronounced "meh-gol-li ee-thay-a"), or "Great Idea"

Making things worse was the rise of an idea that would lead Greece into disaster in the early 1920s. As you can see from the map above, the nation that was Greece immediately after the War of Independence was a much smaller version of modern Greece. Much of the mainland and many islands were still controlled by Turkey or warlords ostensibly loyal to them. Many Greeks still lived under Turkish or foreign control in what they considered their homeland. What's more, perhaps a few million ethnic Greeks lived in parts of the Ottoman and Russian Empires that could not, with the possible and ancient exception of the coast of Asia Minor, be considered a part of Greece proper.

Illustration 18: Ethnic Greeks in Ottoman Empire in shades of purple (Armenians in brown), 1900. There were also small numbers of Greeks along the Russian Black Sea.

Nationalism in Europe was spawned in the French Revolution and its aftermath. Rather than think of themselves as subjects of a monarch, people began to think of themselves in terms of their ethnicity, culture, and language to a much greater degree than previously.

For the Greeks, whose distant ancestors were the focus of a new interest in Europe and America in the 18th and 19th centuries, nationality took on a new meaning. Many Greeks at the time of independence and thereafter began to feel that they were the inheritors of the glories of ancient Greece. It makes sense that they would, as the last time that the Greeks could say they were truly independent and not part of a larger entity was the time of the ancient Greek city-states. Like many nationalists, especially ones in search of an identity after centuries of foreign domination, Greeks looked back to a "Golden Age" when life was as perfect as life on Earth can get. In the case of the Greeks, they literally could look back on what people all over the world called and still call the "Golden Age of Greece," which gave so much to the world.

In the chambers of the Greek parliament, in cafés, the parlors of the well-off, and in the mountain strongholds of the klephts, the idea that all Greeks should be included in the new nation was born. Never mind that the new nation was barely independent, rife with corruption, and under the watchful eyes of the greatest powers in Europe, which included the Ottoman Empire.

Though the "Megali Idea" never really took on the biological aspect of the Nazis in Germany in the 1930s, proponents of it did ignore almost two thousand years of history and assume that all Greeks were direct descendants of the ancient Greeks, which, of course, was not true.

One relative positive to the Megali Idea was that it united many Greeks, at least on one issue, at a time when unity was hard to come by. The idea that the Greeks were inheritors of the ancient Greek ideal did have some positives. One of them was a large building program that expanded the capital city of Athens, and some of the newer buildings, including the building that parliament was housed in, were designed on ancient lines.

Greek students in Greece and in the homes of Greeks in Ottoman lands (and, later, Greeks in the diaspora as far afield as the United States and Australia) were taught about the glories of ancient Greece and the supposed birthright of Greeks to be united under one banner and within the same borders. Unfortunately, a side effect of this was that a "new" version of what was believed to be the ancient Greek language was taught in upper-class homes. This language, called *Katharevousa* ("clean," meaning theoretically free of foreign words), was made the language of the press, religion, and government. The problem was that the majority of Greeks, who did and do speak *demotiko* or "demotic" Greek, did not speak it and did not want to learn it. Even until recent times, the change in language divided Greeks, with some political and socioeconomic factions supporting one or the other. These factions saw each other as "enemies" at times, for example, during the Greek Civil War, which followed WWII, and the military junta of

1967 to 1974 (the end of which ended *Katharevousa* seemingly for good).

The Megali Idea was used by Otho I as a distraction from both his disastrous policies and personal unpopularity in an attempt to unite the Greeks in 1839 when the Greeks of Crete rose up against the Turks and nationalist Greeks attempted to cause trouble in Asia Minor (both were put down harshly by the Ottomans). The same held true in 1854 when the Ottomans, along with the English and French, who were now Turkish allies against Russia in the Crimean War (1853–1856), were distracted in their fight to the north. The badly led and disorganized Hellenic Army invaded European Thrace only to be pushed back by the Ottomans. The British and French then invaded and controlled the major port of Piraeus near Athens and forced Otho to allow them to "supervise" Greek politics and internal affairs for the next few years. The first two Greek adventures attempting to promote the Megali Idea were disasters, and it would get worse in the next century.

It was only Otho's support of the Megali Idea that allowed him to remain on the throne. At home, his rule had become more authoritarian, and economic development had been slow, sporadic, or nonexistent, depending on where in Greece one lived and who one was.

In the 1850s and early 1860s, the independent states of Italy fought with each other and other powers to become a united and politically liberal country, at least for the time. In Greece, students and younger members of the army looked to Italy as a model for what they wanted Greece to be. In 1862, rebellions against Otho and his policies took place throughout Greece, which eventually forced him to abdicate after thirty years of rule.

A popular vote resulted in the replacement of Otho with a grandson of Great Britain's famous Queen Victoria, Prince Alfred, but the other powers of Europe, which were facing an already powerful British Empire, would not allow this, at least not peacefully. Eventually, the kingship was offered to Prince William of Holstein-Sonderburg-Glücksburg (on the German-Danish border—his father would become the king of Denmark the next year). Prince William became George I, King of the Hellenes—this last word is important. It signifies that George wasn't becoming king to the Greeks, those people who lived within the borders of Greece. Rather, he was the king over *all* Greeks; in other words, he was showing his acceptance and support for the Megali Idea.

Under George and in fits and starts throughout the rest of the 1800s, Greece slowly began to establish the makings of a modern state. Railways were laid down, shipping was improved, an economically powerful merchant fleet was built, much land was reclaimed for development, and agricultural techniques were improved. Revisions in the tax code and the way money was spent meant that the debt was eased, and the government was made more effective and responsive, though it was still a far cry from that of England or other western European countries. Still, improvements were made, and generally speaking, the life of many Greeks improved in the latter part of the 1800s.

Unfortunately, the one area that lagged might have been the most important: industry. By the latter part of the 1870s, less than ten thousand people in the country worked in factories, and at the outbreak of WWI for Greece in 1917, there were only about forty thousand. Still, with the help of foreign investment, Piraeus became one of the great ports of Europe, and the opening of the Corinth Canal greatly reduced shipping times from west to east.

By the late 1800s, Greece had shown signs of advancement, and in at least one area—shipping—it was one of the world's leaders. Still, though it seemed to many Greeks to be a positive and a uniting notion, the Megali Idea persisted, and unfortunately, a number of small successes allowed many Greeks to believe that uniting all Greeks (at least in the Mediterranean, the Aegean, and Asia Minor) was a real possibility. In the late 1800s, Greece was torn by factionalism. For the most part, this was limited to politics and did not extend into violence. On the question of Greece's borders and who should be within them, there were three main factions. We've already discussed one of them, the "Megali Idea," which appealed to most Greeks. The opposite of this was the "Mikro Idea" ("mee-kro ee-they-ah"), or, as you can probably guess, "The Small Idea." Proponents of the true Mikro Idea were content, for the time being, on Greece remaining as it was after the War of Independence, believing that the nation should establish itself on a secure footing politically, economically, and militarily before attempting any expansion of its borders. Others believed that Greece should grow but not to the extent of the Megali Idea. They believed that it was possible to identify and form a Greek nation where Greek was and had been the dominant culture and language and Greek Orthodoxy the dominant religion. These people realized, rightly, that any attempt to expand Greece's territory into the Balkans, for example, would be met with great hostility, not only by the people there but also by the Great Powers.

The proponents of the Megali Idea and those who believed in a larger but contained Greece could at least agree that many of the islands of the Aegean should lay within Greece's borders, and the first among those was Crete, the largest island of them all.

The Cretans themselves had rebelled against Ottoman rule periodically throughout the Turkish occupation. There was an uprising during the War of Independence, which was quashed with brutality by the Ottoman forces. From 1829 through 1866, the vast majority of the people of Crete called for *enosis*– ("union") with Greece.

In 1866, a massive uprising began on Crete, calling once again for *enosis*. Not only were many thousands of the island's people demanding union with Greece but so were Greek officers (supposedly against orders but with the knowledge and aid of the Greek government) and soldiers on the Greek mainland. They rallied to the Cretan cause and went to fight the Turks and other Ottoman troops on the island. Philhellenes in Europe and America raised money and even outfitted a warship to aid the Cretans. The

Greek government also tried to form a military alliance with the Serbs in order to form a possible second front to both aid the Cretans and perhaps gain territory in Europe at the sultan's expense.

Within Crete, as you can probably imagine, things took a bloody toll, as the island was also home to a significant and wealthy population of Greek Muslims, who mostly lived in the central highlands and ports on both ends of the large island. Crete was one of the very few islands where Greeks had actually converted in any sizable numbers, and during the uprising, the result was not only a political but also a bloody religious war.

However, as it was obvious that at this point in time, Turkey had no intention of relinquishing one of its most important and last remaining outposts in the Mediterranean, the Great Powers once again stepped in and forced the Greek government to stand down. This resulted in not only much bitterness but also the deaths of hundreds of Cretan civilians, as the Ottoman forces went on a rampage at the end of the uprising in 1869. For their part, the Greeks and Cretans were only given a vague promise, which was secured by the Great Powers, that Turkey might one day reform its rule on Crete to allow for more autonomy.

For the rest of the 19th century, both Greeks and Cretans were frustrated in their hopes for both the Megali Idea (or some form of it) and *enosis*. In 1876/77, the Serbs and Montenegrins rose up against the Ottomans in the Balkans, hoping to push the Turks out of the Balkans for good and to enact their own version of the "Megali Idea" by including more Serbs and Montenegrins within their own small borders. At the same time, the Bulgarians rose up against the Turks, and all of these uprisings had support and aid from Russia. In 1877, the Russians had actually declared war against Turkey, and for a short while, it seemed as if they might take Constantinople.

It seemed to the Greeks that the time was right for them to rise up again against the Turks, and uprisings broke out once more in Crete, as well as Thessaly, central Greece, and the mountainous border areas of Epirus. Unfortunately for the Greeks, the Russians were actually supporting the idea of a "Big Bulgaria," which meant that the idea of a Greek nation jutting into the Balkans and along the Black Sea could not happen. The Russians had sided with their ethnic Slavic brothers at the expense of the Greeks, with whom they shared only a religion. Once again, the revolts were put down harshly by the Ottomans.

Fortunately for the Greeks, however, the peace treaty that ended the war between Turkey and Russia was completely unacceptable to the other powers of Europe, which now included a new "Great Power," a united Germany. An international conference in Berlin was called, and the Russians were forced to back down and give up their support of "Big Bulgaria." However, when the Greeks brought up their own ideas about Greece's borders expanding in the north, they were rejected out of hand.

Over the next few years, the position of Turkey in the region, both due to external and internal problems, weakened. In Crete, the Turks did appoint a Greek governor and allowed some matters to be decided by the Cretans.

In 1885, the Bulgarians went against the decisions of the Berlin Conference and declared independence once again, concerned that the growth of Bulgaria might halt Greek ideas of expansion. Greek Prime Minister Theodoros Deligiannis, worried over the fate of Greeks north of Greece's current borders, ordered a mobilization of Greek forces and prepared them to move north into the mountains of the Balkans to secure territory for Greece. Once again, the British, wishing to maintain the balance of power and stability in the region, interfered. This time, they sent a fleet to blockade Greece and forced them to stand down. Interestingly enough, the British fleet was commanded by Prince Alfred, who had turned down the Greek throne just a few years prior.

The Cretans rose again in 1897/98 and proclaimed the Cretan Republic and demanded *enosis* with Greece. Once again, the mainland Greeks whipped themselves into a state of frenzy, and even the usually cautious royal family got caught up in the call for *enosis*. Greek troops crossed the border with Turkey in Thrace, and for a short time, they occupied Turkish European territory. Greek troops also moved into Epirus but were stopped cold in the mountainous region. A Greek fleet under Prince George (the heir apparent) sailed toward Crete, where most Greek volunteers and Cretan rebels were holed up around the area of Chania (or Hania) and the Akrotiri Peninsula on the northwest coast of the island.

Illustration 19: Crete, which lies about two hundred miles south of the Greek mainland. Courtesy Lonely Planet.

The entire campaign was a disaster for Greece. The Turkish troops in the east and west pushed the Greeks back and approached Athens. Once more, the Great Powers of Europe stepped in, and a naval and marine force from six nations bombarded the Cretans on Akrotiri into surrender. By the late 1800s, the international climate in Europe was tense, to say the least, and the Great Powers did not want the constant Greek uprisings to upset the status quo in the region. They proclaimed Crete an international protectorate, made the Greeks give back all Ottoman lands still in their hands (which was little), pay an indemnity to the Ottomans, and accept an international commission to both supervise the Greek economy to prevent runaway national debt and ensure the nation didn't erupt into chaos. This was a humiliation the Greeks would remember, and they still do, especially since it came from their supposed "friends." The Greeks were reminded of this when the financial crises of the 2000s and onward struck them, forcing them into a similar situation.

Another problem confronting the Greeks was the growth of Slavic nationalism on its northern borders. A few years prior to the Cretan uprising, the Turks allowed the Bulgarians to set up a Bulgarian exarchate (a particularly Orthodox word similar to a bishopric) and an exarch (a high official) who had always been Greek. This further unified Slavic people in the Balkans and seemingly put Bulgaria in a position of power.

For the Greeks, their main concern was the region that is today no less of a crisis point—Macedonia. The ancient Greek word *maćedoine* refers to the mixture of peoples in the area: ethnic Greeks, Turks, Jews, Albanians, Vlachs, and Bulgarians, some of whom were one ethnicity by blood and identified as another by custom or religion. When the Turks set the Bulgarians up in their own high Orthodox office, many Greeks worried that Bulgaria would either claim Macedonia or attempt to seize it either openly or in secret. To the Greek mind, this might also allow the Slavic people to encroach further on land that was traditionally dominated by Greeks, especially around the wealthy city of Salonika.

Illustration 20: Modern map, though the dotted lines indicate the historical region of Macedonia.

Aside from the ethnic and religious problem, the question of Macedonia and who would claim it also brought up a historical question that we will return to toward the very end of the book: the question of Alexander the Great, Prince, then King, of Macedon.

Even before the Cretan uprising in 1897/98, the Greek government had funded expeditions of Greek volunteers and klephts to wage a guerrilla war in Macedonia against similar bands of non-Greeks in the region. Between this, the Cretan uprising, the failed campaign against the Turks, and the costs of governing the nation, Greece was broke when the Great Powers stepped in to get their economy (and their seemingly endless military schemes trying to enact the Megali Idea) under control. All of this brought down a relatively popular government led by Prime Minister Charilaos Trikoupis, who at least had been able to tamp down the factionalism that Greece had been beset by since its independence. For a couple of years after the end of the Cretan rebellion, factionalism tore at Greece.

By 1908, the Balkans were the place where many people believed a major war would start. This eventually happened, although it was not in the Greco-Turkish area of the peninsula, which many expected, but far to the north in Sarajevo.

In 1908, the situation in Macedonia and the area around it got so bad that the Great Powers of Europe once again felt they had to step in to keep the peace. In a number of cities of the European part of the Ottoman Empire, French, Italian, Russian, and British troops landed to keep control. By this point in time, the Ottoman Empire was in such decline, especially in Europe, that the Turks had no choice but to submit.

This submission and the constant loss of territory, combined with the corruption of the empire and much else, led to a revolution in Turkey, which was so profound and shocking to the world that it lent part of its name to the English language. This was the Young Turk Revolution of 1908, which brought younger men from the army, politics, and business together in an attempt to reform the Ottoman Empire and make it more of a constitutional monarchy and less of an absolute one. Prior attempts at reform, along with a more liberal constitution, had been promised and ignored, but the Young Turks succeeded in making the sultan a figurehead, placing the country in the hands of a cabal of officers and a new legislature. In 1912, during a losing effort in the First Balkan War, a more serious coup put the Young Turks in charge of all Turkish affairs. It was the beginning of a move toward Germany and Austria-Hungary.

The rise of the Young Turks also gave new life to a movement that had been boiling just below the surface for years—Turkish nationalism. The Young Turks, generally speaking, felt that too much of the empire was governed and/or populated by non-Turkish people, which had caused innumerable problems over the centuries, especially since the 1800s. These nationalist feelings would end up costing both the Ottoman Empire and many of its people, especially the Armenians and Kurds, dearly.

Reform should have been a good thing for many in the empire, but in actuality, the openness of the rebellion brought home the weakness of the Ottoman state, and one of the main concerns of the Young Turks, the loss of territory, actually got worse.

Bulgaria, which had really been independent for some time, declared its nationhood on October 5th, 1908. The next day, the Austro-Hungarian Empire, which had not been a part of the peace-keeping forces in Greece, seized Bosnia-Herzegovina, along with its capital city of Sarajevo. Elsewhere in the empire, various ethnic groups called for a more representative government and autonomy, which were opposed by the Young Turks.

Once again, the Cretans rose in rebellion against the Turks there. This time, the Greek government was struck by paralysis and took no action, which, in the long run, was a good thing, for shortly after their revolt began, the Great Powers forced the Cretans to back down. Both the submission of the Cretans and the paralysis of the Greek government added to the unhappiness and factionalism of Greece.

Within all of this, however, a man who is still revered among many in Greece and in Greek expatriate communities today came to the fore. His name was Eleutherios (pronounced "Ee-lef-teri-ohss") Venizelos (1864–1936), a Cretan who had played a leading part in the uprisings on the island in 1889 and 1897. Tall, with piercing blue eyes and white hair, Venizelos was charismatic and by all accounts an amazing speaker and debater. Even David Lloyd-George of Britain, who had a similar and much greater reputation in European politics during and immediately after WWI, found Venizelos both hard to argue with successfully or resist.

Illustration 21: Venizelos in the 1920s.

In 1910, Venizelos became the prime minister of Greece, and over the next four years, he built a sense of unity among Greeks that they had not experienced in recent memory. His Liberal Party had won 80 percent of the vote, which allowed Venizelos to push forward with relative ease. One of Venizelos's first and most popular actions was to install a progressive income tax, which eased the tax burden on the poor. Education became both free and compulsory for elementary students. The civil service installed a system of tenure, which cut down on bribery and the effects of political influence. Formerly harsh laws against unions were reformed, a minimum wage for women and children—sadly, child labor was rampant throughout Europe at this time—was instated, a primitive form of worker's compensation began, and sick pay and pensions for retirees were worked on. The great estates in the north of the country, which were inefficiently run by absentee landlords or former "Turkish Greeks" (Greek families who had become wealthy under Turkish rule), were broken up.

Unfortunately, despite all of his domestic success, Venizelos, like virtually all Greek politicians of the time, at least the ones who wished to succeed, was an adherent of the Megali Idea. This eventually would become his downfall.

The Balkan Wars

The Balkan Wars of 1912 and 1913 had their roots in the war between Turkey and Italy, which began in 1911 over Italian claims to Turkish territory in North Africa and its desire to include Albania within its borders, which at the time ran down the Adriatic coast, opposite mainland Italy. Eventually, Italy won control over most of modern-day Libya and the Dodecanese Islands south of Asia Minor (of which Rhodes is the most famous). This only added to the already huge number of problems in the area, as the region was populated by Greeks.

Not only were the Greeks now concerned about the Italians encroaching on what they believed should be their territory, but they also had reason to believe that the Bulgarians were now attempting to unite the Slavic people of the Balkans in an attempt to seize or control Macedonia and the other lands of the Ottoman Empire in Europe. The king of Bulgaria, Ferdinand, who outrageously claimed Bulgaria was the true inheritor of the Byzantine Empire, not Greece or Russia, signed a defense treaty with Serbia. Part of this treaty called for the division of Macedonia between them, and it excluded Greece.

The more effective collection of taxes had allowed Venizelos to begin reforming the military and purchase modern equipment from overseas. Adventurous soldiers from overseas, including many French and British officers, helped train the Greeks on both land and sea. Other military reforms helped both the nation and the institution.

A trip overseas gained Venizelos and Greece an ally in the British Chancellor of the Exchequer, David Lloyd-George. In just a few years, Britain had begun to move away from the Ottomans since their empire was racked from within and without. In addition, an increasingly powerful Germany had developed close relations with the Young Turks.

With some behind-the-scenes aid from the British, Venizelos was actually able to approach both the Serbians and the Bulgarians about a defense treaty against the Turks, as well as action against them. Even tiny newly independent Montenegro, which had designs on areas of northern Albania, joined in.

The First Balkan War

During the first week of October 1912, the Montenegrins attacked Turkish outposts in northern Albania. In ten days, the Greeks, Serbs, and Bulgarians all joined in against the Turks. Most of the fighting on land was done by the Bulgarians, who believed they could seize Constantinople and place themselves in a position of strength. While their attempts at seizing the ancient city failed, the Turks in Europe were driven back to the small area of Thrace, which they still control today. The Greeks, eager to seize the wealthy and important city of Salonika, which was populated mainly by Jews and Greeks, moved in just before Bulgarian troops and claimed the city as part of Greece, which it has been since. The Greeks also moved into the Epirus region and announced that Crete was now part of Greece, inviting Cretans to the Greek parliament. Greek troops also entered the city of Janina (today's Ioannina), which had been the headquarters of Ali Pasha before and during the War of Independence.

Illustration 22: The surrender of Salonika to Greek forces by the Ottomans, October 26ʰ, 1912.

Most people at the time knew that with the Turks driven out of most of Europe, another conflict was likely to erupt among the victors, all of which, as has been described above, coveted areas of the Balkan Peninsula. That conflict was not a long time coming.

Although the Greeks had taken Salonika, united finally with Crete, and pushed the Ottomans out of the Janina/Epirus area, they were concerned with the Bulgarian occupation of Thrace and its position threatening both Constantinople and Salonika. The Serbs and Montenegrins were also concerned about the growing strength and size of Bulgaria, and in the north, Romania had designs on contested territories on its border with the Bulgarians.

The Bulgarians, for their part, felt that they had taken the majority of casualties of the first war, which was true, and that they had not gotten their fair share of the spoils. What's more, they recognized that their former "allies" were now actively plotting against them, especially Macedonia.

The Second Balkan War

On June 1st, 1913, the Serbians and Greeks signed an alliance with each other, which provoked an attack by Bulgarian forces on June 29th, which aimed to push the Greeks and Serbs out of Macedonia. At first, the Bulgarians were successful, but with both Greek and Serbian resistance stiffening and long supply lines, the Bulgarians were soon driven back. On July 2nd and 3rd, the Serbians and Greeks, respectively, attacked the Bulgarians. The Serbians held Bulgarian troops in the center, and the Greeks began to move around the Bulgarians' left flank, which threatened to completely cut them off from their homeland and reinforcements. Making matters worse, on July 11th, the Romanians in the north declared war on Bulgaria, and the Bulgarians were faced with a two-front war they couldn't hope to win.

The war came to a swift end on August 10th, 1913. The Greeks had gained most of southern Thrace (it would gain more at the end of WWI) and southern Macedonia. Serbia gained the region of Kosovo, which they claim as their homeland and is still a bone of contention today. The Serbs also gained most of northern and central Macedonia. Albania became independent under the rule of a German prince, and Romania gained territory in the north. The results of the Second Balkan War pushed Bulgaria into the arms of Germany during WWI and, oddly, with the Ottoman Empire as well.

Illustration 23: The Balkans 1913–1914.

Between the time Venizelos first became prime minister and the end of the Second Balkan War, Greece both knew a degree of internal stability and had more success in expanding its borders than it had seen since the end of the War of Independence in 1832.

To many Greeks, this was not good enough. The Megali Idea demanded that *all* Greeks in the region be brought under one flag, and ideally, Constantinople should be Greek as well. With Turkey weakened and many Greeks still living within its borders, the Serbs and Bulgarians dominating the rest of Macedonia, and the Italians occupying the Dodecanese Islands, the most vocal proponents of the "Big Idea" pushed even harder. Venizelos, agreeing, for the most part, with the Megali Idea and knowing that his political life demanded support for it, continued to push and work for a "Greater Greece."

The years from 1910 to 1913 had seen both stability in government and success at war, but that was all about to end.

Chapter 6 – Much Sadness and Turmoil: The First World War and the Greco-Turkish War of 1921–23

Greece was under no obligation to enter the First World War. Indeed, there were great arguments for not joining either side. It seemed highly unlikely that Greece would join the Turks and their German and Austro-Hungarian allies, but on the other hand, Great Britain and France had not exactly been Greece's friends since the end of the War of Independence. In fact, they had taken the Turks' side far more often than they had the Greeks'.

In addition to all of that, in 1913, the popular King George I (originally from Denmark and the grandfather to Prince Philip of England, late husband of Elizabeth II of England) was assassinated by Alexandros Schinas, who shot the king in the back on a royal visit to Salonika, claiming that the king "owed me some money." Schinas was later made out to be a socialist by the press, but he was more than likely to have been mentally disturbed. The Greeks attempted to make lemonade from lemons by claiming that the accession to power by George's son, Constantine I, was a "sign from heaven" that the Greeks were to reclaim the city of the original Constantine, Constantinople.

Constantine I had led the successful Greek seizure of Salonika, known in Greek as "Thessaloniki," but he was more authoritarian in outlook than his father and was much more apt to use his power.

The First World War began in August 1914, and Greece remained neutral. However, Venizelos pushed for Greek entry into the war on the part of the Allied Powers. He believed that, in the end, the Allied Powers of Great Britain, Russia, and France would be victorious.

Venizelos also realized that Greece's position was quite dangerous. In the north, the Bulgarians had allied themselves with Germany and Austria-Hungary. The Serbs were decisively defeated by the Austrians and sent running south toward Albania and the Adriatic coast, which meant there was nothing except mountains between the Central Powers (Germany, Austria-Hungary, Bulgaria, and the Ottoman Empire) and Greece. In the first half of the war, the Turks were busy fighting the Russians and their allies in the Caucasus area, as well as the British and their allies in the Middle East. In 1915, the United Kingdom and Commonwealth troops landed on the Dardanelles, south of Constantinople. This battle eventually ended in disaster for the Allies, but it kept the Turks from attacking Greece.

Additionally, for historical reasons, it was difficult to foresee any alliance that Greece could make that would have included the Ottomans. The best the Central Powers could hope for from Greece was neutrality, which was what King Constantine and many Greek military officers wanted.

Venizelos was aware of all of the reasons why Greece should stay neutral, but he felt that this would be impossible for a number of reasons. Firstly, Greece had a long coastline, and its economy was dependent on the sea, meaning Greece was quite susceptible to both blockades and attacks from the water. With the Greek economy barely functioning, a blockade by the Allies, who were uncontested in the Mediterranean (even more so after Italy joined them in 1915), could quickly starve Greece into submission. An embargo on Greek exports, which were mostly semi-luxury goods not needed by anyone, would also be disastrous. And lastly, of course, the Allies could swiftly dispatch the Greek navy and bombard Greek fortresses, bases, and cities.

Those were the negatives. Venizelos also believed that there were positives to joining the Allies. He fervently believed they would win, and back in 1914, that was still a big question for most. Thus, Venizelos felt that when the time came to discuss and create the post-WWI world, Greece needed to be at the negotiating table. Neutrality would not do that, but actively joining the Allies would. Being part of the victorious alliance might mean that the Greeks might gain those last significant parts of the "Greek nation" included in the Megali Idea: the coast of Asia Minor, the last remaining part of Thrace, which belonged to the Turks and Bulgarians, perhaps the Dodecanese Islands that was then controlled by Italy, and a number of Turkish-controlled islands in the Aegean. Some of Venizelos's supporters even dreamed of Greek control of Constantinople.

Venizelos went as far as to offer control of the Greek army (also known as the Hellenic Army) to the British and make offers of recently won Greek territory in the north to Serbia in exchange for later gains after the war had ended in their favor. When the king and many of the top army brass found out about this, they were outraged.

However, Venizelos's hand was not the strongest, especially if he wanted so much in return. The Greek army was not as strong as it had been before the Balkan Wars, and the Greek navy, while enough to keep the Turks out of Greek waters, was also small. In order for Greece to profit from the peace treaty Venizelos expected would be the Allies to dictate, he sweetened the pot, and this was where much trouble within Greece began. We'll return to that in a moment.

For his part, King Constantine I pushed for neutrality, even though he was secretly in favor of the Central Powers. The king was a powerful political figure, and he had the power of veto in many cases, as well as the ability to order the resignation of the prime minister and call elections.

In June of 1915, the elections in Greece gave Venizelos, his party, and his platform a majority of the votes. Within a very short time after the election, he allowed the retreating Serbian Army to cross the border into Greece and be shipped to safety in Corfu under the shield of the British Royal Navy. He then accepted a plan by the British and French to land troops at Thessaloniki (Salonika) to forestall any Bulgarian or Turkish moves into the area and perhaps launch an offensive into their territory. Under a treaty signed between Greece and the Great Powers in 1833, the British and French had the right to do this, but that did not mean that all Greeks, especially in the military and those close to the king, liked it.

For their part, the Allied Powers made vague offers to Greece about territorial gains after the war, including parts of southern Bulgaria and, most importantly, the coast of Asia Minor, where many ethnic Greeks lived. (Under the Young Turk regime, many ethnic Greeks found that they were becoming more and more persecuted, and this, combined with historical claims on the area and Allied "promises" of territory there, pushed Venizelos and his followers toward the Allies.) In the end, it turns out that the British and French had made similar promises to the Italians: land immediately to the north of Greece, perhaps the Ionian Islands, undisputed control of the Dodecanese, and control of Albania. This all came out after the Greeks had entered the war in 1917, as Vladimir Lenin in Russia gained possession of Allied communications and released them to the world. Back in 1915 and

1916, however, this was all in the future. Between that time period, the Allies took advantage of Venizelos's offer and his popularity among the Greeks to land troops and ships on Crete and other Greek islands in Aegean, take control of a fortress inside Thessaloniki, and destroy a vital communications hub linking north Greece to the south because they feared the Bulgarians might seize it. This was all done without Greek permission. The king and the military, on the other hand, felt that by aligning themselves with the Allies, Greece would perhaps be giving away territory for good, as well as the control of its own army and land, at least for the duration of the war.

Allied troops in Thessaloniki also added to the problem. The British and French soldiers there were quickly given a nickname by the Greeks: "The Gardeners of Thessaloniki." All they seemed to do was dig, not fight.

In 1915 and 1916, the elections were boycotted by Venizelos and his followers, who simply carried on governing, explaining to anyone who would listen that they had already won elections before that showed overwhelming support for their platform. However, as time went by, more Greeks came to resent the attitude of the Allies for all of the reasons mentioned above. In the spring of 1916, the generals in command of the Greek army announced that they would not allow the Serbs on Corfu to move to Thessaloniki, where they were supposed to link with British and French troops. Even worse, from the standpoint of Venizelos and his followers, who were called "Venizelists," there were a number of incidents in the north of Greece where Greek officers had simply evacuated key border points and given them to Bulgarian and German troops. Within Greece in late 1915, many Venizelist officials were purged; in this case, they were removed from their positions and exiled. (Later in Greek history, political purges often took an exceedingly violent turn.)

To Venizelos, this was treason, and he was determined to do something about it. Because of the strength of the pro-German officers, he fled the mainland for his homeland of Crete in October 1916 and announced a new Greek government. Essentially, there were two Greeces. The king enjoyed support in what was known as "pre-1913 Greece," which consisted of its old borders, and "New Greece," which included many of the islands and territories gained in the wars from 1912 to 1913.

This was the beginning of what is known to Greeks as the National Schism, which pitted authoritarian, right-wing factions, often including the top ranks of the military from colonel on up, and corporations against more liberal factions, which included much of the middle class, poor, and urban population. This "schism" was felt in Greek politics through the 1970s and perhaps beyond.

With the division of Greece and the possibility that the king might join the Central Powers, the Allies acted quickly. In November 1916, the French issued a series of demands to the Greeks. All personnel of the Central Powers in Greece were to be expelled (ambassadors, diplomats, military attachés, journalists, etc.), the Greek navy was to be disarmed, the main north-south railway was to be put under Allied control, and artillery installations were to be given to the Allies.

Illustration 24: Constantine I of Greece.

All of this, of course, caused great anger within Greece, even among some supporters of Venizelos. When a sizable British-French force landed at the leading Greek port of Piraeus south of Athens, they were met with fierce Greek resistance. They sustained heavy casualties and were forced back to their ships. In response, the numerous Allied naval ships off the coast began to shell the city and bombard the royal palace in Athens, which was not far away. They then began a blockade of southern Greece and the Peloponnese, which, by January, had impacted Greece's economy and caused mass hunger.

By January 1917, the king had had enough and agreed to the Allies' terms. Royalist army units were ordered to leave Athens and the Peloponnese, and Constantine was pressured to abdicate and leave the country. His second son, Alexander, was made the new king of Greece (his first son, George, was unacceptable to the Allies for pro-German sympathies). Five months later, Eleutherios Venizelos returned with what was called the "Lazarus Parliament" of his followers (named for rising from the political dead).

When Venizelos returned, two things occurred. Greece joined the Allies, and a cycle of political revenge began, which continued far into the 20th century. In response to Constantine I's removal of the Venizelist officials in 1915, the Venizelists removed many royalist officers and officials and sent many of them into exile on Corfu, where they could be prevented from escaping via the British navy.

Greece's entry into WWI was somewhat anti-climactic. In the spring of 1917, Greek troops took part in an offensive in Macedonia that achieved nothing but heavy casualties. It was not until almost a year later, in May 1918, that Greek troops were involved in heavy fighting, this time against the Bulgarians. This offensive restored some pride to a divided Greek army and pushed the Bulgarians back a considerable distance from the Greek border in Thrace. In September, the Greeks, many of whom were from Crete, joined a British force in a fierce battle of attrition against the Bulgarians near Lake Doiran, north of Thessaloniki. After a prolonged battle, the Bulgarians moved out of their positions to avoid being outflanked to the east.

Illustration 25: Greek volunteer militia, 1917.

In October 1918, Greek and British troops in Thrace were given orders to march eastward toward Constantinople. This motivated the Greeks, who hoped to retake "their" city after five hundred years of Ottoman rule, but as the Allied forces approached the Turkish border, they received word of the Ottomans' surrender. Now, the only way that Greece could move toward the goals of the Megali Idea was at the conference table at Versailles, France, where the victorious Allies prepared to create a "new" Europe.

Despite the personal popularity of Venizelos among the diplomats at Versailles, especially among the British, whose delegation was led by Venizelos's friend and admirer David Lloyd-George, the Greeks emerged with very little after WWI. Venizelos lobbied anyone who would listen to him, and he was both well armed with "facts," which very clearly skewed in Greece's favor, and persuasion but to no real avail.

Venizelos knew that Greek possession of Constantinople would never happen, but he hoped that an international administration would favor the Greeks. He wanted the return of the Dodecanese Islands to Greece, but Italy kept them. The Italians also began making claims on mainland Turkey, which was in disarray with the fall of the Ottoman regime and the Young Turks that the war engendered.

Other than keeping the Dodecanese and some minor concessions on the Adriatic coast of what is today Croatia, the Italians, who lost hundreds of thousands of men in the war, left Versailles with very little. What's more, the "Big Three" of France, Britain, and the United States had treated Italy as a minor partner, insulting Italy's honor. By April 1919, the Italians were preparing to take matters into their own hands. They walked out of the remaining talks going on in France and sent ships in the direction of the major city of Smyrna (today's Izmir in Turkey), directly opposite the Greek island of Chios and home to a majority Greek population.

This alarmed Venizelos and most Greeks, and he asked the Allies—meaning the British and French—if they would not interfere if Greece landed a force in Smyrna (ostensibly to protect the Greeks from the Italian troops) before the Italians could get there. Not wanting to see an over-powerful Italy in the Mediterranean, they agreed, and before terms of the Greek occupation in Smyrna could be discussed, the Greeks had sent troops to occupy the city and the surrounding area.

The Greco-Turkish War, 1919–1922

With the Greeks in control of part of Asia Minor for the first time in five hundred years, it seemed to many Greeks that the culmination of the Megali Idea was at hand. In France, Venizelos had presented his ideas of the lands in Asia Minor that should be given to Greece, seen in the picture below:

Zone claimed by Greece ━ ━ ━ ━
at the Paris Peace Conference

As you can see, Venizelos's plan was quite ambitious. It was also extremely unrealistic. Even on the coast, Greeks were only the majority in the area just south of Smyrna, north to around the town of Ayvali, and a few miles inland. In other places along the coast, Greeks and Turks were relatively evenly balanced, but the farther south and inland one went, the greater the number of Turks and the fewer number of Greeks. Even many adherents of the Megali Idea were skeptical of Venizelos's claims farther inland.

But in August of 1920, the Treaty of Sèvres between the Turks and the Allies gave Greece almost all of what Venizelos had wanted. The Greeks would get Smyrna and a large area around it for five years, at which point a plebiscite would be held, asking the residents which nation they wanted to belong to. And since most residents of the area were Greek, it was pretty obvious what would happen. The Greeks also received the northern coastline of the Sea of Marmara, including the Gallipoli Peninsula, and all of

Thrace, pushing the Bulgarians out forever and moving the Greek border up to the historic defensive lines outside Constantinople. On top of that, they obtained two islands at the mouth of the Dardanelles Strait, which Venizelos didn't even mention, and the Dodecanese Islands were to be negotiated on by the Italians and Greeks (the Italians refused, though, and held the islands until after WWII).

Everything seemed to be going Greece's way, but both Venizelos and many Greeks of all political stripes got greedy. Greek troops began to push into the interior of Asia Minor, and the farther they went, the fewer people were Greek. Needless to say, the non-Greeks they ran across were not happy to see them, but at least, at first, things remained reasonably peaceful.

One of the men who were worried about the tenability of the Greek push into Asia Minor was a general named Ioannis Metaxas (1871-1941), the acting chief of staff of the Greek army. Metaxas believed that Greece's position in Asia Minor was altogether indefensible militarily. Any geographic feature that would allow the Greeks to construct a strong defensive line was deep inside Asia Minor, much deeper than the Greeks wanted to go and certainly deeper than the Allies would permit, not to mention the millions of Turks who lived there. The problem was that the Greek majority area was really indefensible. Even if the Greeks could hold Smyrna and its peninsula, which was possible, it would likely cost more in both lives and money than it was worth. But though Metaxas was absolutely correct, at this point in time, euphoria in Greece was at an all-time high, and no one who advocated leaving Asia Minor was listened to.

The Greeks and Venizelos should have because within Turkey, over the course of 1919 to 1920, a new movement led by one of the 20th-century's greatest statesmen was gaining strength. The party was the Republican People's Party, and its leader was Mustafa Kemal, better known to history as Kemal Atatürk ("Kemal, Father of the Turks").

Kemal had risen to fame as a military officer during the Turks' victory over the Allies at the Battle of Gallipoli. At a point when Turkish fortunes were low, Kemal ordered his men to seize an Allied strongpoint, the capture of which could change the course of the battle. The last phrase of his order is still famous in Turkey: "I am not ordering you to fight. I am ordering you to die." This inflamed the Muslim Turks, and they swept the position of the Allied troops and eventually won the battle.

Since the end of the war, Kemal and his growing number of followers had proclaimed the former Ottoman regime illegal. To them, it was a betrayal of the Turkish people, and they called for a new nation of Turks for Turks. By late 1919, Kemal was in a position to meet with the Allies, and he informed them that all treaties signed by the former Ottoman Empire or the Young Turks were null and void. He would decide what constituted Turkey, not them.

Illustration 26: Atatürk in the 1920s

Naturally, the Allies did not take kindly to this and attempted to blockade Constantinople, which included Greek ships. Atatürk simply moved the capital to a new location, a small city named Ankara in the central part of Asia Minor, which is still the capital of

Turkey today. To get to Kemal, the Allies were going to have to invade the Turkish mainland, something that none of them was willing to do. As a matter of fact, it was around this point that the Allies realized that Kemal and his movement weren't going anywhere. After Kemal's defeat of a French force that had been left in a small part of Turkey at the end of the war, the Allies began to negotiate slowly with the new Turkish leader. This left Greece and the Greek troops in Turkey extremely isolated.

Venizelos was at the height of his power in the fall of 1920 when things began to go wrong. First, the king, Alexander I, was bitten by a pet monkey. He developed blood poisoning and died. The king had been firmly under Venizelos's control. His death was unfortunate because, with the seeming success of the Megali Idea, politics in Greece had become slightly less rancorous. With his death, those against Venizelos called for the return of Constantine I from exile. An election was held in November 1920, which was essentially a referendum on Constantine. Venizelos surprisingly lost. The issue of the king's return and the high taxes and costs of WWI had left the Greek economy in trouble.

Venizelos went into exile in Paris, and Constantine returned in December 1920. The memory of both his not-so-secret pro-German stance in WWI and the killing of French and British troops at Piraeus was fresh in the minds of the Allied Powers, which by this time were beginning to worry more about the rise of communism and the Soviet Union than the concerns of Greece. Among them was Winston Churchill, who had been the first lord of the admiralty during the first part of WWI, then the minister of munitions, and was chancellor of the exchequer by December 1920. He argued that a strong Turkey, Russia's historical enemy, would be a bulwark against Soviet expansion. Greece's position got weaker by the day.

Seeing the writing on the wall and hoping to gain some leverage at future negotiations, the new Greek government launched an assault against the new Turkish capital, Ankara, in March 1921.

Although they fought bravely and effectively, the Turkish position was simply too strong for the Greek forces to break through. A Turkish counterattack pushed the Greeks back to their starting point, where things remained at a stalemate until the next year.

On August 26th, 1922, the Turks launched a massive counterattack, which began to push the Greeks back toward Smyrna. As they advanced, they found evidence that the Greeks had committed atrocities against the population, which was true. As the Turkish position strengthened and Kemal's government became more popular, more Muslims rose up behind Greek lines, provoking a harsh response from the Greeks. Naturally, especially as the Turks advanced, most Greek soldiers who were taken prisoner or trapped behind the lines could expect harsh treatment in return. Though many Greek prisoners were eventually repatriated, thousands more were killed in executions.

By September, the Greeks asked the Allies to interfere. They hoped that they could at least get the Allies' promises for the protection of the Greeks in the area around Smyrna and elsewhere, but their pleas fell on deaf ears. The Turks were winning, and they weren't about to stop until the Greeks were gone from Asia Minor—now Turkey—for good.

The Turkish attack on Smyrna came at a great human cost. Thousands of Greek refugees flooded into the city from surrounding areas. Between the shelling and food shortages, casualties ran high. When the Turks entered the city and its immediate surroundings, massacres of Greeks took place. Within Smyrna, panicked crowds swarmed the docks and piers, hoping to get aboard a ship. Some Allied ships did pick up people in the water; according to survivors, these were mostly French. Others simply steamed away. Many hundreds drowned. Those who could not leave were killed. Hundreds of thousands of "Turkish Greeks" did manage to make it to Greece, where their assimilation proved another great challenge to the Greek government.

Correspondingly, Turks who still lived in Greece were forcibly expelled from the country. So, as the Turks were sealing their control of Smyrna, approximately one million "Greek Turks" were being expelled from Greece, and given the temper of the time, atrocities occurred more often than the Greeks care to admit even to this day.

The Greco-Turkish War of 1919–1922 was a horrific experience for both sides. Estimates of Greek civilian deaths run from 300,000 to 750,000; the lower number is probably closer. It is not known how many Turks were killed by Greeks, but it is likely it runs at least 100,000 or more.

Chapter 7 – Yet More Chaos and Another World War

The Turkish expulsion of the Greek army and the removal of the Greek population of Asia Minor through death or forcible expulsion brought the Megali Idea to an end, seemingly for good. Most Greeks at this point realized that the "Idea" had been and probably always was a pipe dream and that modern Greece, far from being a new power in the region, was simply a small and relatively poor and backward state in a Europe dominated by the Western powers.

At the end of the war with Turkey, Greece was in shambles. The army had been terribly beaten. The economy was barely functioning, and it now had to absorb hundreds of thousands of refugees. The political life of Greece had split between right and left with the National Schism, and this would continue until late in the century.

Between 1923 and 1936, when a fascist-style regime under General Metaxas took power, Greece suffered through a near civil war, the making and unmaking of governments, and, along with everyone else in Europe and much of the world, the Great Depression, which began in 1929.

Even before the ascension of Metaxas in 1936, Greece experienced a brief military government between 1922 and 1924. In 1924, even as the military attempted to intimidate the populace, an election was held that overwhelmingly called for the next Greek government to be a republic. Despite their defeat in 1926, the military interference in government that began in 1922 continued off and on until 1974.

Venizelos became the prime minister again in 1928, and the programs he set in motion might have had a greater effect in another time. He introduced a massive land reclamation project and a series of reforms intended to expand agricultural production, encouraged the purchase of new grain types from America and Canada to increase yields, helped farmers with low-interest loans, and introduced a program of practical education since Greece was short of engineers, scientists, machinists, and others that would bring the country into the 20th century, especially outside of Athens.

One of the more interesting aspects of Venizelos's later prime ministership was his determination to build a respectful relationship with Turkey. And remarkably, throughout the 1920s and 1930s, the Greeks and Turks were able to sign a number of trade agreements and diplomatic treaties.

Unfortunately for Venizelos and many other world leaders, the Great Depression happened in the fall of 1929. It hit Greece particularly hard, as most of its foreign exports were still semi-luxury products, like currants, olives, and mastic, all things that countries stopped importing almost immediately. A significant chunk of the people in the country relied on money sent from Greek emigrants overseas to supplement their income or, in many cases, keep them from going hungry. Since the Depression was worldwide, these remittances almost disappeared. Worst of all, like many countries, Greece began to default on foreign loans.

Within Greece, Venizelos and his supporters kept the bureaucratic jobs for themselves and made sure that supporters of the former military regimes were kept out of the military. These actions, which were just another step in a series of actions and reactions, kept Greece at war with itself.

The Depression spurred the rise of the Greek Communist Party ("KKE"), and although it was still small, it grew during these hard times. Along with the communists, there were social democratic parties modeled on those in Germany, France, and England. Despite their relatively small numbers, Venizelos and successive Greek government leaders persecuted known and suspected communists and socialists, which would lead to a reckoning during and after WWII.

From 1933 to 1936, Greece was racked by political violence. On the one side were right-wing monarchists. On the other were the liberals who supported Venizelos. Then there was the military. An assortment of small parties threw their lot in where necessary to achieve some sort of political gain. In 1933, Venizelos attempted to include the smaller parties in his government to broaden support for his programs, but the situation was so bad that no unity could be achieved. In March, one of Venizelos's supporters in the military attempted a coup, which the old politician tacitly supported.

As a result of this failed coup, a political foe of Venizelos, Panagis Tsaldaris, became the prime minister. However, his time in office was to be short. The monarchists, who sought to replace the republic with an absolute monarchy, became violent. An attempt was made on Venizelos's life, and in response, he and his supporters used violence in return.

On March 1st, 1935, Venizelos and his supporters revolted against the government. This was defeated by the government and military, and Venizelos fled to Paris, where he died in exile almost exactly one year later.

With Venizelos gone and many of his followers rounded up, put on trial, imprisoned, and oftentimes executed, Greece entered a new phase. Tsaldaris was not able to rule effectively, as one of the reforms introduced by the monarchists was proportional representation. Tsaldaris was not able to build the needed consensus—at least not without the small KKE, and that was something both the military and the monarchists would not accept. The deputy chief of the General Staff of the Hellenic Army, Alexander Papagos, who would command the army in WWII, proclaimed that the army would not allow communists to be a part of the government. At this point in time, the king, George II, who had been unacceptable to the Great Powers before WWI, named former chief of staff Ioannis Metaxas as the prime minister, and with that, the Greek experiment with democracy ended.

Illustration 27: Metaxas in the late 1930s.

The Metaxas Dictatorship

Metaxas was born in the city of Ithaca in 1871. He joined the army at a young age and distinguished himself despite the Greek defeat in the war with the Ottomans in 1897. He then went to Germany for advanced training; at the time, many foreign army officers trained in Germany, as it was considered the finest in Europe if not the world. Metaxas's rise was rapid, and he played a significant role in the Greek planning in the Balkan Wars. Despite his rank of colonel, he was appointed chief of staff in 1913 and was made a general in 1916. Like many monarchists, he was exiled to Corfu during the war, but he returned to Greece in 1920 when Constantine was reinstated after the death of his son from the infamous monkey bite.

Along with the monarchist politicians before and during the first part of WWI, Metaxas pressed for Greek neutrality, and as you read earlier, he opposed Venizelos's and others' plans for the Greek occupation of Asia Minor. In 1928, he was a minister without portfolio in the government. During the first years of the Great Depression, Metaxas strongly supported the monarchy and was the head of a small royalist party when the king appointed him the new commander in chief of the military.

Though it was clear to many that a dictatorship was a very real possibility, no one could put together a coalition to either to govern or preempt the placement of Metaxas as the prime minister by the king on April 13th, 1936. On the same day, under not-so-veiled threats from the military, the Greek parliament voted overwhelmingly to end its own existence.

The only group to oppose the rise of Metaxas, whose only support came from the king (he was not a popular nor charismatic man), were the communists, who announced a general strike on May Day (May 1st) 1936. This gave Metaxas, the king, and the military, who were all extreme anti-communists, an excuse to clamp down. They decreed the censorship of the press, suspended many rights that were "guaranteed" by the constitution, and announced that parliament would not meet again until sometime in the unknown future.

Metaxas is a hero to many Greeks today, but that is not because of his policies during his time in power. Metaxas was a fascist, plain and simple. He modeled much of his regime on the same type of symbols as Benito Mussolini and Adolf Hitler, though, to his credit, he did not practice or initiate any sort of ethnic prejudice or persecution against the Jews or other minorities of Greece.

However, he did champion "Greek Civilization" as the cornerstone of modern Western culture and announced the arrival of what he called the "Third Greek Civilization" (the ancients, the Byzantines, and 1936, respectively).

Metaxas was rabidly anti-communist, as were his followers, though, at this point in time, most Greeks had barely heard of communism and likely could not have described it in any great detail. Although he did not practice racial politics as Hitler did, his time in Germany did make him an admirer of that culture, and he wished to install what he deemed a more "disciplined, purposeful and Germanic" ethos into the Greek culture in the hope of making it more efficient, among other things. Like Hitler and Mussolini, Metaxas organized a movement for the young that was literally called the "Youth Movement" and set about censoring schoolbooks and curricula for any sign of liberalism or communism. He even called himself the "First Peasant," "First Worker," and, of course, "Leader."

As you can probably imagine, civil rights within the country suffered greatly under Metaxas, and many were thrown into prison for supposed "communist sympathies," which included protection of workers and farmers against abuse by industrialists and large landowners. Though Metaxas decreed a minimum wage for the first time in Greek history and canceled peasants' debt, these were mostly for public appearance, and these and many other programs supposedly in favor of the poor of Greece were only honored *if* the powerful chose to do so. Naturally, this drove more people into the arms of the KKE or at least made them sympathize with communist ideals, but anyone expressing these was punished severely.

Though Greece enjoyed some stability under Metaxas, it was, of course, imposed. His programs benefited the wealthy as opposed to the poor (there was only a relatively small middle class in the country). The economy moved forward in fits and starts as the

Depression continued into 1940—and that's when Metaxas's reputation was saved.

By the fall of 1940, WWII in Europe had been going on for a year. Hitler was the master of the Continent from the Atlantic to the Arctic Circle in Norway to the border of the Soviet Union, which he was preparing to attack in the spring. In North Africa, the war was going badly for the Italian forces under Mussolini, whose reputation as a "tough guy" was suffering both from Hitler's successes and the lack of his own. In April 1939, Mussolini invaded the small nation of Albania, opposite Italy on the Adriatic Sea. He hoped that success in North Africa and the Balkans might help him establish a new "Roman Empire," with him as Caesar.

One of the prerequisites in becoming a new Caesar was control of the Mediterranean. In 1940, the Italians boasted quite a strong navy and were competing with the British for control of the sea. To further his naval goals and grow his empire, Mussolini drew up a series of demands, which were presented to Metaxas during the night/early morning of October 28th, 1940. Mussolini wished to march and land his troops at various strategic points throughout Greece in order to "protect them" from the British, whom the Greeks were leaning toward in their neutrality.

Metaxas had attended a friendly reception at the Italian consulate earlier in the evening where nothing but good wishes were announced by the Italians toward the Greeks, but now, sick and awakened in the middle of the night and dressed in a nightshirt, robe, and slippers, the Greek leader was given a note by the Italian ambassador, Emanuele Grazzi, which, though in flowery and polite diplomatic language, demanded the right to march through Greece and for Italy to take possession of numerous sites on the Greek coast. What happened next is a legend in Greece; in fact, an entire holiday is based on it. According to Metaxas's widow and others, the Greek dictator simply uttered a firm "No!" and had the Italian escorted out. Others who were there reported that the conversation, which took place in French since it was the language of diplomacy at the time, simply ended with Metaxas saying, "Then it is war!"

Either way, the message to the Italians couldn't be clearer—Greece would fight. Every year on October 28th, Greeks celebrate the *Epéteios tou Óchi* (the "Anniversary of the No") or Oxi (Ochi) Day.

Illustration 28: Recent Oxi Day celebration in Greece.

For Mussolini, the invasion of Greece, which he launched the same day, was a horrendous failure and humiliation. Not only was the timing of the operation poor, which took place in the late fall during the rainy season, but his troops, like many Italian troops throughout WWII, were poorly trained and poorly motivated. Hitler was not informed about this; it was said he was enraged about being left of the loop, and he correctly feared the Italian operation might affect his planning for the invasion of the USSR (the Soviet Union).

The Greeks, on the other hand, were united, as most people would be when their land is invaded. After a fierce fight against the stronger Italian forces, the Greeks began to push the Italians back into Albania. By December, important Albanian ports were seized by the Greeks, and the Italians, at threat of being cut off before winter weather hit, ground things to a halt.

Unfortunately for the Greeks, their success meant that Hitler, who was always strangely loyal to Mussolini, was going to come to his ally's aid. Another factor was the position of the Greeks vis-à-vis Great Britain, which now saw Greece as an ally. The British pushed Metaxas to allow British troops to take positions in Greece, which he refused, still hoping Hitler might be dissuaded from invading his country. However, Metaxas died suddenly from a burst internal abscess and the blood poisoning it caused. His successor, General Papagos, agreed to British requests, believing a German-Italian invasion was coming no matter what.

The British and Greeks were not able to come to an understanding about defensive plans, which was mostly due to difficulties in language and communications systems, so when the Germans and Italians invaded Greece and Yugoslavia on April 6th, 1941, they put up an uncoordinated defense. At best, the Anglo-Greek force might have held up the Axis longer than they did, forestalling Hitler's other plans, but as soon as the Germans got involved, an Allied defeat was a foregone conclusion.

A number of Greek units in the north surrendered to the Germans, and one of their officers, General Tsolakoglou, eventually became the head of a German puppet regime in Greece. A number of Greek troops and about fifty thousand British Imperial troops (mostly New Zealanders) made their way to Crete, where on April 26th, they were subjected to the last German parachute attack of the war. Though the Germans quickly took Crete, the fight was much more costly than Hitler had imagined. In quite a few instances, German airborne troops, whose weapons were dropped in canisters that they had to retrieve upon landing, were literally beaten to death and, in some cases, torn apart by Cretan peasants before they could arm themselves. Of course, German retribution was swift, and hundreds of Cretans were killed in reprisals. Throughout the war, the Cretans, aided by the British, kept up an active resistance to the occupation.

By the beginning of June, all of Greece was occupied by the Axis, which included Bulgaria. Greece was divided into occupation zones, with the Germans controlling major cities, ports, certain islands, and strategic passes linking Greece with Yugoslavia and beyond as they deemed necessary throughout the war. The Italians controlled most of the country, and the Bulgarians oversaw their former territory in Thrace.

The Triple Occupation of Greece by the Axis Powers (1941-1944)

Legend:
- German Occupation Zone
- Italian Occupation Zone (occ. by Germany after Sept. 1943)
- Bulgarian Occupation Zone
- Bulgarian occupation (under German control) from July 1943
- Dodecanese Islands (Italian possession since 1912)

Historically, the consensus has been that in a horrible situation, the Italians were less horrible (though recent studies have begun to refute that), the Bulgarians worse, and, of course, the Germans worst of all. Throughout the war, any acts of resistance or attacks on occupation troops, especially Bulgarians or Germans, almost always led to reprisal killings, and many Greeks who had been imprisoned for minor offenses knew that they might be facing a death sentence when the next reprisal occurred.

Throughout Greece but especially in Thessaloniki, which was still more than half Jewish in population, the Germans began their persecutions. This happened in the Italian and Bulgarian zones too, with Greek Jews being handed over to the Nazis. Within weeks, the Jewish population of Greece almost completely ceased to exist.

The Axis forces sent much of the food grown in Greece to their own homes or troops, and within a short time, hunger began to grip Greece. Throughout the war, thousands upon thousands of Greeks died from hunger or weakened immune systems. In the middle of the war, the Red Cross petitioned the Axis to allow aid packages to come into Greece, but outside of the cities, this did not have much effect. An exodus from the cities began as Greeks attempted to find food in the countryside or with families on farms in the interior. On the islands, it was particularly bad, and fishing fleets were tightly controlled.

The Resistance

After the war, successive Greek governments, virtually all of whom leaned far to the right, attempted to downplay the role of the largest resistance group that existed in Greece during the war. They successfully marginalized them as being 100 percent communist and taking orders directly from Moscow.

This group, the National Popular Liberation Army, was known by its Greek acronym of "ELAS." Throughout most of the war, it was made up of not only communists but also republicans, socialists, and patriots of all stripes who simply wished to help end the occupation of their land. Another group, the National Liberation Front or "EAM," often worked with ELAS, and the two were almost always lumped together in both speech and history books. In fact, they still are known as "ELAS/EAM" today. EAM was a smaller and more radical group, and it did have ideas about the communist reshaping of Greece after the war.

ELAS/EAM was by far the largest of the Greek resistance groups, though a smaller right-wing group called the National Republican Greek Army ("EDES") did get a large share of publicity due to its monarchist beliefs and its colorful leader, Napoleon Zervas.

Like many other nations conquered by the Axis, the occupation engendered not only resistance but also civil war and collaboration (in Greece, by the fascist "X" militia). During WWII, it seemed to many Greeks that the resistance spent as much time fighting each other as they did the Germans, Italians, and Bulgarians.

However, the resistance and the needs of the occupation did require that hundreds of thousands of Axis troops be stationed in Greece. Organizing fights in the mountains and running secret printing presses and intelligence-gathering operations meant that the occupation forces could not fight elsewhere. The most spectacular and effective action of the Greek resistance during the war came on November 25th, 1942, when ELAS and EDES, along with British agents, cooperated to blow up the crucial Gorgopotamos railway viaduct in northern Greece, which cut German supply lines south and had a serious effect on the German campaign in North Africa.

Illustration 29: Gorgopotamos Bridge today. You can see a memorial and history of the Greek resistance operation at the bottom left.

By late 1943, the Greeks and nearly everyone else in Europe, with the possible exception of Hitler, knew that the war was going to end with an Ally victory. Despite the Italians dropping out of the war and the Germans occupying Greek zones and installing their harsh regime, the Greek resistance movements began to increasingly fight among themselves, jockeying for positions when the war ended.

When the war did end, a new round of violence began. Toward the end of the war, British Prime Minister Winston Churchill went to Moscow on his own and met Soviet leader Josef Stalin. During this meeting, Churchill took out a scrap of paper and wrote down the names of various countries in eastern Europe and the Balkans. Next to each, he wrote what he deemed the percentage of control that the Soviets and the Western Allies (meaning Britain and the United States of America) were to have in each. Next to Greece, which he considered vital for the security of the Suez Canal that Britain controlled, he wrote "90%." To this and to all of the proposals made by Churchill, Stalin put a large checkmark in agreement. The post-war world was made. Throughout the rest of his life, Stalin, who was not really known for keeping his word, kept to his part of the bargain in regards to Greece, probably knowing that a naval battle against the United Kingdom and the United States would go badly for him since his power was based on land. Greece and the Black Sea could be easily blockaded by the west.

This left Britain ostensibly "in charge" of what happened in Greece after the war or rather once the Axis Powers left, which happened in October 1944. Churchill was virulently anti-communist, and despite being told that aside from EAM, much of the Greek resistance was not communist, though they might lean toward the left, he believed that any group not supporting the return of the king (who was unpopular) and some sort of republican government under him was a communist.

King George and General Papagos spent much of the war being moved from one place to another, attempting more to wage war against the communists than fight the Germans, though sizable contingents of Greek troops fought in North Africa and Italy. They also whispered in Churchill's ear and inflated the risk of communism in Greece.

The next years of Greek history were spent in a civil war. In 1944, the British landed troops in Athens and installed the king and Papagos. ELAS/EAM, which by then numbered nearly 100,000 men and women, set up a rival government in the north and ran much of the countryside.

On December 3rd, 1944, a huge demonstration against the government and the British took place in Athens. Violence ensued, and British troops fired into the crowd. The protestors claimed hundreds had been shot and/or killed; the number is far less, though it is still tragic. Civil war broke out in Athens between ELAS/EAM, the British, the formerly fascist Greek militia, and some units of the Greek army. In Athens, ELAS was driven out, and mass killings of ELAS prisoners were carried out on the outskirts of the city by members of EDES and the king's government. However, the only parts of Greece under the control of the government and Britain were Athens and Thessaloniki.

For the next two months, battles went on between the government and ELAS/EAM in Athens. However, with much of the city in ruins and no one making any real advances, both sides took part in negotiations sponsored by Great Britain. These negotiations resulted in the Varkiza Agreement of February 1945. Throughout the negotiations, the Greek king remained in exile, and the British-supported prime minister resigned. Both sides needed to make peace. ELAS, now somewhat divorced from the more radical EAM, needed Athens to govern and was eager to avoid the threat of a British blockade. The British were becoming aware that the end of the war and the occupation and administration of Greece and other formerly occupied countries were more expensive than they could afford.

The Varkiza Agreement, named after the town where the talks took place, called for the restoration of civil rights, a plebiscite on the monarchy, and a general election under Allied supervision.

These were the demands of ELAS. General Nikolaos Plastiras vowed that he would jail and try all accused collaborators, grant national amnesty for ELAS fighters, and promised there would be no attempt by the army to go after left-wing organizations (like unions) or political parties. ELAS was also required to give up its arms and withdraw its troops 150 miles from Athens.

The Varkiza Agreement, which was signed by both sides, never came into effect. While most ELAS units gave up their arms, some remained in the mountains and small towns and villages of Greece, believing the government would not live up to its promises, which it did not.

Within a very short time, the army moved against ELAS, unions, and anyone else deemed a communist or leftist. Many completely non-political people were also arrested for allegedly having "communist" beliefs. Worse, many former collaborators and the former fascist militia was armed and sent after ELAS/EAM members throughout the country. Rigged elections in 1946 put former Prime Minister Tsaldaris back in power, and he proved to be even more conservative than he had previously been. In September 1945, after a series of rigged elections, King George II returned to Greece as a figurehead.

By 1946, a full-scale guerrilla war was taking place in Greece. By the middle of the year, the British unilaterally announced that they were leaving Greece and that the Americans had better step in, which they did. President Harry Truman announced his Truman Doctrine, which, simply put, stated that any nation resisting communism would have the help of the United States. The first two countries to receive aid were Greece and Turkey, the latter of which the US saw as the more important partner since it bordered the Soviet Union. The US never sent troops to Greece, though political and military advisers did aid the government.

The Americans also pumped massive amounts of economic and military aid into the country. Even with the financial help of the Americans, the Greek Civil War lasted until 1949, though by early

1948, ELAS and the communists were limited to an area bordering Albania and the new country of Yugoslavia. In October 1949, the communists announced the end of their struggle. Many of them fled to Albania and Yugoslavia, where many of them lived until amnesty was declared in the 1980s.

The Greek Civil War of 1947-49 was vicious, as most civil wars are. Both sides were guilty of the most heinous crimes: torture, mass killings, mass imprisonment, the intentional starvation of areas opposed to them, and even the kidnapping of children for indoctrination. The scars of the Civil War lasted a very, very long time.

Chapter 8 – Greece from 1950

Relatively speaking, Greece in the 1950s was stable, and for a short time, its economic growth actually outpaced that of other post-war European countries, though it must be admitted that these nations had seen much greater destruction during WWII than Greece.

There were two main characteristics of the Greek political scene between 1950 and 1967: communism and its cousin, socialism. These parties would not be permitted political power, and the military would play a significant role in the political life of the country. Stability seemed to come to the country, and Greece, along with Turkey, became part of the North Atlantic Treaty Organization (NATO) for the defense of western Europe against the USSR. Even violent anti-Greek riots in Istanbul (formerly Constantinople) did not cause the two nations to go to war, which was seen by many as not only a sign of stability but also a miracle.

However, below the surface, tensions still existed in Greek society. Simply speaking, this placed more liberal-leaning republican governments against the army, the king (Paul II until 1963, then his son Constantine II until 1973) against the military (in the case of Paul) as well as against the left, and the left against right-wing parties and the idea of a monarchy.

On top of all the political infighting, the 1960s saw the same types of changes to Greek society that happened elsewhere in the Western world. One of the by-products of this was growing anti-Americanism, which led to large protests against both the Americans, who had established naval bases in Greece, and governments that supported it. Additionally, the culture wars that broke out as a result of the changes of the 1960s pitted younger urban dwellers against people from the country and the powerful Greek Orthodox Church. All of the changes led to frequent switches in government, as there was one prime minister after another. Usually, it was one of two men, Constantine Karamanlis (right) or George Papandreou (left).

By the mid-1960s, many Greeks expected the generals in the army to take over, but when the coup did happen, it was a group of three extreme right-wing colonels who had direct command of units in Athens and other important cities. They also had the support of a number of politicians and business leaders.

The "Colonel's Coup" turned into a military dictatorship that lasted from 1967 to 1974. A counter-coup by King Constantine II failed, and his exile ended the Greek monarchy, seemingly for good. During this time, virtually all civil rights were extinguished from Greece, the "clean" language of *Katharevousa* was again made the language of journalism and politics, and Greek history—meaning ancient Greek history—was the focus of history courses. (As a side note, *Katharevousa* has been made all but extinct today, as it has been replaced by *demotic* Greek—the "language of the people.") Anything deemed "anti-Greek" was attacked.

Under the colonels, some parts of the Greek economy thrived, mainly those who were already rich. Others stagnated. One problem that plagued Greece since before the time of Venizelos and was actually made worse by him was giving peasants their own land to work in exchange for political loyalty. In the long run, this harmed the Greek economy, for most agriculture remained small-scale, and Greece had remained dependent on food exports to varying degrees since before WWII. However, the idea of a pastoral Greece appealed to the colonels, particularly their chief, Colonel George Papadopoulos, who began the coup. He ran the dreaded secret police and ended up as the dictator of the entire country. He once publicly beat a journalist to a pulp for suggesting that a piece of ancient Greek art depicted male homosexuality, which the colonel insisted did not exist until communism developed. You get the idea.

The end of the colonels' dictatorship came in 1974 when they, like most dictators, overreached themselves. In the 1950s, 1960s, and early 1970s, the question of *enosis* with Greece came to the fore, this time from the large island of Cyprus, some five hundred miles from mainland Greece to the south of the Dodecanese Islands. For many centuries, Cyprus had a majority Greek population (77 percent in 1960, mostly in the capital of Nicosia and in the western part of the island) and a sizable minority Turkish population (mostly in the capital and in the east). In 1878, the island had been placed under British administration and protection, and it was annexed by the British in 1914.

After the war, Greek Cypriots would periodically call for a union with Greece, but this was resisted not only by Turkey (naturally) but also by the US and the UK, which did not want to see a war between its NATO partners or instability in the area. In the 1950s, violence between nationalist ethnic Greeks and Turks took place, often on the island. In 1960, after long negotiations in London and Switzerland, the island became an independent nation with a power-sharing agreement between the Greeks and Turks.

However, this was not enough for many of the more militant Greeks on the island, who were led by a charismatic and politically clever Greek Orthodox archbishop, Makarios. With the connivance of the colonels, Makarios urged the Greek nationalists to rise up, and the colonels sent arms and were preparing to send a contingent of troops when the Turks decided they had had enough.

On July 20th, 1973, the Turkish Army attacked Greek Cypriot positions, its jets bombed their positions, and the Turkish Navy cut the island off from the rest of the world. An international agreement was swiftly concluded to avoid a growing conflict, which Greece at this time would have easily lost, and to avoid further ethnic and combat bloodshed on the island. Today, Cyprus is a divided island, with an unrecognized semi-independent Turkish state in the north and the internationally recognized Republic of Cyprus in the south. The demilitarized zone between the two parts of the island stands as it did in 1973, and it is only populated by occasional United Nations patrols.

Illustration 30: The Cypriot Demilitarized Zone (DMZ) today.

The Turkish "victory" in Cyprus spelled the end of the military regime in Greece. International pressure, the turning of former allies against the colonels, and huge anti-government demonstrations (some of which involved mass fatalities) caused the colonels' dictatorship to end. Papadopoulos was sentenced to death, as were many in his government. This was commuted to a life sentence, and he died in custody while in an Athens hospital in 1999.

Though the road has been rocky for Greece since the end of the dictatorship, thankfully, nothing like it has occurred since.

Conclusion

In the years since 1973, Greece has remained, at least in comparison with prior years, relatively stable and at peace. From the mid-1970s to the first decades of the 21st century, Greek politics remained as animated and contentious as ever, but it was violence-free. Governments and their policies have shifted to the left and the right, with the 1980s and much of the 1990s actually seeing a left-leaning government in power.

In the early 1990s, the nation of Yugoslavia broke apart and saw its various ethnic groups go to war with one another. The conflict was marked by much suffering and the return of genocide to the European continent for the first time since WWII. When the United States and NATO finally put an end to the war, an entirely new group of nations had come into existence. One of them was made up of people who called themselves "Macedonians." Right away, there were problems with Greece. By calling themselves Macedonians and their new nation Macedonia, which lay between Greece and Serbia on Greece's north-central border, many Greeks feared that at some time in the future, these "Macedonians" would make claims on the region of Greece that the Greeks themselves called Macedonia. Aside from the potential problems about the border, the Greeks believed the Slavic people were attempting to usurp the Greeks' claim on the legacy of Alexander the Great, an intense point of pride in Greece (intense may not actually describe it correctly).

Huge protests broke out in Greece, and some extreme nationalists even called for punitive military action against the new nation unless they changed their name. It appeared for a time that there was going to be an international crisis in the Balkans once again. Talks eventually established a new provisional name for the nation that was at least somewhat palatable to the Greeks: the Former Yugoslav Republic of Macedonia, widely known by its acronym of FYROM. In a way, this name established that the new country had existed north of Greece's present-day borders as a province of Yugoslavia. Though this settled the matter for a while, the people in FYROM were not happy with constantly being reminded that they had been part of a failed state, and many Greeks still had problems with the nomenclature. Finally, in 2019, Greek Prime Minister Alexis Tsipras and his counterpart in FYROM announced an agreement on a new name, North Macedonia, which seemed to satisfy most people in both nations.

While the arguments about the name of its newest neighbor were raging, the Great Recession of 2008–09 occurred. It hit Greece particularly hard. It was already running deficits and barely keeping up with repayments on loans from the European Economic Community (EEC), of which it is a member, the International Monetary Fund (IMF), and individual nations, specifically Germany and the United States. This was partially because of massive tax evasions from the bottom of the economic food chain to the top. Greece's economy went into a tailspin as a result. Greece was hit worse than almost any other nation in Europe. Massive layoffs of government workers, including police, which naturally means a large rise in crime, and unemployment in the rest of the country ensued. Unemployment reached over 30 percent at one point. Banks failed by the score. Protests against the successive governments took place virtually every day for years. Parties on both the extreme right and the extreme left gained members, and political violence occurred, thankfully not at previous levels.

For years, Greece had been essentially governed by the fathers, sons, and grandsons of existing political dynasties, but in the 2000s and into the 2010s, these families and their political parties seemed to be out of answers.

The entire situation was made worse by two things. First, the international community, led by Germany, demanded that Greece change the way it governed, collected taxes, and created budgets if it was to secure more loans to stay afloat. This was met with violent opposition by many groups, including a union of left-leaning political parties, one of which was known by its acronym **SYRIZA**, from its Greek name meaning "from the roots" and which came to power at various times throughout the first part of the 2000s. However, given the alternative, even **SYRIZA** eventually had to agree to a program of fiscal austerity in Greece, of which the government (as of this writing in 2021) is still feeling the effects.

The second major problem, which reached critical mass in 2015 and which was discussed in some detail at the beginning of this book, is the Middle East refugee problem. In 2015, the problem consisted of massive numbers pouring into Greece, hoping to make it to Germany and other parts of wealthier northern Europe. Today, the problem is the refugee camps in Greece, which came as a result of various countries closing their borders to the refugees, mostly those from Syria. As you read earlier, tensions along the border with Turkey over the refugee question are on the rise.

Let's end on a happy note, though. Greece, almost inexplicably, seemed to get a handle on what to do about the COVID-19 pandemic of 2020–21. Comparatively speaking, Greece had a lesser rate of both infection and death than almost any other developed country. Part of that was the close feeling of community that still exists in much of Greece. Take a look at the article on the island of Chios in the bibliography for details on how this happened. As of this writing, Greece has opened its borders to tourists of most countries, including the United States. Perhaps time will tell, but for now, things seem to be looking up.

Here's another book by Captivating History that you might like

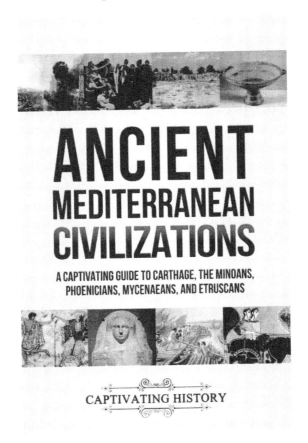

Free Bonus from Captivating History (Available for a Limited time)

Hi History Lovers!

Now you have a chance to join our exclusive history list so you can get your first history ebook for free as well as discounts and a potential to get more history books for free! Simply visit the link below to join.

Captivatinghistory.com/ebook

Also, make sure to follow us on Facebook, Twitter and Youtube by searching for Captivating History.

References

Bury, J. B. (2015). *A History of Greece: To the Death of Alexander the Great*. Cambridge: Cambridge University Press.

Cartledge, P. (2016). *Sparta and Lakonia: A Regional History 1300-362 BC*. Place of publication not identified: Routledge.

Everitt, A. (2017). *Rise of Athens: The Story of the World's Greatest Civilization*. New York: Random House.

Grote, G. (2008). *History of Greece: From the Earliest Period to the Close of the Generation Contemporary with Alexander the Great*. Place of publication not identified: Hesperides Press.

Henderson, B. W. (1973). *The Great War between Athens and Sparta: A Companion to the Military History of Thucydides*. New York, Arno Press.

Herodotus, Godley, A. D., Herodotus, & Herodotus. (2004). *The Persian Wars*. Cambridge, MA: Harvard University Press.

Martin, T. R. (1996). *Ancient Greece: From Prehistoric to Hellenistic Times*. New Haven: Yale University Press.

Osborne, R. (2000). *Classical Greece: 500-323 BC.* Oxford: Oxford University Press.

Pickard-Cambridge, A. W., Gould, J., & Lewis, D. M. (2003). *The Dramatic Festivals of Athens.* Oxford: Clarendon Press.

Robinson, C. A., & Greenberg, L. (1984). *Ancient Greece.* New York: F. Watts.

Starr, C. G. (1991). *A History of the Ancient World.* New York: Oxford University Press.

Thucydides, Hammond, M., & Rhodes, P. J. (2009). *The Peloponnesian War.* Oxford: Oxford University Press.

Beaton, Roderick. *Greece: Biography of a Modern Nation.* Chicago: University of Chicago Press, 2021.

Beevor, Antony. CRETE: THE BATTLE AND THE RESISTANCE. London: John Murray, 2011.

Brewer, David. THE GREEK WAR OF INDEPENDENCE: THE STRUGGLE FOR FREEDOM AND THE BIRTH OF MODERN GREECE. New York: Abrams, 2011.

"Chios Massacre: The Worst Atrocity Committed by the Ottomans Against Greeks." GreekReporter.com. Last modified February 6, 2021. https://greekreporter.com/2020/03/29/chios-massacre-the-worst-atrocity-   committed-by-the-ottomans-against-greeks/

"Controversial New Labour Laws Set to Shake Up Working Life in Greece." The Guardian. Last modified June 17, 2021. https://www.theguardian.com/world/2021/jun/17/greece-controversial-new-labour-law-reform-shake-up-working-life

Contoudis, John. CHIOS: A HISTORY. River Vale, NJ: Cosmos Publishing, 2009.

Durant, Will. THE LIFE OF GREECE: THE STORY OF CIVILIZATION. New York: Simon & Schuster, 2011.

"Exploring Greece's Unseen Corners." The New York Times - Breaking News, US News, World News and Videos. Last modified June 15, 2021. https://www.nytimes.com/2021/06/14/travel/greece-traditions.html?smid=em-share.

Gage, Nicholas. ELENI. New York: Ballantine Books, 2010.

"The Greco-Italian War: One of Benito Mussolini's Biggest Failures." Warfare History Network. Last modified September 25, 2020. https://warfarehistorynetwork.com/2017/07/20/the-greco-italian-war-one-of-benito-mussolinis-biggest-failures/

"Greco-Turkish War, 1919-22." HistoryNet. https://www.historynet.com/greco-turkish-war-1919-22.htm

"Greek Nationalism, the 'Megale Idea' and Venizelism to 1923." Redirecting. Accessed July 12, 2021. https://staff.lib.msu.edu/sowards/balkan/lect14.htm

"HOW A SLAVE GIRL BECAME AN OTTOMAN QUEEN." (2019, January 17). OZY. https://www.ozy.com/true-and-stories/how-a-slave-girl-became-an-ottoman-queen/88876/

"Katharevousa Vs. Demotiki: The Unknown History of Modern Greek." Nicholas C. Rossis. Last modified December 6, 2019. https://nicholasrossis.me/2014/11/21/katharevousa-vs-demotiki-the-unknown-history-of-modern-greek/

"List of Massacres During the Greco-Turkish War (1919–22)." Wikipedia – Encyclopedia.

"Macedonia and Greece: Vote Settles 27-year Name Dispute." BBC News. Last modified January 25, 2019. https://www.bbc.com/news/world-europe-47002865

Mazower, M. (2007). SALONICA, CITY OF GHOSTS: CHRISTIANS, MUSLIMS AND JEWS 1430-1950. Vintage

The New Arab & agencies. (March 2020). "*TURKEY FIRES TEAR GAS AT GREEK BORDER GUARDS AS REFUGEE STANDOFF CONTINUES.*" The New Arab. https://english.alaraby.co.uk/news/turkey-fires-tear-gas-greek-border-guards

"On This Island, Everyone Knows Your Name (if You Have Covid-19)." The New York Times - Breaking News, US News, World News and Videos. Last modified September 18, 2020. https://www.nytimes.com/2020/09/17/world/europe/greece-chios-coronavirus.html

Psaropoulos, John. "How Poetry Won Independence for Greece." WSJ. Last modified April 8, 2021. https://www.wsj.com/articles/how-poetry-won-independence-for-greece-11617906113?mod=flipboard

Ureneck, Lou. SMYRNA, SEPTEMBER 1922: ONE AMERICAN'S MISSION TO RESCUE VICTIMS OF THE 20TH CENTURY'S FIRST GENOCIDE. New York: HarperCollins, 2015.

"*WAS COLUMBUS GREEK?*" (n.d.). Matt Barrett's Guides to Greece and the Greek Islands. https://www.greecetravel.com/history/columbus/

Appendix A: Further Reading and Reference

A Traveller's History of Greece. Tim Boatswain. 1989.

The Unification of Greece: 1770-1923. Douglas Dakin. 1972.

Ancient Greece: From Prehistoric to Hellenistic Times. Thomas R. Martin. 1996.

Greece, the Hidden Centuries: Turkish Rule from the Fall of Constantinople to Greek Independence. David Brewer. 2010.

Made in the USA
Coppell, TX
05 November 2022

85823689R00223